D0810204

THE BIBLE'S LEGACY
FOR WOMANHOOD

BY THE SAME AUTHOR

All the Women of the Bible
Great Women of the Christian Faith
Family Living in the Bible

EDITH DEEN

The Bible's Legacy for Womanhood

DOUBLEDAY & COMPANY, INC.
Garden City, New York
1969

Preface

In giving lectures all over the country for several years after my first book, All of the Women of the Bible, *was published, I learned there was an imperative need for a book highlighting biblical precepts regarding womanhood as a whole.*

In THE BIBLE'S LEGACY FOR WOMANHOOD, *I have tried to show that women through the centuries have been inheritors of a priceless heritage from the Bible. In one sense, legacy means anything handed down from the ancient past, and woman's legacy from the Bible is not limited but boundless, not material but spiritual. Although written in the context of my first book, this one is not biographical but interpretative.*

As I have researched and written for more than four years on my subject, I have been amazed to see how patterns have unfolded, never easily but always purposefully, and especially so this last year. If I grew weary or discouraged, the faith of these noble women of the Bible came forth to inspire me.

I needed biblical inspiration, for many problems and responsibilities often drew me from my task. Among these were my husband's long illness and passing in May

1967, and months of public service that required more
time than I had from home and family responsibilities.

But my blessings were manifold, a spiritual light that
often seemed to cross my path when I thought it was impossible to continue writing, also loving helpers all about
me. One of these was Ella Higginbotham, a neighbor, who
did more than type. She inspired me with her faithfulness
over many revisions, when another might have grown im-
patient. In typing all four of my books, she has become my
indispensable helper.

Another person to whom I shall be eternally grateful is
Dr. William L. Reed, chairman of the Department of Religion at Texas Christian University here in my home city
of Fort Worth, Texas, and a trustee of the American
School of Oriental Research in Jerusalem. Millar Burrows,
in his first book on The Dead Sea Scrolls, tells that "Father
de Vaux and Professor William L. Reed, who was serving
that year (1951–52) as Director of the American School
of Oriental Research at Jerusalem, directed the enter-
prise," that of making "a systematic exploration in the
whole region within a radius of about five miles in each
direction of Khirbit Quamran" (p. 59), where the Dead
Sea Scrolls were found in 1947. Authorities recognize Dr.
Reed as one of this country's eminent Bible scholars, and
his suggestions here and there have greatly strengthened
this manuscript.

One of the difficulties of writing a book on the Bible
today is the new knowledge that is pouring forth from research in archaeological discoveries and new translations.
I have chosen to use the King James Version as my basic
text, largely because some of the most conservative faiths

still prefer it, and also because of its beautiful prose and poetry. On the other hand, I have quoted from the Revised Standard Version and the New English Bible when the dialogue was clearer and controversial questions had to be cleared up by newer scholarship. I also have referred occasionally to the James Moffatt translation.

As I was making revisions and needed a woman for a sounding board on certain matters of good taste, in walked a very discerning and interested friend, Marion Hodgson, who has given me excellent suggestions. I am indeed grateful for her keen insight and helpfulness.

Mrs. Sarah Blum, head of the reference department at the Fort Worth Public Library, has also generously aided me in my search for facts. Also I have enjoyed marvelous co-operation from my editor, Alex Liepa, Senior Editor at Doubleday. He has given constructive co-operation from his first letter and contract after the prospectus reached him, on through to my visit with him in his New York office, and his subsequent correspondence.

Other blessings have been many. Among these are a tranquil garden, which my husband designed during his illness. Frequently when I needed inspiration I had but to listen to its redbirds and mockingbirds and walk amid its redwood, bay, red oak, and cherry laurel trees, and its white blooming abelia, barberry, and red Nandina bushes. Our garden made me realize we never do anything alone. Even nature sings of its dependence upon God.

I have had other inspiring areas in my environment. One is a home library of more than four thousand books, and some of these have become my best companions as I have researched and written. Most of the materials for this book were under my own roof, so I have had many pleasant and exciting hours as I have gone about my task in my own home, faithfully assisted by Versie Roberts, our housekeeper of eighteen years, who lost her husband, a minister, a few weeks before this manuscript was to go to the publisher.

Although my labor has been long and strenuous at times, I have kept before me Arnold Toynbee's statement, "Books are expendable, like the man hours that go to the making of them. A book that has been weathered away will have served its purpose if it provokes other minds to write other books that may perhaps prove less vulnerable. The one thing that matters is that inquiry shall go on; for so long as it continues there is hope that it will go farther" (Arnold Toynbee's Story of History, vol. 12, p. 7). *I have realized better too what the writer of Ecclesiastes meant when he said, "Of making many books there is no end; and much study is a weariness of the flesh"* (12:12).

As I now conclude my task, I rejoice that I shall no longer have to discipline myself to interminable reading, research, and writing. And yet in a little while I know I shall feel as lost as a mother who has seen her child marry and leave home for good. And so I send forth this child into the world, praying that it will lift the minds and hearts of readers in this complex and fast-changing world, when basic values, our richest legacy from the Bible, have been seriously threatened. I hope that readers will feel as I did as I wrote, that God, the supreme power of the universe, is very much alive in our world, just as he was from the time of the Creation on through the New Testament Church.

Table of Contents

PREFACE   V

Section One
WOMAN'S HIGH DESTINY

Chapter One   IN THE CREATION   3

    The Significance of His Likeness   5
    The Artist and His Enduring Creations   5
    Man's Masterpiece Indefinable   6
    God's Creation Unexplainable   7
    Woman as Man's Inspirer   8
    A Summons to Decency, Greatness   10

Chapter Two   IN HER COMMUNICATION WITH GOD   12

    Ministers to the Righteous   13
    Guardians of Welfare   14
    The Angels in Mary's Life   16
    Other Beings Beyond Solar System   17
    Ever in the Presence of His Spirit   18

Chapter Three   IN HER RELATIONSHIP TO GOD   20

    Wonders Amid Heartache, Temptation   21
    A Mother's Close Walk with God   22
    Rejoicing in the Lord   23
    God's Abundant Supply   25

His Omnipotence and Omniscience 26
A Woman Saint's Walk with God 27
On Building the Kingdom of God 29

Chapter Four IN THE STREAM OF THE GENERATIONS 31

An Inspiring Portrait of Womankind 32
No Old Testament Woman So Ideal 34
The Influence of the Noble Wife, Mother 35
A Part of Life's Universal Stream 36

Chapter Five IN HER ROLE AS "KEEPER OF THE SPRINGS" 38

Bread of Idleness Untasted 39
Her Flowers, Trees, and Herbs 41
Her Kitchen Equipment and Foods 42
Her Lamps of Special Significance 43
Her Home, a Hospitable Place 44
Homemaker's Role, a Sacred One 45

Section Two
A MAGNA CHARTA FOR WOMANHOOD

Chapter Six THEIR GOD-GIVEN RIGHTS 51

Status of Wives of Patriarchs 51
Thoughtful Regard for Daughters 52
Other Honors to Hebrew Women 54
Good Test of Nation's Culture 55
Equality of Man, Woman Not Likeness 56
Instant Equal Opportunity Impossible 57

Chapter Seven THEIR STATUS IN THE SANCTUARY 59

The Service of All the Women 60
The Gift of Their Talents 61

Their Treasured Bronze Mirrors 63
Their Other Services and Stewardship 63
Their Part in Temple Music 64
Blessed Are Those Who Serve 66

Chapter Eight THEIR OCCUPATIONS AND CREATIVITY 68

Expert as Midwives 69
Skilled as Nurses from Early Times 71
Their Agricultural Duties 72
The Builders of Towns and Walls 73
A Diplomat from Southern Arabia 74
Queens of the Hebrew Monarchy 75
The Spinners and Weavers 76
Their Knowledge of Fabric Arts 78
Tentmaking, an Old Vocation 79
Teachers and Doorkeepers 80
Labor, the Basis of a Good Life 80

Chapter Nine THEIR STATUS AS NATIONAL LEADERS 82

Miriam, One of Founders of Hebrew Common-
  wealth 83
Deborah, the Motherly Helper in War 85
Huldah, the Wise Prophetess to King Josiah 88
Esther, a Liberator of Her People 89
Status, a Product of Achievement 91

Chapter Ten THE RESPONSIBLE ROLE OF LITTLE, OBSCURE
ONES 92

The Seven Shepherdess Sisters 92
The Faithful, Nameless Nurse 94
The Maidservant of En Rogel 96

A Plain Farm Woman   97
The Far-Sighted Woman in a Little Town   97
A Little Hebrew Maid   99

Section Three
THE ETERNALLY FEMININE

Chapter Eleven   THEIR NEVER CHANGING CHARACTERISTICS   103

A Good Wife, a Crown to Her Husband   104
The Noisy, Brawling Woman   105
On Wickedness in Woman   106
The Unlovely and the Wise   107
Ruth—the Woman of Worth   108
Apocryphal Adjectives on Women   109
Women More Powerful Than Kings   110
The Women of High Principle   111

Chapter Twelve   THEIR EMOTIONAL CONFLICTS   114

An Ambitious Mother but a Disloyal Wife   115
Resentment, Deceit in a Patriarch's Wife   116
Moses's Wife and Her Bad Temper   117
Miriam's Prejudice in a Race Matter   118
Sin's Relationship to Bodily, Mental Ills   119
One Woman Who Taunted Another   120
The Impatience of Two Wives   120
A Woman's Face, a True Barometer   122

Chapter Thirteen   HOW THEY LOOKED AND WHAT THEY
WORE   123

Their Appearance   123
Their Many Colors   125

Their Fabrics of Wool, Silk, Linen 126

Their Jewelry, Ointments, etc. 127

Their Hair, Eyelashes, Sandals 129

Meaning of Modesty, Simplicity 130

Chapter Fourteen BEAUTY IN WOMANHOOD 132

Real Beauties: Five Maidens, Four Women 133

Sarah, One of Beauties of the Ages 134

Rebekah and the Master Artists 135

The Ever Radiant Rachel, Wife of Jacob 136

Artists' Acclaim of Patriarchal Wives 137

A Daughter Who Is All Glorious Within 138

Bath-sheba, Beautiful of Form and Face 139

The Beautiful Vashti and Her Courage 140

Artists' Conception of Esther's Loveliness 141

New Testament Definition of Beauty 142

Chapter Fifteen ROMANTIC LOVE IN WOMANHOOD 143

Romance in Patriarchal Times 144

Romance in a Second Marriage 146

Personal Togetherness in Love 147

In an Atmosphere of Love 148

The Consummation of Married Love 149

Chapter Sixteen SEXUAL SANCTITY IN WOMANHOOD 151

Sex, a Part of the Divine Plan 151

How Sex Can Bring Reverence for Life 153

Safeguarding Woman's Sexual Sanctity 154

"Such a Thing Ought Not to Be Done in Israel" 155

Chastity—Its Significance to Civilization 157
Monogamy, the Ideal in Marriage 158
The Decline of Energy in Lower Standards 159

Section Four
HER DENIAL OF HER LEGACY

Chapter Seventeen THOSE WHO DO NOT HEAR THE WORD 163

When Woman's Seed Is Bad 164
Murders Involving Women 165
Wicked Women in New Testament 167
Woman's True Destiny for Good, Not Evil 170

Chapter Eighteen THE INFLUENCE OF PAGAN GODDESSES 172

The Sensual Fertility Cults 173
Solomon, First King to Erect Pagan Shrines 175
Queens Who Maligned Israel's Womanhood 177
Baalism's Destruction of Womanly Ideals 180

Chapter Nineteen THE HARLOT (PROSTITUTE) AND THE
ADULTERER 181

Adultery, a Violation of Commandment 182
Harlotry, a Denial of Love 182
A Mother's Warning Against Both 184
The Guilty Adulterer 185
David and Bath-sheba's Adultery 186
God's Forgiving Grace 187

Chapter Twenty AMOS—THOSE WHO NEVER HAVE ENOUGH 189

Those in Ivory Houses 190
Those in Large Harems 191

His Plea for Justice and Righteousness   192
The Luxuries of the Greedy   193
Amos's Influence on History   196

Chapter Twenty-one   ISAIAH—THE FASHIONABLE AND
FRIVOLOUS   197

State of Samaria, Judah   198
The Proud, Pampered Women   199
His Warnings Unheeded   201
A Call to Women to Rise Up   202
Moral Decay, Spiritual Decadence   203

Chapter Twenty-two   JEREMIAH—THOSE WHO WORSHIP
FALSE GODS   205

His Feminine Imagery   205
A Call for Mourning Women   207
Prophet's Suffering Over Evils   208
His Cries to All the Women   210

Chapter Twenty-three   EZEKIEL—THE LEWD AND THE
WORSHIPERS OF FALSE CULTS   212

The Unstable Women   213
The Foundling Girl and the Unfaithful Wife   216
The Harlotries of Two Sisters   217
His Own God-Loving Wife   218
How Woman Achieves Moral, Spiritual Rebirth   219

Chapter Twenty-four   WOMAN'S INESCAPABLE MAN-MADE
DISABILITIES   221

Attitude of Pagan Cultures Toward Women   222
Biblical Laws Safeguarding Women   223

No Religious Influence in Babylonian Laws 225
Woman's Rights Under Old Hebrew Laws 227

Section Five

WOMAN'S LEGACY FROM CHRIST AND HIS CHURCH

Chapter Twenty-five   HIS MOTHER, A TRUE HANDMAID OF
LORD 231

Servanthood Akin to Priesthood 232
Mary's Understanding of Servanthood 232
Her Influence on Other Women 235
Other Noble Handmaids in History 235
Those Who Still Suffer for Christ 237

Chapter Twenty-six   HIS EXAMPLE OF PRAYER AND
WORSHIP 240

A Reverent Belief in God 240
The Praying Women About Him 241
His Prayer Fellowship with God 243
His Prayers for and in the Home 245
The Power of Prayer 246

Chapter Twenty-seven   HIS EXAMPLE OF STEWARDSHIP
AND WITNESS 249

Loyal and Disloyal Stewards 250
Eloquent and Effective Witnessing 252
A Twentieth-century Witness 253

Chapter Twenty-eight   ON BRINGING THE VISIBLE FROM
THE INVISIBLE 256

The Honored Heroines of Faith 256

The Healing Light of Jesus   258
Another Blessed Recipient   260
Others of Great Faith   261

Chapter Twenty-nine   HIS SPIRITUAL REVELATIONS TO
    WOMEN   263

The Woman of Samaria—"God Is a Spirit"   264
Martha—"I Am the Resurrection and the Life"   265
Mary Magdalene—"I Ascend Unto My Father"   268
The Benefits to Womanhood   269

Chapter Thirty   HIS OTHER GIFTS   272

His Discourses on Their Daily Lives   273
Woman, Not Subordinate to Man   274
His Restoration of Outcast Women   275
His Thoughtful Concern for Widows   277
His Ageless Morality   278

Chapter Thirty-one   THE MINISTERING WOMEN ABOUT HIM   280

The Many Who Served Him   280
A Womanly Spirit All the Way   282
The "Certain" Women with Him   283
"A Great Company of Women"   284
Those "Beholding Afar Off"   285
The Evidence of Those at the Tomb   286

Chapter Thirty-two   THEIR HARVEST FROM BEARING HIS
    CROSSES   289

Those Who Embraced His Cross   289
Saints Who Endured for Him   291

The Blessings of Suffering 294
The Radiance in a Constant Cross 295

Chapter Thirty-three   THEIR SERVICE TO HIS CHURCH 298

Woman's Home, a Cradle for Church 299
Women Among First Converts 300
Those at Thessalonica, Tyre 301
Those at Seaport of Joppa 301
In the Church at Philippi 302
Helpers in Athens, Corinth, Ephesus, Rome 303
"A Helper of Many" at Cenchreae 304
The Faithful Household of Apphia 305
Other Believers in Roman Church 306
Philip's Daughters at Caesarea 307

Chapter Thirty-four   IMPERISHABLE LEGACY—The Fruits
  of the Spirit 309

Love, the Seed of All Others 310
Joy and Its Indefinable Strength 311
Peace, the Spirit of Acceptance 312
Patience, a Special Need of Women 314
Unwavering Gentleness (Kindness) 315
Goodness, Next to Godliness 316
Faithfulness, an Inheritance from God 316
Meekness, an Indestructible Jewel 317
Self-Control, an Exceptional Quality 319

BIBLIOGRAPHY 321

INDEX 327

THE BIBLE'S LEGACY
FOR WOMANHOOD

Section One

WOMAN'S HIGH DESTINY

CHAPTER ONE

IN THE CREATION

God's legacy to womanhood is both lofty and inexhaustible. This is revealed in the great themes of the Bible and the standards set by the noble women who march through its pages.

Woman's chief legacy is her divine destiny as outlined in the Genesis story of the Creation. She is born to rise toward spiritual perfection until at last she is united with God, her Creator. All the imaginative art and technical genius in the world could never develop a creature of such lofty dignity, beauty of spirit, and loveliness of face and form, as woman in the beginning. But Eve's early transgression illustrates how woman is prone to lose sight of her divine destiny and deny her God-given legacy.

One of the magnificent themes of the Bible is the orderly process of creation, the work of a personal intelligence, harmonious in every concept, and moving ever onward and upward. The creative acts of God, outlined in the first two chapters of Genesis, corroborate this sense of order.

The wonder of the Bible is that it constantly unfolds new vistas of the revealing activity of the living and personal God of the Creation. An older account of the formation of the cosmic universe appears in Psalm 104. This proclaims God as the creator of a boundless universe, one who is "clothed with honour and majesty." Portions of Job and the Second Isaiah, who was influenced by Job, sing the same praise to God, the Creator. In his suffering and despair, Job questioned God's justice, but God answered Job out of a whirlwind and asked, "Where wast thou when I laid the foundations of the earth?" (38:4). In Isaiah we find God's answer on the wonders of man and space further clarified. "I have made the earth, and created man upon it: I, even my hands, have stretched out the heavens, and all their hosts have I commanded. I have raised him up in righteousness, and I will direct all his ways" (45:12–13). This was the Bible's poetic way of describing man and the supernatural wonders above, and modern man has not found a better way to describe them.

Another inspiring Genesis theme of the Creation is that God has made us "after his image." This concept fills us with awe, for we know that we could not exist without God, who is within us. In the knowledge of such mysteries reposes the secret of our own divine destiny.

The story of the Creation seems to say that only as we seek to live by the ideal that God set for us can we fully comprehend his exalted and harmonious plan for the universe. For man and woman's creation is even more wonderful than all his other creations, and only they actually resemble God and have the ability to communicate with him.

To describe our likeness to God in finite terms is impossible. But when we remember that our being is rooted in God who created us, we can press forward to the heart of God himself. He alone can determine and resolve the whole mystery of the unique nature of woman.

The Significance of His Likeness

Because of our limited concept of God, we cannot fully comprehend what God's likeness in (man and) woman fully signifies. But we ask, "Who but God could create a form so lovely, a spirit so rare as that of Eve in the beginning?"

We know the answer. Only God's hand fashioned her, just as he has fashioned us. Only God's wisdom, as declared in the Book of Proverbs, can lead us to make the right choices. In this, Eve failed miserably. Her example of eating the Forbidden Fruit teaches us what happens if we disobey God.

He has made us "upright," says the writer of Ecclesiastes; it is we who have "sought out many inventions" (7:29). It is we who have turned in the wrong direction, forgetting that our lives and our days come from God.

Who are we to think that if we draw away from God we can continue to identify with him and receive his boundless benefits of strength and grace? Who are we to try to live by bread alone, and in so doing, forget our Creator? Only as we strive to live in accord with his divine will (as Jesus did perfectly)—only then can we learn what this likeness to him truly signifies.

The Artist and His Enduring Creations

Michelangelo, says Thomas Craven in his *Men of Art,* "knew how to get his ideas and feelings into marble—to think, one might say, in three dimensions; to endow stone with meaning and vitality; to create a form that thrills . . .

and invades our whole being like a fresh and powerful experience" (p. 151). "Michelangelo's decorations in the Sistine Chapel constitute the greatest single-handed work of art that man has ever produced," according to Craven (p. 143).

Yet Michelangelo, better than anoyne, knew how far he fell short of God's perfection, but in striving for this perfection, he seemed to strive for something that is God.

In his *Pieta*, a marble creation of Mary holding her crucified son on her knee, Michelangelo not only combines the two figures into a harmonious unity but he breathes an ethereal loveliness into the mother, Mary. Her purity and youthfulness linger on in the mind of the beholder, as if they were miraculously wrought to convince the world of the virginity and perpetual purity of the mother.

Man's Masterpiece Indefinable

Leonardo da Vinci created in his *Mona Lisa* a different type of womanhood. This woman with the strange, uncanny smile bespeaks a puzzling serenity, a subtlety and refinement. She seems immortal, and in a sense she is, for she has lived through more than four and a half centuries since Leonardo painted her.

The *Mona Lisa*'s inscrutability stands apart from the paint, color, and canvas from which Leonardo created her. Great lady that she is, she seems to possess an emotional life which, like all life, seems insoluble.

Leonardo, the foremost genius of the Italian Renaissance and perhaps the most versatile genius that ever lived, often asked himself as he painted, "What is soul?" Then he left this aside, along with other unprovable things.

Although Leonardo was also an architect, sculptor, and a pioneer of designs for the first flying machines, based on the flight of birds, he realized better than anyone how far short he was of God's own creativity. Reflecting on his own human inadequacy, Leonardo asked God's mercy for not using all of the resources of his spirit and his art.

God's Creation Unexplainable

Like the master artist's, God's Creation can be no better explained than the flight of the birds, the curve of the tendrils of the vine, the symmetry of leaves and snowflakes, or the whirl of the eddy and hurricane. An art canvas or a sculpture is never perfect but it is nearer God's likeness than any of man's creative expressions.

"A thing is perfect," says Aristotle, "when it lacks nothing in respect to goodness or excellence and cannot be surpassed in its kind." Because God is perfect in knowledge and creation, we can never equal him in anything we try to become, just as the master sculptor or painter can never create a vibrantly alive young maiden. In the graceful beauty of her neck and shoulders, the gentle curve of her breast, the textured beauty of her face, the mobility of her mind and heart, in her emotions, dreams, and ambitions, she represents "the perfect workmanship of God."

The pastor and author Dr. Charles L. Allen, writing on the wonders of the body, describes its electrical and air-conditioning systems and thermostat with its own nervous system connecting every part, and the eyes attached to the brain by three hundred thousand separate and private "telephone" lines. And he makes this penetrating comment, "All the mechanical genius in the world could never develop a hand that could play an organ, paint a picture, or perform a delicate surgical operation. Yet most of us have not one but two."

How can we conceive of the handiwork of the master artist God? It is difficult enough to explain how the master painter creates on canvas and in marble a likeness of palpitating life. Through his God-given talent, he learns somehow to endow stone and canvas with emotion and vitality. He must of course have boundless energy and a mind that perceives lucid grandeur: then he seems to be able to breathe into inanimate materials both life and spirit.

But God's creation is more wondrous than any man ever conceived in his fondest imagination. It is impossible for human beings to duplicate truly even God's simplest forms such as a butterfly with wings that will carry it skyward or a mountain canyon with glints of sunshine reaching into its deepest recesses at given moments of the day. Man, however, will go on reaching for the stars, but never entirely realizing his dreams unless God's hand is upon him.

Woman as Man's Inspirer

In his noblest achievements, woman is man's most mystical inspirer. In *The Divine Comedy* Dante, the great prophetic exponent of the heart of the Middle Ages, leaned heavily upon Beatrice. She was his ideal through Paradise, and Dante saw God because Beatrice's eyes were upon God.

In his eulogy to his saintly mother, Monica, St. Augustine tells how by her example she rescued him from sin, how by her influence she directed his mind from things transitory to things eternal. In religion Jerome, Father and Doctor of the Roman Catholic Church, was aided and inspired in his translation of the Bible by the noble Roman woman Paula and her daughter Eustochium. Paula often worked right beside Jerome as he did his translation from the original Hebrew and Greek text into the Latin Vulgate in the Holy Land, where she is buried. Jerome dedicated some of his Bible books and commentaries to Paula and Eustochium, whom he called his spiritual daughters. Michelangelo had for encouragement one of the noble spirits of the Italian Renaissance, the lovely Vittoria Colonna, who increased his religious faith and inspired him with an ideal of womanhood.

In science the Italian physicist and astronomer Galileo was stimulated by his loving daughter Celeste. Pasteur, the French bacteriologist, had his devoted wife. Jean Louis Agassiz, the celebrated Swiss-American naturalist, had his wife, Elizabeth Cary Agassiz, who was president of Radcliffe College and also remembered because she held her students to the highest ideals of womanhood. John Stuart Mill, the English writer, logician, and economist, spoke from experience when he declared, "Hardly anything can be of greater value to a man of theory and speculation who employs himself, not in collecting materials of knowledge by observation, but in working them up by processes of thought into comprehensive truths of science and laws of conduct than to carry on his speculations in the companionship and under the criticism of a really superior woman."

A Summons to Decency, Greatness

Most of the world's unique achievements represent the combined talents of both men and women. Leon Bloy, the instigator of the French Catholic Renaissance, understood this when he said, that "the holier a woman is, the more she is a woman." What a noble concept of and what a constant challenge to womanhood! How then is woman to exert her birthright and realize that she is "fearfully and wonderfully made?"

Isn't it possible to summon us again to greatness and decency, despite the developing and debased pattern for womanhood as mirrored in the new sex standards (or lack of standards), in pornographic literature, lurid sex films, and other decaying modes of morality which accentuate the most depraved instincts in womanhood? Has woman lost sight of her divine destiny as set forth in the Bible? Has she denied for too long her unlimited God-given legacy? Are excellence and goodness outdated in this century? Or has our concentration on science and technology caused us to lay aside permanently the ageless formulas, such as those that guided America's strongest characters in its frontier days? Has woman, the true inspirer of man in all that is good and true, forgotten how to cast her gaze Godward?

Although America has evolved in this century from an agrarian to an urban civilization, with complex new problems, God has not changed. It is we who have changed in our relationship to him. How can we again better communicate with him? What can we do to better equip ourselves in our own sphere as women? What are our God-given rights and privileges—yes, and our responsibilities?

In the two succeeding sections of this book, we shall attempt to give the Bible's answers to these and other penetrating questions when, as the Psalmist says, God's word once more can become "a lamp unto my feet, and a light unto my path" (Ps. 119:105).

CHAPTER TWO

IN HER COMMUNICATION
WITH GOD

Varied are the Bible records of men and women who saw celestial creatures fly down out of space, appear as intermediaries from God, and then vanish as suddenly as they came. Whether these were allegories told to present a spiritual experience we do not know, but the Bible does reverently refer to angels who seemed to represent the highest conceivable mode of communication between Creature and Creator.

Although the Bible never gives the source of their origin, it does depict these celestial creatures as appearing in mortal form and speaking in human voices, as if they represented a special communication system between God and those who sought a filial relationship with him.

The devout in Bible times had an abiding faith in angels, who either appeared to convey the mandates of God, to protect the faithful, or to usher in special events. Sometimes, the scriptures tell of angels who appeared suddenly as if from a cloud. Clothed in celestial light, to these primitive people, angels seemed to travel on wings of magic or through prisms of light. Sometimes they appeared to be exactly like other human beings, but their bodies were transitory and they vanished almost as quickly as they came.

MINISTERS TO THE RIGHTEOUS

The Bible describes angels as "an innumerable multitude," superior to man in power and intelligence. It pictures them as ministering to the righteous, as delivering those in need of God's protection, such as going before them in battle and leading them to victory, of bringing food out of nowhere to the hungry, of forming a protecting arm around the afflicted, of opening prison doors, and of executing judgment upon the wicked.

Finally, it refers to angels as "ministering spirits, sent forth to serve, for the sake of those who are to obtain salvation" (Heb. 1:14, RSV). Whatever their mission they always seemed to have knowledge of and interest in earthly affairs.

More than two hundred Bible passages allude to angels who perform the work of his spirit. Many of the God-loving believed with the Psalmist that "he shall give his angels charge over thee, to keep thee in all thy ways" (91:11). Sometimes these divine beings were not called angels at all, but spokesmen for God from the unknown, who were concerned with the ordinary everyday relationships of his people.

From the door of her tent, when she was old and past the age to bear children, Sarah saw three strange men (beings of a supernatural character) appear quite unexpectedly before her husband, Abraham, to announce that she would conceive a son who would be born in the natural way. The miraculous birth of Sarah's son, Isaac, exemplified God's wondrous power, because both she and Abraham were past the age to have children, a fact as unexplainable as creatures from outer space.

How can such mysteries be accounted for? As the visitors told Abraham, nothing is "too hard for the Lord" (Gen. 18:14). Although Sarah was more childlike in her response to these divine beings than was Abraham, the Father of the Faithful, her trust in what they told implies her faith in the unseen.

GUARDIANS OF WELFARE

Angels appeared to the worthy and the unworthy alike, for God is no respecter of persons. Abraham's concubine, the "bond woman," had an experience with an angel after she was cast into the wilderness with Ishmael, her son by Abraham. As the child was dying from starvation,

> God heard the voice of the lad; and the angel of God called to Hagar out of heaven, and said unto her, What aileth thee, Hagar? fear not; for God hath heard the voice of the lad where he is.
>
> Arise, lift up the lad, and hold him in thine hand; for I will make him a great nation. (Gen. 21:17–18)

The guardian angel, who had watched over Hagar in her distress, served as the intermediary to bring her closer to God and to save her and her son from starvation and death. Hagar's experience reassures us that in moments when we seem neglected and forsaken, God is ever close at hand, if we only seek him. We too can learn that these unseen intermediaries, call them angels or celestial spirits or whatever you may, can become guardians of our welfare.

Samson's mother had a similar experience to Sarah's and not unlike Hagar's. An angel of the Lord appeared to her and said, "Behold, you are barren and have no children; but you shall conceive and bear a son" (Judg. 13:3, RSV). And Samson's mother rushed forward to tell her husband, Manoah, that "a man of God came to me, and his countenance was like the countenance of the angel of God, very terrible; but I did not ask him whence he was, and he did not tell me his name" (v. 6).

Manoah and his wife offered food to this man of God, but instead of accepting it, he suggested that they burn it for an offering. While Manoah and his wife looked on, the messenger ascended in the flame, and Manoah said to his wife, "We shall surely die, for we have seen God" (Judg. 13:22, RSV), but his wife assured him that he need not fear, for God's promise would be fulfilled. And it was miraculously accomplished in the birth of their son Samson, one of the early heroes of the Hebrew people.

Although this story comes out of the folklore of a primitive people, as do some of the others, this one teaches that Samson's mother was a woman who feared God, helping us to understand better the words of the Psalmist, "the angel of the Lord encampeth round about them that fear him, and delivereth them" (34:7). We, like the Psalmist, learn to see that the Lord is God and that if we sufficiently trust in him he will guide and keep us no matter how many are our afflictions or how desolate we may seem.

THE ANGELS IN MARY'S LIFE

Angels surrounded Jesus from the moment of his conception until his Resurrection. Luke records that an angel sped from the court of heaven to the city of Galilee to announce to a meek virgin the Messiah's approaching birth.

What would the Christmas story be without the presence of angels? Or how would we know Mary, in whose life there were so many miracles and wonders such as the approaching birth of her child? Young and not sure of herself, Mary questioned the angel who told her, "The Holy Spirit will come upon you, and the power of the Most High will overshadow you: and for that reason the holy child to be born will be called 'Son of God.' . . . Then the angel left her" (Luke 1:35, 38, NEB).

What woman, exploring for an answer to her questioning, ever had a more profound answer? The angel's explanation makes us know that we are not computers receiving mechanical equations which are available to anyone punching a button, but we can be God-attuned individuals, who too can learn that with God nothing is impossible.

Mary saw her own child grow under the watch and guardianship of angels, one of whom warned her husband, Joseph, in a dream to flee into Egypt with the young child and his mother, to escape Herod's persecution. Through the years of Christ's childhood, angels invisibly attended him and marveled at the mystery which humbled him to such a destiny. They were even witnesses to his Resurrection.

OTHER BEINGS BEYOND SOLAR SYSTEM

We know little more today about life on other planets than these primitive people knew about angels, but no doubt a great unfoldment awaits when science delves deeply into a study of these and other unexplainable cosmic forces. Recent findings, however, give considerable support to the idea that intelligent civilizations exist beyond our own solar system. Angels are believed to be conscious of the secrets of the cosmos, called "extraordinary mysteries" in the Dead Sea Scrolls. It is also perceived they sometimes are conjoined with cosmic "powers and principalities."

The great John Milton felt the presence of angels when he declared, "Millions of spiritual creatures walk the earth unseen, both when we sleep and when we wake." The nineteenth-century clergyman Edwin Hubbell Chapin believed that "the angels may have a wider sphere of action and nobler forms of duty than ourselves but truth and right to them and to us are one and the same thing." At Pope John's famous 1962 Ecumenical Council, church fathers privately discussed the potential actuality of angels, it was reported.

A few imaginative individuals today theorize there do exist on other planets beings of another form, probably of a higher degree of intelligence than our own. And they intimate that we shall learn how to tune in with these other beings, now far removed and invisible, just as we have learned how to radio to an astronaut hanging in the hazeless clarity of space, where his day is only minutes from dawn to dusk and where his spacecraft glides as if by magic.

Ever in the Presence of His Spirit

The believing women of Bible times and later arouse in us a sense of the miraculous we cannot explain. Through their faith in their ability to communicate with God, we too can learn how to do the same. Even during sleep, a nightly journey more mysterious than a flight to the moon, we have experiences that are far removed from our daily lives. Later, we can only question this state of consciousness which we do not yet fully understand.

Of this we can be sure. Thoughts are magnetic forces, as unexplainable and powerful as electricity. If dreams do suggest other degrees of consciousness not comparable to our own, who are we to say that angels are only figments of the imagination? In a world filled with uncertainty, it is refreshing to take childlike flights of fancy with angels, in whose realm we can wing our own thoughts to where dwell those who seek communication with God. Then we better understand these words of the Psalmist:

Whither shall I go from thy spirit? or whither shall I flee from thy presence?

If I ascend up into heaven, thou art there: . . .

If I take the wings of the morning, and dwell in the uttermost parts of the sea;

Even there shall thy hand lead me, and thy right hand shall hold me.   (139:7–10)

Or this one which the astronauts on Apollo 10 considered of special significance as they returned from a near pass over the moon and set forth to earth on a Sunday morning, thinking of their own church on their home planet:

When I consider thy heavens, the work of thy fingers, the moon and the stars, which thou has ordained;

What is man, that thou art mindful of him? and the son of man that thou visitest him?

For thou hast made him a little lower than the angels, and has crowned him with glory and honour.

(8:3–5)

As the Apollo 11 astronauts passed the halfway mark of their starlit journey home, Edwin E. Aldrin, Jr., brought to mind the same praise from Psalm 8. And, again, an enthralled world became less earthbound because he and Neil A. Armstrong had left footprints on the moon and had brought to life a new age for mankind.

As Von Braun, one of the pioneers in the space program, said, man too gained a certain kind of immortality, for he had left the earth planet and begun a realistic exploration of the heavens. Suddenly they had become too infinite for man's comprehension. Now man began to talk of Mars or other planets where could dwell other creatures who might have a closer communion with God and who might understand some of the mysteries of God's creation that we do not yet comprehend.

CHAPTER THREE

IN HER
RELATIONSHIP TO GOD

Although the women described in the preceding chapter were far removed in time from miraculous mass communications, their means of contact with the invisible God excelled ours. Primitive though the women of Israel seemed in their beliefs about God, the vital thing to them was that he was ever present. They saw him in the changing forms of rain clouds, in the sunshine over flower-dotted hills, in the sunset's flash of crimson splendor, and in the stillness of flocks and herds slowly wending their way to watering troughs.

They never forgot, either, God's part in the miracles of their own national history, the thunder and lightning over Mount Sinai, the transfiguration of the face of Moses, and the fall of manna in their desert wanderings. They saw all events, whether supernatural or commonplace, as revelations of God; and in their constant awareness of the miraculous, they nurtured faith which they passed on to their children and their children's children.

Unfathomable are some of today's miracles, namely, computers, superhuman in their skills, and spaceships that fly to the moon. Man himself alone could not conceive of or achieve such wonders. And yet there are those who say, "God is dead."

But to the God-loving women in Bible times God was never dead. He could not be, for they kept him alive in their hearts. Only the foolish would say, "There is no God" (Ps. 53:1). Such fools, continues the Psalmist, "Corrupt are they, and have done abominable iniquity: there is none that doeth good."

With those who continually sought a closer relationship to God, the theme of the Bible, we can hear the echo of the Psalmist: "O God . . . send out thy light and thy truth: let them lead me; let them bring us into thy holy hill, and to thy tabernacles" (43:3). Their demonstrations make us confident that God does hear the supplications of those who conscientiously seek and serve him.

WONDERS AMID HEARTACHE, TEMPTATION

Even Eve, who first fell far short of God's plan, through conflict and hardship gradually drew closer to God. At the birth of her first son, Cain, who afterward brought her so many heartaches, she realized the miracle of birth itself when she said, "I have gotten a man from the Lord" (Gen. 4:1). But this first son was not to have the good qualities of Eve's second son, Abel, who gave generously of the best that he had to the Lord, while Cain kept the best for himself and afterward, out of jealousy, killed Abel.

Abel's life was not in vain. His score for goodness was never lost. Even in the New Testament it is written that "through faith he continued to speak after his death" (Heb. 11:4, NEB).

Eve no doubt grew closer and closer to God in the later years of her motherhood, for in the remarkable record of her words at the birth of her last son, Seth, she declares, "God hath appointed me another seed instead of Abel, whom Cain slew" (Gen. 4:25). When Eve's grandson Enos (Enosh, RSV) was born to Seth, "then began men to call upon the name of the Lord" (4:26).

It is comforting to know that even after temptation and disobedience, Eve turned back to God. Her later revelations, centering around her life as a mother, confirm that God is ever present when we need him most and when he may seem farthest from us.

A Mother's Close Walk with God

Jochebed, the mother of Moses, was the member of a priestly family (Num. 26:59). This godly woman probably did not live to see her son become one of Israel's spiritual giants, but she recognized that he was born to a high destiny when he was only a young babe. And what a fore-ordained future! He it was who talked with the Lord on Mount Sinai and who, after praying there for forty days and nights, came down with Israel's basic laws, which contain clues to the good life. In her fondest imagination, however, Jochebed, could never have dreamed that she would produce a son who would fill such a remarkable place in God's plan.

It was Jochebed no doubt who summoned her other children to excellence, her son Aaron, the first head of the Hebrew priesthood, and her daughter, Miriam, who sang to God as she led the women of Israel across the Sea of

Reeds as if it were dry land, just as had her brother Moses when he led the men of Israel in the advance guard.

Like the resourceful Jochebed and Miriam, who saved Moses for his historic role, we can learn through them that God is ever present when we seek him. Through many tribulations, including bondage, an unjust Pharaoh, a new Egyptian law that would have killed Moses at birth, this mother and daughter pressed on in the knowledge that God would deliver all of them. And he did, much more miraculously than they could have ever imagined, and all because they bore a unique relationship to God.

REJOICING IN THE LORD

Ruth's mother-in-law, Naomi, also had an intimate contact with God. When she learned how kindly her kinsman Boaz had treated her son's widow, Ruth, on the first days she worked in his field as a gleaner, Naomi prayed out loud, "Blessed be he of the Lord, who hath not left off his kindness to the living and to the dead" (Ruth 2:20), meaning that God had shown faithfulness, kindness, and mercy to her daughter-in-law as well as to her son's memory. Through Naomi's rejoicing, we come closer to a God whose goodness and truth know no bounds.

Hannah, the woman with a sorrowful spirit because she had had no son, never forgot God in her many trials. We can hear her praying in the house of God at Shiloh:

My heart rejoiceth in the Lord. . . . There is none holy as the Lord, for there is none beside thee, neither is there any rock like our God. . . . The Lord is a God

of knowledge, and by him actions are weighed. . . .
The Lord maketh poor, and maketh rich, he bringeth
low, and lifteth up. He raiseth up the poor out of the
dust, and lifteth up the beggar from the dunghill,
to set them among princes, and to make them inherit
the throne of glory: for the pillars of the earth are the
Lord's and he hath set the world upon them. He will
keep the feet of his saints, and the wicked shall be
silent in darkness; for by strength shall no man pre-
vail. The adversaries of the Lord shall be broken to
pieces . . .   (I Sam. 2:1–3; 7–10)

This, one of the Bible's most positive affirmations of
what God is, shows that Hannah never doubted God's
goodness, even through her many trials. So fervent was her
desire to live closely to God that we begin to understand
that only one as devout as she could have given birth to
such a marvelous son as Samuel, the last of the judges, a
seer and a priest and the first of the prophets after Moses.

What would Hannah have been had she not maintained
a close relationship to God, the unseen power of the universe? And what would her son have become without such
a mother?

Abigail, another God-loving woman, restored David's
belief in God when he was young and when he needed to
be reminded of the importance of seeking closer relationship with him (I Sam. 25:28–31). In so doing, Abigail
helps us to declare with confidence that God lives, that he
is a "preserver of life," and that our souls are as immortal
as God, our Maker.

God's Abundant Supply

From the prophet Elijah, the widow of Zarephath discovered that God will supply his children abundantly, even in the midst of lack. Elijah had been without food once himself, and the ravens had miraculously fed him. So he could say confidently to this widow without food, "Fear not." After her last meal and oil were gone, she learned that God would not fail her from his infinite source.

Sometime afterward, when the widow's son died suddenly, probably of malnutrition suffered earlier, Elijah performed a second miracle, that of raising the son from the dead. Now she could say to him with assurance, "I know that thou art a man of God, and that the word of the Lord in thy mouth is truth" (I Kings 17:24), for the old prophet had given her a new knowledge of God, one who sustains in time of famine and one who raises the dead to life again.

Elijah's protégé, Elisha, revealed to another poor widow that God can bring forth plenty in the midst of scarcity. Her husband left so many debts at his death that his creditor had already come to take her two sons to be his slaves. As a last resort the widow appealed to Elisha, who had known her husband, and who gave her a marvelous demonstration of plenty as revealed in II Kings 4:3–7. Her experience helps us to declare with positive assurance that "the Lord will be a refuge for the oppressed, a refuge in times of trouble" (Ps. 9:9).

In direct contrast to this poor widow's experience with God's demonstration of plenty is that of the woman of

Shunem, who knew no poverty but had plenty of other trials. Twice Elisha renewed the latter's faith in the impossible, once when she and an aging husband had a son and again when Elisha raised that son from the dead. A third time her faith in the impossible was fulfilled. During a later famine, before her storehouse was empty, Elisha advised her to depart with her household from Shunem and live in the land of the Philistines, which she did for seven years. When she returned, the king, learning of the miracles surrounding her life, appointed an official to "restore all that was hers, and all the fruits of the field since the day that she left the land, even until now" (II Kings 8:6).

This woman of Shunem, who had experienced the sorrow of childlessness, plus death and famine, now fully understood that as a child of God she could always take refuge in him.

In moments of peril, fear, and dismay, these women tell us that God does not cast us out but sustains, controls, guides, and uplifts us, if we remain obedient to him.

His Omnipotence and Omniscience

We can never doubt God's omnipotence, either. Our knowledge of him, gained by those mentioned above and other great men and women of the Bible, strengthens our understanding of his marvelous power. We sense his omnipresence too and come to understand better Jacob's dream of heaven at Bethel, when he said, "Surely the Lord is in this place; and I knew it not" (Gen. 28:16). With

Jeremiah we also hear God's searching question, "Am I a God at hand . . . and not a God afar off" (23:23).

Of his omniscience we can be certain too, for he is a wise God. By wisdom he "made the heavens" (Ps. 136:5). His "understanding is infinite" (Ps. 147:5). He reveals deep and secret things, as Daniel (2:22) learned so well. Also as we seek to draw nearer him, we hear an echo of Job's plaintive words, "Lo, he goeth by me, and I see him not: he passeth on also, but I perceive him not" (9:11). Through the experiences of all of these we come to know a God who is also changeless, invisible, infinite, holy, just, one who is filled with light, love, power, righteousness, truth, and wisdom, a being wondrous, a power incomprehensible.

A Woman Saint's Walk with God

God-loving women all through history have sought a closer communion with God, and in the transmission of their thoughts with him, we too can learn how to walk with him. One of these was the Blessed Angela. The Blessed Angela was born in the thirteenth century, twenty-four years after the death of St. Francis. Until Angela became imbued with the ideals of St. Francis, a true man of God, she had lived a frivolous social life in her provincial town of Foligno, Italy. She thought a lot about fashionable clothes, about dyeing her hair and styling it correctly, so that she might attract attention as she went from one meaningless pursuit to another.

After the death of her husband and sons during the bubonic plague that swept Italy, Angela detached herself

from materiality. Love for God and Christ so filled her
heart that her old love for things dropped away little by
little. And she began to have great visions of God, in one
of which, according to Lucy Menzies in her *Mirrors of the
Holy*, Angela said:

> Immediately the eyes of my soul were opened and
> I beheld the plenitude of God, whereby I did com-
> prehend the whole world, both here and beyond the
> sea, and the abyss and all things else; and therein did
> I behold naught save the divine Power in a manner
> assuredly indescribable, so that through excess of
> marvelling the soul cried with a loud voice, saying,
> "This whole world is full of God!" Wherefore did I
> now comprehend that the world is but a small thing!
> I saw, moreover, that the power of God was above all
> things, and that the whole world was filled with it.
>
> (Pp. 75–76)

An educated woman for medieval times, Angela became
a skilled writer and dictated her revelations in a spiritual
biography, *The Book of Divine Consolation*. This was lost
for several centuries, but the light she had received in her
vision of God could not remain hidden indefinitely. Evelyn
Underhill tells us that:

> In reading Angela's biography we seem to be pres-
> ent "at veritable outpourings of the Divine Mind,
> crystallized into verbal form on their way through the
> human consciousness." We feel on the one hand a one-

ness with the Absolute, on the part of the mystic which has made her really, for the time being, the "voice of God," while on the other we recognized in her the persistence of the individual—exalted, but not yet wholly absorbed in the Divine—whose questions, here and there break in upon the revelation which is mediated by the deeper mind.   (*Mysticism*, p. 277)

The Blessed Angela so trained herself in the disciplined, selfless way of the spiritual life that she began to realize more fully God's wonders. Such a divine change began to take place in her soul that she discerned she possessed God in such fullness that she was now a new being. She had learned to accomplish the miraculous, not through herself but through God. Most of all she had learned that rather than make endless supplication to him for personal blessings she first must learn to serve him, and when she did, she walked in such perfect peace of mind that she was content in all things.

On Building the Kingdom of God

The Blessed Angela and other God-loving women have handed down to us a priceless legacy. Through their recorded communion with God, we too can learn how to build a reservoir of spiritual strength with which to meet life's crises, which come to all of us.

We have to discover how to be wise enough to take things as they come and to know that God works through all of them. However, we cannot buy this serenity of spirit at a counter like a loaf of bread or apply it hurriedly like rouge to the face. We have to work and most of all be willing to suffer for it.

To experience God as did these great souls of the past is to learn those values with which he is identified and which they found workable. To reverence God is to venerate the order in which his values are incarnate, otherwise our adoration of him has little meaning. Thus, in seeking a closer relationship with God, we are helping to build the Kingdom of God.

CHAPTER FOUR

IN THE STREAM
OF THE GENERATIONS

It took the wisest of the Hebrews to exalt womanhood to the eminence achieved in the excellent woman of Proverbs (31:10–31), who typifies all of the best qualities in womanhood. This twenty-two-verse acrostic has probably done more than any single work in either biblical or classical literature to elevate woman to her high destiny and her spiritual capacity.

The marvelous aspect of this is that it faithfully guards one of woman's most valuable legacies, her womanliness, and highlights as well her noblest qualities: virtue, feminine tenderness, strength, honor, trust, diligence, foresight, ingenuity, compassion for the poor and needy, wisdom, kindness, creativity in the homemaking arts, and a love for God. Most of all it accentuates her foremost role, that of wife, mother, and homemaker, and sets her apart as a shining example to her children and her husband, who have implicit trust in her.

Although the word ideal is never used to describe a woman in any of the Bible translations, its counterparts, righteous, blameless, and excellent, occur often. Elisabeth, the mother of John the Baptist, for example, is described along with her husband, Zacharias, a priest, as "righteous before God, walking in all the commandments and ordinances of the Lord blameless" (Luke 1:6).

The adjective excellent (precious in RSV but not nearly so descriptive) has many beautiful connotations in the Bible. The woman who strives for perfection is an excellent woman. For example, the Psalmist exclaims, "How excellent is thy loving kindness, O God" (36:7). God, we come to realize, has love and kindness for us, even when we fall short of what he would have us be.

An Inspiring Portrait of Womankind

It is interesting to note that this twenty-two-verse portrayal in Proverbs, as shown below, first pays tribute to the maiden and wife (10–12), then to the homemaker (13–22), to the wife again (23), once more to the homemaker (24–27), then to the mother and wife (28), and finally to the woman herself in the three verses of the finale (29–31).

In its superb delineation of excellency in womanhood, this portrayal never grows old or monotonous but actually more beautiful with time. It is no wonder that it is literature's most superb description of the best in womanhood both now and then.

10. Who can find a virtuous woman? for her price is far above rubies.
11. The heart of her husband doth safely trust in her, so that he shall have no need of spoil.
12. She will do him good and not evil all the days of her life.

13. She seeketh wool, and flax, and worketh willingly with her hands.

14. She is like the merchants' ships; she bringeth her food from afar.

15. She riseth also while it is yet night, and giveth meat to her household, and a portion to her maidens.

16. She considereth a field, and buyeth it: with the fruit of her hands she planteth a vineyard.

17. She girdeth her loins with strength, and strengtheneth her arms.

18. She perceiveth that her merchandise is good: her candle goeth not out by night.

19. She layeth her hands to the spindle, and her hands hold the distaff.

20. She stretcheth out her hand to the poor; yea, she reacheth forth her hands to the needy.

21. She is not afraid of the snow for her household: for all her household are clothed with scarlet.

22. She maketh herself coverings of tapestry; her clothing is silk and purple.

23. Her husband is known in the gates, when he sitteth among the elders of the land.

24. She maketh fine linen, and selleth it; and delivereth girdles unto the merchant.

25. Strength and honour are her clothing; and she shall rejoice in time to come.

26. She openeth her mouth with wisdom; and in her tongue is the law of kindness.

27. She looketh well to the ways of her household, and eateth not the bread of idleness.

28. Her children arise up and call her blessed; her husband also, and he praiseth her.
29. Many daughters have done virtuously, but thou excellest them all.
30. Favour is deceitful, and beauty is vain: but a woman that feareth the Lord, she shall be praised.
31. Give her of the fruit of her hands; and let her own works praise her in the gates.

This radiant tribute to womanhood immediately follows observations on "the adulterous woman," who "eateth and wipeth her mouth, and saith, I have done no wickedness" (30:20), and the "odious woman" (30:23), who when she is married, disturbs everything around her.

This clever application of contrast, first the bad and then the good, is one of the many reasons why the Bible continues to make a tremendous contribution to our intellectual, moral, and spiritual life, as well as to give perpetuity and unity to our civilization. The Book of Proverbs itself, never surpassed as a masterpiece of reflection, has a dynamic power over our way of life and a potential for great reactions within our souls.

No Old Testament Woman So Ideal

Not a single woman in the Old Testament epitomizes all of these good qualities, but we do find one or several of them idealized in individual women. For example, we can imagine that this woman in her maidenhood would have been like the chaste and thoughtful Rebekah, whose admirable qualities were immediately apparent to Abraham's steward when he chose her for Isaac's bride. It is also easy to imagine that this ideal woman in her maidenhood would be cast in the same mold as Jephthah's daughter, who was willing to sacrifice all for what was morally right.

She might resemble too the well beloved Rachel and the worthy Ruth. The latter retained her noble qualities through widowhood and her second marriage and never forsook the good and the true. Like Deborah, this excellent woman could be called "a mother in Israel." Like Sarah, the wife of Abraham and the mother of Isaac, her husband would be known in the gates and her children and grandchildren would call her blessed. Like Huldah, she would fear the Lord. Like Hannah, the mother of Samuel, she would be clothed with strength and honor, which is of far greater significance than to say she was the richest woman in Israel, or that she ruled over it with an iron will, as did the hated Athaliah.

The Influence of the Noble Wife, Mother

The wife and mother who possesses even a few of these noble qualities, as exemplified in these Old Testament women, is able to face life with dignity, imagination, modesty, tact, compassion, and reverence. People respect her so highly that she has no need to seek honors. Old people find comfort in her faith. Handicapped people find courage in her strength. Young people, through her, renew their allegiance to that which is beautiful and good and true. Women rejoice in the things she stands for, and men find new strength and security in her presence.

Such a woman is never desolate or destitute because she has God to sustain her. She learns that only in upholding that which is good can she attain that for which God intended her. Only in love for her fellow man, even for those who despitefully use her, can she achieve true excellence.

A Part of Life's Universal Stream

The Bible seems to say to us that only in the elevation of woman, especially mothers, can womanhood accept its divine place in God's plan. When a mother falls from grace, the whole family of mankind suffers, for a mother is the silent carrier of those great, historically effective talents. Man spends his talents but woman transmits them.

This is why it is so dangerous to a nation's welfare when large numbers of women, especially its mothers, turn to dope addiction, alcoholism, atheism, adultery, and other demoralizing modes of behavior. Because woman in her motherhood represents the continuity of the race, she must be its standard-bearer.

In her significant book *The Eternal Woman*, Gertrud von le Fort, German author, describes a mother's role this way:

As woman primarily denotes not personality but its surrender, so also the endurance that she is able to give to her descendants is not self-assertion, but something purchased at the expense of submerging herself into the universal stream of succeeding generations. . . . Even the experience which is most fundamentally her own, the passing on of life and heritage of blood, remains nameless and concealed as far as she herself is concerned. The great stream of all the forces that have made and will continue to make history proceeds through the woman who bears no other name than that of mother. Our time does justice to this elemental fact when it values woman first of all as mother.   (P. 18)

CHAPTER FIVE

IN HER ROLE
AS "KEEPER OF THE SPRINGS"

As we study the spiritual as well as the physical aspects of the life of the ideal homemaker, so well portrayed in the Book of Proverbs and quoted in the preceding chapter, we come to understand that the home such as she fashioned was more than its members. She created a spiritual entity built out of the imponderable things of the spirit, where her husband, her children, and her household helpers obtained a foretaste of the heavenly kingdom, because in such a home, more than anywhere else in all the world, everyone counted. For everyone loved and everyone led a meaningful and responsible life, most of all this ideal homekeeper herself. Her dwelling place became a sanctuary, and across its portals, like that of a church, could be inscribed, "This is none other but the house of God and this is the gate of heaven" (Gen. 28:17).

She had many talents and she used them all well for the creation of a haven for her husband and children. Like the willing and generous women, who gave of their time and talent to make altar pieces for that first tabernacle built by Moses and Aaron, she sought wool and flax and worked willingly with her hands. We can think of her too as a "great woman" like the Shunammite, superior in mind and heart and spirit, and like Abigail, "the woman of good understanding."

We see her also as a woman of tremendous energy as well as a devotee to beauty. She was so adept in all of the homemaking arts that all who came into her home were refreshed in body and spirit.

BREAD OF IDLENESS UNTASTED

Although her days were filled with hard work, they also held beauty and drama from morning until night. She arose while it was yet dark, laid out tasks for her maidservants and started the preparation of food before her family awakened. Probably she had brought some of it from afar the day before, either by a cart drawn by an ass or atop a donkey.

This woman comes into clearer perspective after a careful study of the Proverbs' acrostic along with a wide variety of books on home life in Bible times, several of which are listed in the bibliography. She spun wool and flax from which she fashioned clothes for all of her household. In addition she wove other garments and girdles (sashes), which she sold in the market place and delivered in person. Since there was much barter and trade in these times, she probably exchanged her handcrafts, poultry, and garden produce for foods she did not raise.

Her largest field was a vineyard where she raised grapes that she either sold or made into wine for ceremonial or health purposes for her household. We can imagine that she went through all of the processes that Isaiah describes of God's activity for his children in his parable of the vineyard (fifth chapter). If so, she chose a fertile hill, had it dug and cleared of stones, planted it with choice vines, and hewed out a wine vat in the center of it. After the tender plants appeared in April, she had a vinedresser cut away branches, and when the grapes were ripe, she probably directed her own household, her children, and her maids as they harvested the grapes and carried them to the wine press.

This was a joyous vocation for a householder, especially at harvest season, when the new grapes were deposited at the presses, and whole families joined in an autumn festival and the singing of vintage songs. A small segment of one of these in Isaiah 65:8 gives us an idea of what a happy time this was for a household, such as that presided over by this excellent homemaker.

She and her maids tended flocks and herds of goats and sheep, as had Jethro's daughters when Moses came upon them in the Midian wilderness. They might also have gathered honey from the wild bees, as had Samson when he went down to Timnath to call on the Philistine woman he was courting and afterward married. In the spring the women helped with the outside work, for there was much to be done in this agricultural civilization, and it took the efforts of both men and women.

They drew water from a cistern, such as the Bahurim woman had done when she hid David's trusted messengers in her cistern, or from a well, such as Rebekah had done for Abraham's steward. Although the water supply was sometimes short, we can imagine that this homemaker and her maidservants learned to sing with the Psalmist:

Thou visitest the earth, and waterest it: thou greatly enrichest it with the river of God, which is full of water: thou prepared them corn, when thou hast so provided for it.

Thou waterest the ridges thereof abundantly: thou settlest the furrows thereof: thou makest it soft with showers: thou blessest the springing thereof.

Thou crownest the year with thy goodness; and thy paths drop fatness.

They drop upon the pastures of the wilderness: and the little hills rejoice on every side.

The pastures are clothed with flocks; the valleys also are covered over with corn; they shout for joy, they also sing.   (Ps. 65:9–13)

Her Flowers, Trees, and Herbs

We can also imagine that the house of this versatile homemaker, whether she lived in village or country, was surrounded by an abundance of wild flowers in the spring. Among these were the anemone, daisy, asphodel, rose, salvia, lily, marigold, and the star-of-Bethlehem, all common in Bible times. She might also have cultivated closer to her house the rose of Sharon, which resembled a species of narcissus. As winter faded to early spring, she also had crocuses, hyacinths, and gladioli blooming in many colors. She probably could look from her house into an orchard of apricot, apple, pomegranate, date, olive, and almond trees. For shade she might have sycamore, pine, balsam, and bay trees, the latter with lovely white blooms like a magnolia only smaller; also boxwood, cypress, and myrtle bushes.

She also cultivated her own herbs, including leek, garlic, and onions for seasoning her lamb and goat meats, as had Rebekah when she made the savory stew for Jacob to serve to Esau. This homemaker grew other herbs for medicinal, cosmetic, and worship purposes, and wormwood for making hyssop, an antiseptic powder. The latter is referred to in Psalm 51:7, "Purge me with hyssop, and I shall be clean." She also had her own cane, anise, and dill. The anise was used as a healing wash for skin wounds, the cane for making sugar, and the dill for seasoning sour condiments.

She raised her own lentils, too, in several varieties, as well as pumpkins, cucumbers, melons, and greens. Her flocks and herds included pigeons, antelope, gazelles, and fatted hens, as well as sheep and goats.

If affluent enough, she probably had her own press for olives, which she and her maids raised themselves. When the olives turned black, they gathered and crushed them on a large upright wheel made of stone, and used the oil from them for cooking.

HER KITCHEN EQUIPMENT AND FOODS

This homemaker of the time of Proverbs, compiled probably during the fourth and fifth century B.C., baked in a large clay bowl with a removable lid, heated by hot stones. After grinding her own flour, she added to it salt, olive oil, water or milk, and yeast. The latter was made with a little sour milk and some flour, and allowed to stand in a warm place for several hours or overnight. When the bread was removed steaming hot from the oven, it was served with melted butter and honey, or sometimes with ripe olives.

Among other kitchen furnishings were ceramic vessels, twenty-five to thirty inches in height, for storage, cooking, and eating. The storage jars were used to keep water, wine, and grain. Also common were clay cooking pots, most of which held about two quarts.

Other kitchen items were utensils, such as meat hooks or forks, ladles, a goatskin butter churn operated by shaking it back and forth, and skins for cooling water. A necessary accessory was a hand mill of two stones used for grinding grains. In the kitchen, too, which often served as an all-round work area, was the distaff, spindle, and looms for weaving cloth and making clothes.

Her Lamps of Special Significance

This ideal woman not only pressed out oil for cooking but for her lamps as well. She probably had many, for they signified the divine presence, and the woman with a lamp that did not go out by night became one who gave spiritual as well as visible light to her household. The symbolic power is that God is the lamp lighting the darkness (II Sam. 22:29).

The lamps in this ancient home most likely were of clay saucers set in a niche in the wall. These were filled with olive oil, which fed a wick of hemp or peeled rush which rested on the rim of the saucer. The same lamp was used to kindle a fire, either for the cooking vats or the brazier (portable fireplace) for heat in the winter.

HER HOME, A HOSPITABLE PLACE

Household furnishings included stools, legged tables, chests of cedar, and wooden bedsteads. Across the latter were spread carpets or striped covers so that the bed could serve as a couch by day. Other sleeping comforts could include a wool-filled mattress, homemade goat-hair quilts, and coverlets. A wooden cradle used for sleeping and rocking babies hung from the roof beams. The family probably included at least seven children, the average size in these early times.

This homemaker's house was hospitable. Strangers were welcome at all times, and she set nutritious meals before her guests and her family. These might include fragrant, coarse brown bread, dairy products, fish, meat, melons, berries, honey, pistachio nuts, almonds, and dried fruit. She probably served on the floor where she laid mats woven of straw and grass. Dishes placed in the center held large portions of food, and guests dipped into them.

During their nomad days the early Israelites lived in caves or tents, but this homemaker, of the time of the Book of Proverbs, lived in a house of either dried mud or uncut field stone set in mortar. It might also have had a staircase to the flat roof, such as Bath-sheba was seen bathing upon when David caught a glimpse of her from his own roof. Such a roof was reached from a walled court, so that marauders could not enter. At night mats were unrolled, especially in hot weather, and used for roof-top beds.

A few finer houses were made of cedar. Excavations at Ai and many other biblical cities have disclosed impressive houses with thick walls from the early Bronze Age, from about 3100 to 2100 B.C.

An urban house might be a part of the city wall with a window opening to the outdoors, but the ideal homemaker of Proverbs no doubt lived away from the heart of the city, where she had a house surrounded by a vineyard and a garden.

In the center of her house there probably was a courtyard. Storage, work, and living rooms were arranged on two long sides and one short side of the courtyard. The rooms as a rule were about eight to ten feet square. Recessed openings served as windows.

Domestic animals usually stayed inside a central area at night, and there was a central room with a hearth for cooking, and braziers for heating. Smoke went out through open windows. These could be closed with latticework.

Oftentimes the floors were of dirt, stomped hard. The floors of the better houses could be of plaster or stone. The roof surface was of clay, and in the spring grass might grow there (Ps. 126:6). Walls were approximately two feet thick, which meant the houses were warm in the winter and cool in the summer.

It is easy to imagine that they were comfortable, especially when presided over by an ideal homemaker, who like the capable homemaker today, could make the simplest dwelling a joyous place to enter.

Homemaker's Role, a Sacred One

Although we are far removed in time from these excellent homemakers, they rise before us as busy, able, vigorous women, at whose table we could sit and eat delectable food, in whose gardens we could gather many kinds of vegetables, in whose flower beds we could assemble lovely bouquets, and in whose vineyard and orchards we could pick luscious fruits.

Such homemakers are what the late Peter Marshall calls "Keepers of the Springs" in his delightful sermon in *Mr. Jones, Meet the Master* (pp. 147–58). He likens them to an ancient custodian who patrolled the hills and wherever he found a spring, he cleaned its brown pool of silt and fallen leaves, of mud and mold, and took away from the spring all foreign matter so that the water which bubbled up through the sand ran down clean and cold and pure.

Peter Marshall says about our days that "there never has been a time when there was a greater need for Keepers of the Springs, or when there were more polluted springs to be cleansed. If the home fails, the country is doomed. If the Keepers of the Springs desert their posts or are unfaithful to their responsibilities, the future outlook of this country is black indeed."

There is an old Chinese proverb on this same theme: "If there is righteousness in the heart, there will be beauty in the character. If there is beauty in the character, there will be harmony in the family home. If there is harmony in the home, there will be order in the nation. When there is order in the nation, there will be peace in the world."

Peter Marshall adds that "men have recognized that womanhood is sacred and a noble thing, that women are of finer clay . . . are more in touch with the angels of God and have the noblest function that life affords." He says "our country needs today women who will lead us back to an old fashioned morality, to old fashioned decency, to old fashioned purity and sweetness for the sake of the next generation, if for no other reason." And this is the special role, not of "beautiful women, smart women, sophisticated women, career women, talented women, divorced women, but of godly women," who can "come nearer fulfilling their God-given function in the home than anywhere else." This noted twentieth-century minister concludes with the thought that it is "a greater achievement to establish a Christian home than it is to produce a second-rate novel, filled with filth."

He furthermore reminds us that for nineteen hundred years woman has not been equal—she has been superior. It remained, he continues, for the twentieth century "to pull her down from the throne and to try to make her like a man," a far cry from what the Bible intended, as revealed in the next section, "A Magna Charta for Womanhood."

Section Two

A MAGNA CHARTA
FOR WOMANHOOD

CHAPTER SIX

THEIR GOD-GIVEN RIGHTS

Woman's equal rights and privileges extend to the Creation when God gave the first man, Adam, his equal partner, Eve. Like Adam, Eve was created in God's moral and spiritual image but regarded as man's equal in responsibilities toward God and in the care of his creatures. Furthermore, she is endowed equally with man but differently as to the nature of those endowments.

His mission is to protect and lead, hers to soothe, bless, and assist. Since woman is a part of man's own being, she inherits with him God's infinite blessings, because that was their high destiny from the beginning.

Status of Wives of Patriarchs

The wives of the patriarchs achieved equal status along with their husbands. Sometimes these wives exerted too much authority but at least no one questioned this.

Sarah was ill-tempered over the threatened rights of her own son, Isaac, by Ishmael, son of Abraham's concubine Hagar, but she was tolerant. To her own discredit, Rebekah connived and contrived until she had her husband, Isaac, exercising his dominion over the household according to her plan. No one seemed to so much as suspect that

Isaac was putty in Rebekah's hand when she directed a plan for her son Jacob to receive the family blessing in preference to Esau, the first-born twin. Rachel and Leah, wives of the third patriarch Jacob, seemed to have had full status and could do as they pleased, because Jacob, like his father, Isaac, and his grandfather Abraham, respected the God-given rights and privileges of his two wives.

Joseph's Egyptian wife, Asenath, the daughter of a priest in the great temple at Heliopolis, married Joseph when he was prime minister of Egypt, and she inherited many rights as a member of the Egyptian aristocracy. But her husband, Joseph, who was reared under the laws of Israel, would have respected her rights as a wife anyway.

The early Hebrew home was regarded as the temple of the woman. When she created an atmosphere of righteousness, and members of her family were taught to love God with all of their hearts, each knew the value of keeping his covenant with God. In the tradition of this national legacy, Hebrew women discerned better the power of God over all of his people. It is no wonder then that the God-loving women of Israel from patriarchal times loved their faith and nurtured their children in it.

Thoughtful Regard for Daughters

The Mosaic law gave consideration to daughters. A Hebrew father in distress was allowed to sell his sons into slavery but not his daughters (Ex. 21:7–10). A daughter's children could be legally recognized if they used their mother's maiden name rather than their father's name. An isolated case of this appears in I Chronicles 2:35, which tells of the little-known Sheshan, who gave his daughter in marriage to his servant, who was legally adopted into the tribe and by whom she bore a son. Sheshan, it is probable, had no sons, and he did this to protect his family line through his daughter.

Another Mosaic law stipulates that in case of seduction, provision must be made for a daughter's welfare (Deut. 22:28–29; Ex. 22:16–17). Her seducer must pay to her father, according to the dowry of virgins, and he could not "put her away" all of the days of his life.

A father in Bible times, as now, often favored a daughter. Caleb, the conqueror of Hebron under the leadership of Moses, at the request of his daughter Achsah's husband, Othniel, gave land as a dowry to Achsah. When he asked her, "What do you wish?" (Judg. 1:14), she requested her father's most desirable land, the upper springs. Caleb showed his affection for his daughter when he gave her both the upper and the lower springs. She received them in her own right and in a degree exclusive of her husband, and in preference to her three brothers.

Both Ezra and Nehemiah relate the story of Barzillai's daughter, who probably inherited from her father a large estate. She married a little-known priest, who relinquished his own name and took the better-known name of Barzillai (Ezra 2:61; Neh. 7:63).

Daughters in ancient Bible times might declare their own rights, as in the case of the five daughters of Zelophehad: Mahlah, Noah, Noglah, Milcah, and Tirzah. At their father's death they boldly went before Moses and told him that their father's inheritance should not be taken away simply because he had no sons (Num. 27:4–11).

It appears that Zelophehad was rich in land, otherwise his daughters might not have been granted their request to appear before Moses and his court of law. At least their appeal was urgent. In winning their property rights, these five daughters activated into the laws of Israel a new statute and ordinance for women.

OTHER HONORS TO HEBREW WOMEN

Other special honors were bestowed on Hebrew women, thus confirming further their high status as individuals. The Book of Ruth honors Ruth, the humble gleaner in the field of Boaz. The Book of Esther glorifies the humble Jewish maiden, who became the wife of King Ahasuerus of Persia.

The names of women also appear in long genealogical lists in the Bible. At least fourteen are included in the long genealogy in I Chronicles, chapters two through nine. Four, Tamar, Rahab, Ruth, and Bath-sheba, are in Matthew's genealogy of Jesus. Women are given full credit in three of the Bible's most triumphant songs, the Victory Ode of Deborah (Judg. 5:1–31), Hannah's Song of Praise (I Sam. 2:1–10), and Mary's Magnificat (Luke 1:46–55). Whether they wrote these great songs we do not know. At least they inspired them.

Women in Bible times who achieved political distinction in a so-called man's field did it through hard work, though sometimes they belonged in the family of the ruling power, as in the case of certain queens in the Hebrew Monarchy. These represented a small minority and were not typical.

GOOD TEST OF NATION'S CULTURE

In the nation that ceases to build on coercion but patiently approximates the Kingdom of God, as did Israel in the beginning, woman gains her God-given rights and privileges, not as a woman but as a person. The status of woman is a good test of a nation's civilization.

In his essay "Civilization," Ralph Waldo Emerson stresses that the right position of woman in the state is an index to its progress, that "when a state combines antagonism and utilizes evil, women achieve a low status accordingly. For civilization depends on morality. The evolution of a highly destined society must be moral" says Emerson, who further observes:

> Place the sexes in right relations of mutual respect, and a severe morality gives that essential charm to a woman which educates all that is delicate, poetic and self-sacrificing; breeds courtesy and learning, conversation and wit, in her rough mate; so that I have thought a sufficient measure of civilization is the influence of good women. . . . There can be no high civilization without a deep morality. . . . Civilization depends on morality. Everything good in man leans on what is higher. . . .
> (Emerson's *Complete Writings*, p. 628)

In his essay "Manners," written more than a century ago, Emerson wrote that this country was fortunate, in that it excelled in women. And then he commented, "The wonderful generosity of her sentiments raises her at times into heroical and godlike regions . . . and by the firmness with which she treads her upward path, she convinces the coarsest calculators that another road exists than that which their feet know" (Emerson's *Complete Writings*, p. 284). It's woman's responsibility, as man's inspirer, to keep her feet on the right path, and then men as a whole will follow in the direction in which she leads.

Equality of Man, Woman Not Likeness

When a woman achieves full status as a person this does not mean that she ought to be admitted to all the callings of men. There are two barriers to this. One is permanent, because women are not men, and their equality in the Kingdom of Heaven is not likeness. Each has a characteristic perfection, and one perfects the other.

Woman today has achieved a higher status than at any period in history. Tomorrow she may receive greater privileges, but she must merit them.

Woman's great problem today is that she has a diversity of roles to play: wife, mother, chauffeur, nurse, housekeeper, shopper, wage earner, and so on. She cannot achieve excellence in all, for she cannot be everything to everybody in the home and a successful businesswoman as well, unless she is a super person.

Often she has to accept a lesser role in business than she might deserve, especially when her family is young. But through her profound human concerns for her family and a continuing desire to develop her own talents, she can guide others, especially her children, by instilling in them an appreciation of the value of skills in a woman's life.

While the educated woman seeks to advance other learned and qualified women to their rightful place, she cannot forget or neglect those women who stand insecurely and uncertainly on the lower rungs, without even the barest necessities of life or even the emotional support of a husband. Their status as persons is never secure, even in a highly advanced society such as our own.

If a woman is educated and trained in some skill, there is actually no limitation to what she can do. But she must be prepared to work a little harder and do a better job than a man in the same field, for more is expected of the woman who finally reaches the top, especially in those skills where she competes with men. A woman's role today is a difficult one, but she must learn to be gracious yet firm and capable at the same time.

Instant Equal Opportunity Impossible

Today's woman, even amid her ever increasing opportunities, need not think she can demand equal status immediately, because the law permits it. There is no such thing as instant equal opportunity in all areas of living, not even in the Bible. For opportunity is not a potion to which we can add water and then stir in good will and expect immediate results. Our efforts and our education must be continuous as well as our willingness to try new approaches.

Many bars against women that were firmly in place in America in 1900 have been lowered. Although certain restrictions still remain, the woman in America today stands at the threshold of ever broadening opportunity. In 1963 President John F. Kennedy appointed the first Commission on the Status of Women, stating that "it is appropriate at this time to review recent accomplishments and to acknowledge frankly the further steps that must be taken. This is the task of the entire nation." This first commission came forth with this preamble which is in keeping with woman's God-given rights and responsibilities:

We believe that one of the greatest freedoms of the individual in a democratic society is the freedom to choose among different life patterns. Innumerable private solutions found by different individuals in search of the good life provide society with basic strength far beyond the possibilities of a dictated plan.

Illumined by values transmitted through home and school and church, society and heritage, and informed by present and past experience, each woman must arrive at her contemporary expression of purpose, whether as a center of home and family, a participant in the community, a contributor to the economy, a creative artist or thinker or scientist, or a citizen engaged in politics and public service. Part and parcel of this freedom is the obligation to assume corresponding responsibility.

CHAPTER SEVEN

THEIR STATUS
IN THE SANCTUARY

If we could turn back the clock of time to the tent of the Israelites or to the splendid temple of Solomon, we would find women ministering in almost every phase of the worship service. Their duties and their giving run almost parallel to that of women in the church now.

The Bible record of woman's first service to God's holy meeting place dates back to the time when Moses, descending from Mount Sinai, called "all of the congregation together," and announced the building of the first tabernacle to God. This was not a temple but an elaborate, movable tent appropriate to the unsettled life of the Israelites as they wandered from one watering place to another. They had wandered through the wilderness and they would wander some more before they settled in Canaan, but at least they could anchor themselves better to God in this worship center, which could be transported along with their camels, their herds, and their flocks.

In their deliverance from Egypt and in their long journey across the wilderness, the people had experienced what it meant to be borne up on eagles' wings and to experience God's presence. God had now given the Ten Commandments to Moses on Mount Sinai, made a new covenant with his people, and declared that his Holy Presence would abide with them. Their next step was to establish a meeting place in the name of Yahweh (God), where they might house his laws handed down to Moses. These would be kept in what would be known as the Ark of the Covenant and would contain the high priest's ephod (apron) and the urim (yes) and thummin (no), "the oracular media by which the will of God in relation to particular problems was ascertained." The first reference to these unidentified objects, which were probably sacred stones used by the priest when he wished to know God's will under certain circumstances, appears in Exodus 28:30. Later this ark would contain the Decalogue (Ten Commandments). This sacred chest would continue in long use, first in the temple at Shiloh, where Hannah took Samuel to be educated by Eli, the priest there, afterward in the Davidic tent, and finally in Solomon's magnificent temple at Jerusalem.

THE SERVICE OF ALL THE WOMEN

Only in this Mosaic age, the creative period of Israel's religious history, do we have this detailed account of the part women played in building the first ornamented worship center uniting men and women.

> And they came, both men and women, as many as were willing hearted, and brought bracelets, and earrings, and rings, and tablets, all jewels of gold . . .
> And all the women that were wise hearted did spin

with their hands, and brought that which they had
spun, both of blue, and of purple, and of scarlet, and
of fine linen.

And all the women whose heart stirred them up in
wisdom spun goats' hair.   (Ex. 35:22, 25–26)

It is noteworthy that it is twice related that *all the
women* took part in these particular phases of tabernacle
building. Because the altar was trimmed with gold and had
a pure gold lampstand holding fragrant incense and
annointing oils, women gave willingly of their gold
brooches, rings, and other jewels, as well as of their talents,
as stated above. These jewels either were traded for other
serviceable objects and necessary labor or were molded into
the various worship accessories.

Other tabernacle furnishings included a court at the
temple entrance, set apart by a curtain and a mercy seat.
The screen for the gates was embroidered in gold threads
on blue, purple, and scarlet linen. The tabernacle had ten
inside curtains made of fine twined linen. The outside
was covered with hand-woven goat's hair, resembling fine
red leather, to keep out the dust, wind, and rain.

The Gift of Their Talents

Much of the weaving and the embroidery were done by the
women who were clever with handwork. They no doubt
found spiritual renewal as well as joy in spinning, weaving,
and sewing together, especially as they remembered
Moses's promise that God would fill his people with the

ability to accomplish the most difficult tasks. None seemed either trivial or tedious in this period of creativity.

Not since patriarchal times had they had the opportunity for such self-expression. And never before had they had the opportunity to bring glory and beauty into God's meeting place. As they created patterns of thread across hand-woven wool and linen, they likely remembered Moses's reminder that the gifts of small talents used wisely were as important to God as the larger gifts.

Their needlework has its counterpart in the gifts of twentieth-century women to the National Cathedral in Washington, a majestic Gothic structure of stone, wood, silver, iron, and glass, under construction since 1907 and not to be finished until 1985. Through the cathedral's Needlepoint Guild, a thousand women have volunteered their labor for the portrayal of the Christian story in needlework. Twenty-six women in Pittsburgh embroidered the cloth covering the steps of the cathedral's main altar. Women in all fifty states wove the seals of their states and territories into a tapestry for the War Memorial Chapel. Hundreds of others, including the late Queen Mary of England, did the needlework for the nine hundred and sixty kneeling pads.

Two thousand years hence this vast Gothic cathedral, now the sixth largest in the world, will stand as a memorial to the work and gifts of thousands of people, including these dedicated women, who also worked with "willing hearts and generous spirits," just as had these other women in the time of Moses.

Their Treasured Bronze Mirrors

In Exodus we further learn that the tabernacle builders "made the laver of brass, and the foot of it of brass, of the looking glasses of the women . . . assembled at the door of the tabernacle of the congregation" (38:8). These mirrors were fashioned of precious polished bronze, for not until the Roman era about a thousand years later were glass mirrors available. It is reasonable to suppose that these mirrors, originally coated with highly polished silver, came from Egypt and were treasured family possessions from the years of the Exile.

We may conjecture, too, that when the tabernacle was finished, these women who assembled at its door directed other women to their places in the congregation, or instructed them in religious rites. They likely performed certain duties too in connection with the purification rites of other women and visited the sick, caring for both their bodily and their spiritual needs. On occasion they also assisted as mediators in family problems within the tabernacle.

Their Other Services and Stewardship

It is probable that the women sometimes baked the shewbread or showbread (Ex. 25:30). This is also called the bread of the Presence in the same verse in the RSV, and was like that used for the royal table and honored guests (Gen. 18:6), to signify God's continual presence. Each Sabbath twelve fresh loaves, suggesting the twelve tribes of Israel, were baked in a row (with two-tenths of an epah of grain in each), and brought into the sanctuary. The old loaves, according to custom, were eaten by the priests.

Although the Book of Exodus does not tell us, we can imagine that after the service the women served food to the congregation near the door of the tabernacle. We can picture them preparing this around their own hearths, inside a tent or a mud or stone hut. They made unleavened bread from their own grains, which they pounded to fine meal with a stone. With this they served roasted meats, milk from their own goat herds, wines from their vineyards, and raisin cakes sweetened with honey from their own bee hives.

Their service and stewardship reveal that then as now devout women served God's holy meeting place where and when needed, no matter how menial the task. For centuries their fidelity and zeal have inspired churchgoers, helping them to remember that in the midst of indifference and infidelity to God, there always are those who render homage to him in small, seemingly insignificant ways.

The Book of Exodus ends with the triumphant note, "For the cloud of the Lord was upon the tabernacle by day, and fire was on it by night, in the sight of all the house of Israel, throughout all their journeys" (40:38).

THEIR PART IN TEMPLE MUSIC

The part that women played in the music of the tabernacle is not mentioned in the Exodus account, but music was linked to all the concerns of women, from birth to death. Just as we can imagine primitive women crooning to their nursing babies so can we be certain that these ministering women of the tabernacle also sang to God in worship. We can hear their deeply resonant voices caroling such post-exilic Psalms as this:

Whom have I in heaven but thee? and there is none upon earth that I desire beside thee.

My flesh and my heart faileth; but God is the strength of my heart, and my portion for ever.

(Ps. 73:25–26)

The first Bible record of woman's part in temple choirs occurs in the time of Solomon's magnificent temple, about nine centuries B.C.

. . . And God gave to Heman fourteen sons and three daughters. All these were under the hands of their father for song in the house of the Lord, with cymbals, psalteries, and harps, for the service of the house of God. . . . And they cast lots, ward against ward, as well the small as the great, the teacher as the scholar. (I Chron. 25:5–6, 8)

Heman led the temple musicians under David and Solomon. His three daughters, whom he taught to sing hymns, psalms, and doxologies, played harps and lyres, all in joyous exaltation of the Lord.

In Jeremiah's lament for Josiah, it is related again that "all the singing men and the singing women spake of Josiah in their lamentations" (II Chron. 35:25). It is further recorded in Nehemiah's genealogy of the more than forty-nine thousand exiles, who came out of Babylon and back into Judah, that "two hundred forty and five singing men and singing women" (Neh. 7:67) were in the group. This concludes the Old Testament record of woman's service in the tabernacle.

BLESSED ARE THOSE WHO SERVE

In our mind's ear we can hear ringing down the centuries the voices of women, like Heman's daughters and the refugees returning from Babylonia, and some centuries later those first little bands of Christians, all praising God in song:

O give thanks unto the Lord; call upon his name; make known his deeds among the people.

Sing unto him, sing psalms unto him: talk ye of all his wondrous works.

Glory ye in his holy name: let the heart of them rejoice that seek the Lord. (Ps. 105:1–3)

It is heartening to know that from earliest Bible times, women have sung unto the Lord. From them we have inherited our realistic conception of God and our recognition of the priority of God in our daily lives. In the record of these nameless women's devotion, we sense God's greatness, yet nearness, his holiness and his presence, the unspeakable mystery of his hidden being, and his active concern for us.

Happy are all churchwomen who, like these of old, serve the church with "willing hearts and generous spirits," and are not too concerned about their equality of service in high places but how well they serve when and where needed. In such dedication they are a vital part of a luminous light in the Church Universal, where all come together in one Cathedral of the Spirit to shed faith, hope, and love upon a world where darkness too often prevails.

Oliver Wendell Holmes has reminded us that "the nice, calm, cold thought, which in women shapes itself so rapidly that they hardly know it as thought, should always travel to the lips by the way of the heart. It does so in those women whom we love and admire." Such women have illumined worship services dating back to this first written record, and have handed down to us a rich legacy, both a love of God and a desire to serve him.

CHAPTER EIGHT

THEIR OCCUPATIONS AND CREATIVITY

The image of women at work in Bible times has often been overshadowed by that of men. But women then, as now, did more than bear, rear children, and keep house. They also engaged in many of the trades and crafts of their time. A few owned their own businesses. Others were builders, singers, nurses, maidservants, spinners, gleaners, midwives, doorkeepers, shepherdesses, teachers, seamstresses, innkeepers, tentmakers, water carriers, queens, and fortune-tellers.

All through Bible history women found the answer to their desire for creativity, always a great need in a woman's life. They did exquisite needlework. They sang. They played harps, cymbals, and psalters, as mentioned in the preceding chapter. A few like Herodias's daughter were professional dancers. Some played tabrets as they danced. Among these were the young maidens who came out of all the cities of Israel, singing and dancing as King Saul and the young David marched through the cities of Israel celebrating the latter's victory in the slaying of Goliath.

From earliest Bible times women also participated in social welfare work. They cared for the young, the sick, and the aged. They laid out the dead, comforted the sorrowing, quieted the impetuous with gentleness and wisdom, and in some instances chose a life of single blessedness, in order to devote all of their time to God and God's children.

EXPERT AS MIDWIVES

In midwifery they seemed to be especially skilled, carefully caring for mothers at childbirth as they sat on a birthstool, a peculiarly shaped chair of Egyptian origin. They also cut the navel string of the newborn, washed it with water, rubbed it with salt, swathed it with bands, and then laid the babe in a manger of straw or a crib cut out of a cedar log.

Like obstetricians today, midwives sometimes faced difficult problems in deliveries at childbirth. Two mothers we know of died in childbirth. One was Rachel when she gave birth to her second son, Benjamin (Gen. 35:18). The other was Eli's daughter-in-law by his son Phinehas when she gave birth to Ichabod (I Sam. 4:19–20). Each midwife foretold that a son was about to be born.

Midwives handled multiple births expertly. The story is related of the midwife who attended Tamar when she gave birth to twins by Judah. When the time came for delivery of the first-born, the midwife took and bound the baby's hand with a scarlet thread, saying, "This came out first" (Gen. 38:28). And as the child's brother appeared, she labeled and bound his hand with another scarlet thread.

The Bible's best-known midwives Puah and Shiprah of Moses's time had various duties. There is a Jewish tradi-

tion that Shiprah dressed the infant and Puah used arti-
ficial respiration through the child's mouth, the same that
Elisha would later use on the Shunammite's child (II
Kings 4:32–36). Puah and Shiprah no doubt attained considerable influence and skill as related here:

> And the king of Egypt spake to the Hebrew mid-
> wives, of which the name of one was Shiprah, and the
> name of the other Puah:
> And he said, When ye do the office of a midwife to
> the Hebrew women, and see them upon the stools; if
> it be a son, then ye shall kill him; but if it be a daugh-
> ter, then she shall live.
> But the midwives feared God, and did not as the
> king of Egypt commanded them, but saved the men
> children alive.
> And the king of Egypt called for the midwives, and
> said unto them, Why have ye done this thing, and
> have saved the men children alive?
> And the midwives said unto Pharaoh, Because the
> Hebrew women are not as the Egyptian women; for
> they are lively, and are delivered ere the midwives
> come in unto them.
> Therefore God dealt well with the midwives: and
> the people multiplied, and waxed very mighty.
> And it came to pass, because the midwives feared
> God, that he made them houses.   (Ex. 1:15–21)

Scholars ask two questions about this last verse. Did
God raise the midwives up to become mothers themselves?
Or were they elevated to the headship of their fathers'

houses as an honor to the Hebrew people, all because they had willfully disobeyed the Pharaoh's evil edict?

Often midwives were family friends and neighbors. When a son was born to Ruth, neighbors gathered around to congratulate the grandmother Naomi, telling her that this baby would be "a restorer of thy life, and a nourisher of thine old age" (Ruth 4:15). They even gave the baby its name of Obed (v. 17), and one probably served as the midwife.

SKILLED AS NURSES FROM EARLY TIMES

Nursing, like midwifery, was an honored vocation. Since children were breast-fed until about the age of three, Hebrew mothers usually nursed their own children, but occasionally a wet nurse was employed. Such nurses were treated as members of the household.

One of these was Joash's nurse, who was hidden with the child, an heir to the throne, when Jezebel's daughter Athaliah seized the government of Judah. The child and the nurse were concealed in a bedchamber, probably a priest's room in a temple. It is recorded that they remained there for six years (II Kings 11:3).

The earliest nurse on record was Rebekah's Deborah, whom she took with her from Mesopotamia to Canaan when she became the bride of Isaac (Gen. 24:59). This Deborah probably had been with Rebekah since childhood and had remained with her after the birth of her twins, Esau and Jacob. Deborah, who probably never married and who chose to serve several generations of this patriarchal family, is memorialized as one who served well. Nurses like Deborah "probably bathed and dressed young children, played with them or observed their play, and accompanied them on walks and outings; they probably also kept the children's quarters tidy," says Walter Duckat in his *Beggar to King, All the Occupations of Biblical Times*.

Such a nurse was the kindest and gentlest of creatures. In writing to the church at Thessalonica, Paul said, "We [myself, Silvanus, and Timotheus] were gentle among you, even as a nurse cherisheth her children" (I Thess. 2:7).

THEIR AGRICULTURAL DUTIES

Women of Israel also engaged in a variety of agricultural pursuits. They tended and watered their fathers' flocks. Among these were Jethro's daughters in Midian, as already mentioned. It is easy to imagine that the hardier ones tilled the soil while the men cut the grass with sickles, also helped to thresh, winnow, flail, and bind the grain. A Hebrew agriculture law prohibited the owner from cleaning up his own field, vineyard, or orchard, so as to leave provisions for the orphan, the widow, and the alien resident.

Ruth, the gleaner, went to Bethlehem from her native Moab with her mother-in-law, Naomi, a farm migrant, who had lived in Moab but desired to return to her native Judea, following the death of her husband and two sons. In the field of Naomi's kinsman Boaz, Ruth gathered up bunches of wheat, left standing behind rocks or near the boundary walls. The generous Boaz probably permitted the needy Ruth to follow his reapers and pick up the leavings. Ruth supported herself and her mother-in-law

with her labor and became such an industrious and help-
ful gleaner that she attracted the attention of Boaz, whose
wife she later became.

THE BUILDERS OF TOWNS AND WALLS

As early as fourteen centuries before Christ, women engaged in construction work. Sherah, an ancestress of
Joshua, was one of these (I Chron. 7:24). She designed
and supervised the building of three ancient towns. Two
of these were the Upper and Lower Beth-horon, located
on the road from Gibeon to the valleys of Ajalon and
Shephelah, both with great strategic importance. The
third town was the Uzzen-sherah, thought to be three
miles southwest of Lower Beth-horon.

When the walls of Jerusalem were restored during Ezra
and Nehemiah's time, the daughters of Shallum were
among the workers. Their father had charge of half of one
of the five governmental districts into which postexilic
Judah was divided. Their family, it is thought, remained
in Judah after the downfall of the Southern Kingdom in
586 B.C. Because they had witnessed the destruction of
the city walls and the invasion of the enemy, they understood better than others Nehemiah's cry, "Come, and let
us build up the walls of Jerusalem, that we be no more a
reproach" (Neh. 2:17). Along with the other public-
spirited citizens, these daughters responded "Let us rise
up and build. So they strengthened their hands for this
good work" (Neh. 2:18).

The entire wall of Jerusalem was portioned off in short
lengths to different bodies of volunteers. These included

members of the rich city guilds as well as wealthy and
public-spirited citizens. It is commendable that Shallum, a
municipal chief, and his daughters would be among the
first to volunteer when laborers were few and funds
limited.

When the Athenian dramatist Euripides (480–406 B.C.)
stated that "A woman should be good for everything at
home, but abroad good for nothing," he had no knowledge
of the work of the eminent women of Jerusalem.

A DIPLOMAT FROM SOUTHERN ARABIA

The Queen of Sheba, who traveled to Israel from her rich
land of Saba in Southern Arabia, represented a country
where it appears women had attained equal rights. During
the reign of Solomon (962–922 B.C.), some centuries earlier than Euripides, this diplomatic queen set forth with
her formidable caravan to visit the wise and rich king of
Israel, whose fame had spread across the world.

The Kebra Nagast (the Ethiopian account of her journey) relates that her camels numbered seven hundred and
ninety-seven and that she also had mules and asses loaded
with Saba's richest products.

This young and beautiful Queen of Sheba had one purpose in mind as she journeyed the twelve hundred miles
from her homelands to Israel. That was to better trade
relations between her native Saba and Solomon's powerful kingdom of Israel.

When she and her large retinue arrived at his palace,
she was impressed with its magnificence, the splendor of
his table, the seating of his officials, and the ceremonial

apparel of his many servants. But most of all she admired him for the way he went up into the House of the Lord. And she said to the king:

> The report was true which I heard in my own land of your affairs and of your wisdom, but I did not believe the reports until I came and my own eyes had seen it; and, behold, the half was not told me; your wisdom and prosperity surpass the report which I heard. Happy are your wives! Happy are these your servants, who continually stand before you and hear your wisdom! Blessed be the Lord your God, who has delighted in you and set you on the throne of Israel! Because the Lord loved Israel for ever, he has made you king, that you may execute justice and righteousness. (I Kings 10:6–9, RSV)

After extended conferences with the wise Solomon, the Queen of Sheba worked out alliances which were of tremendous advantage to both of their countries. Although she gave King Solomon a fortune in gifts, a fortune came back to her own Saba in its new trade with Israel.

QUEENS OF THE HEBREW MONARCHY

During the Hebrew Monarchy, there were more than a dozen queens who served Israel as consorts to their husbands or as reigning queens. Among the best known of the latter were Queen Jezebel, wife of Ahab, king of the Northern Kingdom of Israel, and their daughter Queen Athaliah of the Southern Kingdom.

Both, especially Jezebel, were among the most powerful in Israel's history. She dominated from behind the scenes, but her daughter was a ruling monarch in her own right. Both, however, had one thing in common. They were as wicked as any two queens in history and left only horror wherever they walked.

THE SPINNERS AND WEAVERS

Vocations of women ran the gamut from queens to spinners and weavers. The latter developed many skills in their menial tasks.

Specifications for the curtains for the tabernacle (Ex. 26:2–8) in the time of Moses and Aaron indicate that four cubits (or six feet) were a standard width used by women weavers. If a woman wanted to weave a long robe with sleeves, for example, she made sure that the warp was twice as wide as the length desired for the robe, much as one would now gauge a sweater size. When she wove from cuff to cuff, the selvage came at the hem and neck openings, where strength was needed.

She would begin work on enough of the center warps to make a sleeve and leave the side warps bare. These were added when the sleeve was woven from cuff to shoulder, to form the tunic length. When the head opening was the size she wanted it, she wove the second shoulder across the whole warp and finished the second sleeve. Then she cut the tunic from the loom and finished the raw edges. Exodus 28:32 tells of a woven binding around the opening of the neck, and Numbers 15:38, of "fringes in the borders of their garments." This was accomplished by beginning the cord at the top and leaving the ends at the bottom.

Because the looms were easy to transport, nomadic women carried them about in their wilderness wanderings. The looms consisted of two beams held in place by four pegs driven into the ground. The Greek vertical loom was the most commonly used in later Bible times. Women embroidered fabrics made on this loom, but those made on the horizontal loom were "skillfully worked."

Rahab had two known vocations, that of innkeeper and weaver. She hid Joshua's two spies in stalks of flax, which lay drying upon her roof. Later she let them down by a scarlet cord through the window. She later no doubt would use the flax for her weaving, and we can imagine that she had spun, dyed, and woven the scarlet cord, heavy enough to hold the weight of these two men.

Rahab is also called a harlot (Josh. 2:1). But whatever Rahab's vices, she later redeemed herself in her love of the God of Israel (Josh. 2:11), and because she was a believer, she is honored as one of the heroines of faith in Hebrews 11:31.

It is interesting to note that while Samson slept, Delilah took the seven locks of his hair and wove them into a web (Judg. 16:13–14). She probably used the horizontal-type loom, where two weavers sat side by side. Samson would have had to sit up while sleeping, had she used the vertical loom. When Samson awoke and Delilah told him that the Philistines were upon him, he rushed forth from his sleep "with the pin of the beam and with the web" (v. 14).

In Delilah's time, weavers sat before the loom, their feet deftly curled beneath them. Threads of goat's hair or camel's hair or sheep's wool or cotton or flax were spread across the loom. This was made with two wooden upright sets placed in piles of mud under trees in the summer; in the winter the loom was set on an earthen floor inside the house. Some of the weaving looms were made of wood and others of clay. Before wool was woven it was twisted and twirled into yarn by spindle whorls, or discs, to steady moving spindles.

THEIR KNOWLEDGE OF FABRIC ARTS

The dyeing of threads, an ancient art, is not described in the Bible, but excavations at various sites reveal sufficient data on the equipment and organization. Dye works seemed to have been quite common in later times. Lydia, the New Testament's kest-known businesswoman, probably owned one of these, for she is described as a "seller of purple" (Acts 16:14) and seems to have been a woman of means. She opened her home at Philippi to the church and also invited Paul and Barnabas to share her hospitality when they came to Philippi. The *Interpreter's Bible* describes a dye plant, such as Lydia might have owned, in this manner:

At Tell Beit Mirsim an estimated thirty homes devoted rooms roughly ten by twenty feet to dyeing showing that it was a domestic, but well-organized industry. The installations excavated (six or seven in number) share a basic plan: each room was arranged with two round stone vats with small openings on top and retrieving drains around the rims; masonry basins and benches were constructed between or in front of the vats. . . . Additional storage jars containing lime or potash—for fixing the dyes—stood close by. As the size of the mouth of the vats indicates, thread rather than the woven fabric was dyed, from which multicolored cloth could be woven. The normal process required two baths, after which the dye was carefully squeezed out and saved. The dyed thread was then laid out to dry.   (Vol. 1, p. 875)

Purple was the most valued of ancient dyes and included hues ranging within the red-purple range. Some of the most famous purples required double dyeing. A garment made of purple linen or wool gave the wearer a mark of distinction, royalty, and wealth. So Lydia, this seller of purple goods, probably dealt with wealthy patrons.

Tentmaking, an Old Vocation

Tentmaking was an old and common vocation for women. Priscilla, a first-century Christian, is the Bible's best-known tentmaker. She and her husband, Aquila, worked side by side and made their tentmaking equipment in the weaving sections of Corinth and Ephesus available to Paul when he visited them at both places.

Tents in these times were difficult to cut and stitch. Many were made out of the felted cloth of goat's hair, which was heavy and hard to handle. From the same material, sails for boats were made also. It is probable that Priscilla helped fashion sails for the boats in which she and her husband and Paul sailed together.

There is evidence that one who made tents and sails also was skilled in leatherwork. If so, Priscilla knew how to design beds, bedsteads, and leather cushions, and made them not only for her own home but for the homes of her fellow Christians.

TEACHERS AND DOORKEEPERS

Teaching was another vocation for women. Huldah, a prophetess, preacher, and teacher in the reign of King Josiah (643–612 B.C.), is mentioned in the succeeding chapter as a prophetess. She was one of the brilliant women of her time and is thought to have taught in a school in Jerusalem.

Teachers of religion were common in New Testament times. The best known of these was Priscilla, who taught the learned Apollos of the things of God. Among others who taught religion were Euodias and Syntyche, eminent workers in the Church at Philippi, and the four unmarried daughters of the evangelist Philip.

Women doorkeepers also are mentioned in New Testament times. Among these were the maid who opened the door for Peter in the High Priest's Palace in Jerusalem when Peter denied Jesus. There must have been many such maids of the court, who performed a variety of tasks in palaces of rulers and in mansions of the rich.

LABOR, THE BASIS OF A GOOD LIFE

The Bible is a fascinating record of primitive people at work. The industrious believed with the Psalmist that

God "guided them by the skilfulness of his hand" (78: 72), and so labor was the basis of the good life. They joyously sang with the Psalmist, "For thou shalt eat the labour of thine hands: happy shalt thou be, and it shall be well with thee" (128:2). Isaiah records that the elect of God "shall long enjoy the work of their hands" (65:22).

Centuries later when Paul wrote to the Thessalonians, he commanded the people to keep away from "mere busy bodies" who lived in idleness, and commended those who work patiently and quietly, not burdening anyone.

The industrious women who were never idle provide an inspiring example for us. Too often we are more concerned with our status and wages than with the service we render, but these primitive women achieved recognition, a natural by-product of service well rendered, in a wide variety of vocations.

CHAPTER NINE

THEIR STATUS
AS NATIONAL LEADERS

Miriam, Deborah, Huldah, and Esther achieved front rank as national leaders. Miriam stood beside her brothers Aaron and Moses in the highest office of the state. Deborah, one of the so-called judges, exercised authority over limited tribal areas and led her people to victory in battle against the Canaanites. Huldah, a prophetess, teacher, and preacher, identified for King Josiah the Book of Law, the brilliant work of a group of prophets and priests who recorded Yahweh's spiritual ideals. Esther averted a general massacre of her people, plotted by the wicked Haman, the prime minister to her husband, King Ahasuerus, and an enemy of the Jews.

It is quite remarkable that all four of these women lived in several of the most critical periods of their nation's history: Miriam, when the law was delivered to Israel (about 1290–1280 B.C.); Deborah, in the twelfth century B.C.; Huldah, during the reign of King Josiah in the seventh century B.C.; and Esther, Queen of Persia, served her nation when the Jews fled there during the Babylonian captivity in the reign of her husband, Ahasuerus (486–465 B.C.).

Though the centuries divide these four women, they were all one in their service to their country, and each in turn rose to eminence in the people's hearts during national stress.

Miriam, Deborah, and Huldah gave God the credit for their opportunity to serve Israel in time of need. God is not mentioned in the Book of Esther, but Esther was a child of the covenant which her people had made with God, and her actions in behalf of its precepts substantiate her faith in him.

Since God had called these women to fulfill their historical and social responsibility within his holy purpose, their exemplary service drew the people of Israel closer to God in wonder, gratitude, and faith. Each seemed to give new meaning to Moses's exhortation, "For what nation is there so great, who hath God so nigh unto them, as the Lord our God is in all things that we call upon him for?" (Deut. 4:7).

MIRIAM, ONE OF FOUNDERS OF HEBREW COMMONWEALTH

Miriam was jubilant as she led the women of Israel, all of them following her voice in the song "Sing Unto the Lord" (Ex. 15:21), as they crossed the Sea of Reeds back into Canaan. Long decades of bondage in Egypt had been lifted.

The prophet Micah afterward paid this tribute to Miriam, along with her brother: "For I brought thee up out of the land of Egypt, and redeemed thee out of the house of servants; and I sent before thee Moses, Aaron, and Miriam" (6:4). She gave new courage to her people, especially the women, in their many trials that followed. As they journeyed into the wilderness, they drew closer in love and purpose as they sang this song of Moses:

> Thou in thy mercy hast led forth the people which thou hast redeemed: thou hast guided them in thy strength unto thy holy habitation.
>
> Thou shalt bring them in, and plant them in the mountain of thine inheritance, in the place, O Lord, which thou hast made for thee to dwell in, in the Sanctuary, O Lord, which thy hands have established.
>
> The Lord shall reign for ever and ever.
>
> (Ex. 15:13, 17–18)

Miriam probably maintained her position as a triumphant leader of the women of Israel through their long years of trial before they went into the Promised Land. As the women journeyed beside their husbands and children into the desert of Shur, they had to prove God's care again, for suddenly they found themselves without water. The only water that they came upon were the bitter waters of Marah, an oasis in the desert, and they could not drink this until Moses, at God's direction, threw a certain tree into this well, and then it was made sweet.

Miriam not only justified her own position by her leadership but she gave women in the succeeding years of Israel's long history new confidence in themselves as women.

DEBORAH, THE MOTHERLY HELPER IN WAR

Deborah, a third major judge and a deliverer of her people, lived in the turbulent period of the Book of Judges, when her people were both complacent and hopeless.

Typical of some of those in power in this period of the Judges was Abimelech, the son of Gideon by his Shechemite concubine (Judg. 9). Whether Abimelech was a contemporary of Deborah or not, there is no certainty, but his story stresses the crying need for able, staunch national leaders in Israel.

Abimelech arrived at his place of power as "judge" over the city-state of Shechem after murdering seventy of his half brothers born to the concubines of his father. Only one brother, Jotham, the younger, escaped by hiding himself.

When the coronation ceremony for Abimelech was about to take place, Jotham climbed to the highest point of Mount Gerizim and addressed the people on the famous parable of the Fig Tree and the Bramble as told in Judges 9. According to the parable, regal honors first were offered to the youthful olive tree but this tree spurned the offer. Then they were placed at the disposal of the full-branched fig tree, which in turn spurned the proposal, then to the vine, which also declined. Finally, the crown was proffered to the worthless bramble, which with considerable pride accepted the overture but not without corresponding demands and thrusts.

Here lies the lesson of this fable. It is absurd for trees to take refuge in the shade of a bramble bush, just as it is absurd for citizens to take refuge with a wicked ruler like Abimelech, a worthless fellow who had hired other reckless fellows in his plot to take over the government. The olive, the fig tree, and the vine stood for the people who let him take over. It was possible that, like the bramble, such a ruler might kindle a fire capable of wiping out not only those who elected him but their neighbors as well. Later, Abimelech cruelly treated all of the people, a just judgment for their acquiescence in naming such an unfit man to rule.

The people were as acquiescent in the time of Deborah as they had been in the time of Abimelech. The men of Israel stood back, afraid of their powerful enemy, so Deborah took the initiative.

She is first introduced as a prophetess, who sat under a palm tree between Ramah and Bethel "and the children of Israel came up to her for judgment" (Judg. 4:5). Her people were afraid of the Canaanites who had oppressed them for twenty years and now had nine hundred war chariots of iron, while they had none.

Deborah, their friend and counselor, had no royal lineage. She was the wife of an obscure man, Lapidoth, and the head of a household, and doubtless was encumbered with many domestic duties. Those in search of a helper in time of trouble might well have passed her by, but even in this age of cruelty, they chose Deborah, not because she was a queen, but because she was a motherly helper and because many of the afflicted and oppressed had found in her judgment a new source of strength.

The spirit of maternity had fallen upon Deborah with tremendous power. She was a mother of Israel, and every son and daughter of Israel were now her own. Her children had a malignant disease, and she knew it must be rooted out, like cancer in a drastic operation.

Sisera, captain of the troops of Jabin, king of Canaan, was the "foreign germ" preying upon the "vital organs" of her family. Her love and sympathy for her people demanded drastic action, the lash on Sisera. Because her people had lost that sense of nationalism and direction in time of crisis, she must act quickly and confidently. And she did.

She summoned Barak to aid her in leading the North Israelite militia in a battle against Sisera, this mighty Canaanite general, who had large forces of men, as well as nine hundred chariots of iron. Barak was fearful at first to march against such strong forces, but he had Deborah to assure him that all would go well, and so he hurriedly assembled ten thousand valiant men from Zebulun and Napthali. With Deborah they all set forth for the plains to face this powerful enemy. When the day came for the battle, Deborah spoke to Barak with authority, "Up, for this is the day in which the Lord hath delivered Sisera into thine hand: is not the Lord gone out before thee?" (Judg. 4:14).

And he had. Not only did Sisera lose both the battle and his life but the swollen waters of the river Kishon swept his army back.

> From heaven fought the stars,
>   from their courses they fought against Sisera.
> The torrent Kishon swept them away,
>   the onrushing torrent, the torrent Kishon
> March on, my soul, with might!
>   (Judg. 5:20–21, RSV)

So sings the Song of Deborah (Judg. 5:1–31), which is considered one of the most beautiful specimens of Hebrew poetry, and was either inspired or written by this motherly woman who became great in Israel. In her victory over a mighty enemy, Deborah achieved national status as a much loved leader during a war that could have destroyed Israel. Praises are still sung to Deborah, this great woman leader in Israel, and echoes of her song can still be heard:

Hear, O Kings; give ear, O princes;
   to the Lord I will sing,
I will make melody to the Lord, the God of Israel.
                            (Judg. 5:3, RSV)

Huldah, the Wise Prophetess to King Josiah

Huldah also was honored by all the people in power because she had great prophetic insight, a quality entrusted only to the deserving. She also had a profound knowledge of the law and a strong perception of the ways of God. It is probable she taught in Jerusalem, either a woman's group or in school. She may have preached also.

Her important connections came through her husband, Shallum, who was keeper of the priests' wardrobes for the great reformer King Josiah. No doubt Huldah was known largely as Shallum's wife until this opportunity to serve her country came. And when King Josiah sent his messengers, including his high priest and scribes, from the temple to Huldah to inquire whether the scroll found there was the lost Book of the Law, they reached Huldah not at some important place but in her own dwelling.

In her miraculous answer to the king's messengers, appearing in II Kings 22:14–20, Huldah reveals that the book they had found in the temple was the authentic record of the people of Israel and that everything it said was from God. She convinced the messengers that God would bring evil upon them because they had forsaken him for other gods. Huldah credited God, whom she loved with all of her heart, with her prophetic power.

So aroused was King Josiah with what Huldah had revealed that he set in motion the words that are written into the Book of the Covenant. First, he and his people went to the house of the Lord, and there they made a pledge to walk once more in God's commandments, statutes, and testimonies, as revealed in this Book of Law, a good part of which appears in the Book of Deuteronomy.

Like her predecessors Miriam and Deborah, Huldah took her place beside Israel's eminent national leaders.

ESTHER, A LIBERATOR OF HER PEOPLE

Queen Esther rendered as notable a service to her people, but it came about in a different manner, for she was a different type: young, timid, essentially feminine, and dependent upon the good graces of a powerful king. She did not live in Israel but in Persia, where thousands of Jews had been carried into captivity by Nebuchadnezzar after the fall of Jerusalem several decades earlier. Many of them had risen to eminence in the state. Among these was Mordecai, uncle and guardian of the beautiful Esther, who became a candidate for the vacant queenship after the deposition of Queen Vashti.

After King Ahasuerus chose Esther for his queen, she discovered through her uncle Mordecai that the king's prime minister Haman had a plot under way to kill all Jews, both young and old, even the little children and women. And these were Esther's own people.

In his fatherly appeal to Queen Esther, Mordecai said to her:

> Think not with thyself that thou shalt escape in the king's house, more than all the Jews.
>
> For if thou altogether holdest thy peace at this time, then shall there enlargement and deliverance arise to the Jews from another place; but thou and thy father's house shall be destroyed: and who knoweth whether thou art come to the kingdom for such a time as this?   (Esther 4:13–14)

Esther seemed to realize that she was born for such a time as this and so she acted on an immediate impulse. First she told Mordecai to gather all the Jews they could find in Susa, the capital, and to hold a fast in her behalf. She promised him that she and her maids would fast also. "Then I will go in unto the king," she said "which is not according to the law; and if I perish, I perish" (Esther 4: 16). No queen in history has shown such willingness to sacrifice herself, nor has any queen exhibited greater fearlessness.

No woman in Jewish history is more loved or has been honored over a longer period. And the five words that she spoke so valiantly, "If I perish, I perish," bespeak a woman's willingness to save her people in the face of impending disaster, even if she dies in the attempt.

STATUS, A PRODUCT OF ACHIEVEMENT

The successful roles played by all four of these women, Miriam, the spiritual leader, Deborah, the commander of an army, Huldah, the prophetess, and Esther, the queen of her people in time of despair, reveal that noble women who are willing to give of themselvs never have to doubt their status. It comes without question to those who occupy a place of destiny and who have an unselfish desire to serve.

All four of these had several qualities in common, an unpretending simplicity, a love of home, family, and country, mental and spiritual superiority, and faith in themselves, but most of all, faith in a power beyond themselves, so that they were given the courage to act at the right time.

Each seemed to excel in woman's natural sphere, which is to influence, not to command, to entreat, not to threaten, to lead more by example than by precept, and to rejoice in unselfish service to others. Each also seemed to realize to the fullest that she was an instrument of God, ready and waiting to do as he commanded.

Their leadership in time of national crisis makes us know that it matters little whether the people are led by a man or a woman. In such periods the sexes do not compete but learn to co-operate and complement one another.

CHAPTER TEN

THE RESPONSIBLE ROLE
OF LITTLE, OBSCURE ONES

There is no status symbol under God. He "made the small and great, and careth for all alike," says the Wisdom of Solomon (6:7) in the Apocrypha. The great often rose to prominence by standing on the shoulders of little, unknown people, who had learned the art of humbly standing by, ready to render menial service.

Some of these—and we shall consider only those in the Old Testament here—emerge only long enough for their names to be called, but because of their humble and faithful dedication, others better known are able to play a more brilliant performance. These unassuming ones suggest the minor actors on a theater stage. Without them the play could not go on. The top cast of big names would be lost without them. So it was that some of these obscure women in the Bible seemed to know they could not be stars in the sky but they were willing to hold a lamp a little while for those whose names would be woven into the loom of destiny.

The Seven Shepherdess Sisters

Among these who made their sudden appearance were the seven daughters of the priest of Midian. Moses saw them as they "came and drew water, and filled the troughs to water their father's flocks. And the shepherds came and drove them away: but Moses stood up and helped them, and watered their flocks" (Ex. 2:16–17). Afterward they told their father: "An Egyptian delivered us out of the hand of the shepherds, and also drew water enough for us, and watered the flock. And he said unto his daughters, and where is he? why is it that ye have left the man? call him, that he may eat bread" (19–20).

This quickly etched profile of these seven shepherdesses has special meaning and purpose. Zipporah—the only one later called by name—afterward became the wife of Moses, Israel's eminent statesman and lawgiver, who led his people from slavery in Egypt to independent, religious statehood in Canaan.

Only a short time before Moses came into this desert country he had killed an Egyptian, whom he had found brutally beating a Hebrew. Possibly the sudden emergence of these lovely shepherdess sisters helped Moses to look toward God, for their beauty and grace lent a delicate glimmer and a mystical charm to the desert landscape at this, the twilight hour, when they came to water their father's flocks.

Six of the sisters are not mentioned again, yet they are as necessary to the scene, in which Moses became an important participant, as the soft shadows in a pastoral painting.

In his biography of *Nancy Hanks, the Destined Mother of a President*, Adin Baber says, "There is an obscurity in the affairs of men that suffers them to struggle on: to continue their monotonous toil; nor do few ever learn that they were a part of the pattern of destiny. It is the privilege of history to seek them out, and set them apart" (p. 6).

This author refers to Abraham Hanks, the frontier father of Nancy, who with thousands of underprivileged, unnamed persons crossed the frontier through Cumberland Gap into territory later to become Kentucky. The long trek of these obscure ones marked "the time, the place and the genesis of the explosive expansion of the settlement of America." The last-named of these unknowns, a blacksmith, was to become the patriarch in the genealogy of an American family who would produce Abraham Lincoln, one of America's most eminent presidents.

History gleams with such stories. The Bible, the greatest of all books, effectively dramatizes many so-called little people. Their lives remind us of what the Roman stoic philosopher Seneca said, "Nothing comes to pass but what God appoints. Our fate is decreed, and things do not happen by chance, but every man's portion of joy or sorrow is predetermined." Thomas à Kempis, the medieval German mystic and ascetic, author of *Imitation of Christ*, reminds us that "Man proposes, but God disposes."

The Faithful, Nameless Nurse

When David's errant son Absalom tried to usurp his father's place as king of Israel, several names loom into the foreground for a fleeting, but unforgettable, moment. The first is a nurse, the second, a maidservant, the third, a farm woman, and the fourth "a wise woman."

The nurse is introduced in the last days of King Saul,

following the slaying of his son Jonathan in a battle with the Philistines at Mount Gilboa. At Jonathan's death, King Saul's household was thrown into a state of panic for fear something might happen to Mephibosheth, Jonathan's son and King Saul's last remaining heir. Out of the shadows of obscurity appears the child's unnamed nurse:

> And Jonathan, Saul's son, had a son that was lame of his feet. He was five years old when the tidings came of Saul and Jonathan out of Jezreel, and his nurse took him up, and fled: and it came to pass, as she made haste to flee, that he fell, and became lame. And his name was Mephibosheth.   (II Sam. 4:4)

The matter of lameness is a little vague. The child must have been crippled from birth. When his nurse nervously picked him up, he fell, and became more seriously handicapped. But she had saved his life and had taken him safely to Lodebar, where he found security in the home of his benefactor Machir, a powerful Transjordanian noble. There the child stayed until King David sent for him.

The nameless nurse disappears after this, but Mephibosheth, whose life she saved, appears again and again as the immediate survivor of King David's friend Jonathan. Because of David's love for Jonathan, he desired to show kindness toward his crippled son.

First we see him eating at David's table. And when he comes for the first time, we hear David say to him,

> "Do not fear; for I will show you kindness for the sake of your father Jonathan, and I will restore to you

all the land of Saul your father; and you shall eat at my table always."

And he [Mephibosheth] did obeisance, and said, "What is your servant, that you should look upon a dead dog such as I?"

Then the king called Ziba, Saul's servant, and said to him, "All that belonged to Saul and to all his house I have given to your master's son. And you and your sons and your servants shall till the land for him, and shall bring in the produce, that your master's son may have bread to eat; but Mephibosheth your master's son shall always eat at my table."

(II Sam. 9:7–10, RSV)

Through this and other touching scenes between David and Jonathan's crippled son, a more admirable David arises, one who is compassionate, tender, and generous to the son of his dead friend. And this nameless nurse lives on as a very worthy servant of a kingly family for whom she was willing to risk her life.

The Maidservant of En Rogel

In the same period is introduced another maidservant, called a wench in the KJV but a maidservant in the RSV. She lived in the valley of the Kidron, near Jerusalem, near a spring called En Rogel, conspicuous because it marked the limit between the tribes of Benjamin and Judah. When David fled from Jerusalem during his son Absalom's rebellion, it is related that "Now Jonathan and Ahimaaz stayed by En Rogel; for they might not be seen to come into the city: and a wench went out and told them; and they went and told king David" (II Sam. 17:17).

A nameless maidservant—how could anyone seem more inconspicuous? And yet she carried a message to a group that formed a connecting link to David's army. Her obscurity brought her into prominence a fleeting moment; then she disappeared down the corridors of time.

A Plain Farm Woman

Another nameless one, identified as the Woman from Bahurim, lived in this small village east of Mount Scopus, near Jerusalem. Two of David's messengers passed by her farm on their way to Jerusalem with vital information to David.

Seizing upon the dramatic opportunity to hide his messengers, this farm woman camouflaged her courtyard cistern with a cloth and a basket of corn. When Absalom's men came looking for them, she not only had concealed them well but she had managed to send Absalom's men back in the wrong direction.

Not identified by name but with an urgent mission to perform, this woman joins the throngs of farm women down the ages, most of whom have cisterns or wells and baskets of corn.

The Far-Sighted Woman in a Little Town

David had many enemies in battle. About this same time appeared a base fellow, Sheba, a Benjamite, who rebelled against him. As Sheba sought to stir up enmity against

David, there came forth a nameless woman, cited briefly in a preceding chapter. She lived in Abel, a fortified town in north Israel. When Joab, David's nephew and also captain of the host, came through with his army, they battered the city wall and threatened death to its people. This woman, learning that her town and all its inhabitants were about to be annihilated, because of the rebellion of this one man named Sheba, went before Joab, saying:

"They were wont to say in old time, 'Let them but ask counsel at Abel'; and so they settled a matter. I am one of those who are peaceable and faithful in Israel; you seek to destroy a city which is a mother in Israel; why will you swallow up the heritage of the Lord?" Joab answered, "Far be it from me, far be it, that I should swallow up or destroy! That is not true. But a man of the hill country of Ephraim, called Sheba the son of Bichri, has lifted up his hand against King David; give up him alone, and I will withdraw from the city." And the woman said to Joab, "Behold, his head shall be thrown to you over the wall." Then the woman went to all the people in her wisdom. And they cut off the head of Sheba the son of Bichri, and threw it out to Joab. So he blew the trumpet, and they dispersed from the city, every man to his home. And Joab returned to Jerusalem to the king.

(II Sam. 20:18–22, RSV)

This discerning woman looked before and beyond this catastrophic moment, first by reminding Joab that her town of Abel was an inheritance from the Lord and then by presenting a solution to save it from destruction. Only a sagacious woman could foresee that it was better to sacrifice the life of one dangerous man than the lives of all of her peaceable and faithful townspeople. And in her logic she had the backing of her fellow citizens.

Who was this woman? She might have borne a prominent Hebrew first name such as Sarah or Ruth or Hannah, or she might have been the wife of a proud citizen. Her wisdom, however, is of far more significance than her name. Because of this she takes her place among the Bible's immortals.

A Little Hebrew Maid

This lovable little maid is etched in a few words which depict her in all of her kindness and sweetness.

> Now Naaman, captain of the host of the king of Syria, was a great man with his master, and honourable, because by him the Lord had given deliverance unto Syria: he was also a mighty man in valour, but he was a leper. And the Syrians had gone out by companies, and had brought away captive out of the land of Israel a little maid; and she waited on Naaman's wife. And she said unto her mistress, Would God my lord were with the prophet that is in Samaria! for he would recover him of his leprosy. And one went in, and told his lord, saying, Thus and thus said the maid that is of the land of Israel.   (II Kings 5:1–4)

Through the intercession of this little maidservant Naaman rode forth in his chariot to Elisha, after the king of Syria and the king of Israel had exchanged letters arranging the visit. And Naaman was miraculously healed in the waters of the Jordan, and later confessed to Elisha that the God of Israel was the God of all. Not only was Naaman healed but he now denied his idolatrous beliefs.

This lowly Hebrew slave girl, a spoil of war taken into the city of Damascus, lives for all time in the Bible by reason of her intercession and her simple faith. She and these other thoughtful, nameless ones wrote their lives into the history of Bible times without title pages but are remembered by what they did for others rather than by who and what they were. Their lives make more meaningful these immortal lines from Rupert Hughes:

Sometimes at night within a wooded park,
Like an ocean cavern, fathoms deep in gloom,
Sweet scents, like hymns, from hidden flowers fume,
And make the wanderer happy; though the dark
Obscure their tint, their name, their shapely bloom.

So in the thick-set chronicles of fame,
There hover deathless feats of souls unknown.
They linger as the fragrant smoke-wreaths blown
From liberal sacrifice. Gone face and name!
The deeds like homeless ghosts, live on alone.

Section Three

THE ETERNALLY FEMININE

CHAPTER ELEVEN

THEIR NEVER CHANGING CHARACTERISTICS

Adulterous, aged, angry; bad, beautiful, brawling; careless, chaste, clamorous, comely, compassionate, complacent, contentious; deceitful, devout, diligent, discreet, dishonest, domestic, drunken; elect, evil; fainthearted, fair, faithful, foolish, foreign, fretful; glorious, godly, good, gracious, grave, great; haughty, high-principled, holy, honest, honorable; impudent, indiscreet; jealous; kind; loose, loving; obedient, odious, outlandish; peevish, peaceable, pitiful, prudent; quarrelsome; reverent, righteous; sensible, serious, shamefaced, shameless, silent, silly, simple, sober, steady, strange, submissive, subtle; temperate, trustworthy; unloved; virtuous; wayward, weak, wealthy, whorish, wicked, wily, worthy; young.

The adjectives used to describe womanhood have not changed too much since the Bible began to be compiled because human nature has not altered much either. We still have the chaste and the unchaste, the faithful and the unfaithful, the prudent and the indiscreet, the wise and the wicked.

The Book of Proverbs has more vivid adjectives than any book in the Bible. Assembled for instructional purposes for the young, it could have served as a manual in academies attended by sons of patricians, for it is filled with advice on moral behavior, especially that dealing with the relationship between men and women. Other expressive adjectives are woven, however, in and out of the Bible and come to a meaningful climax in the New Testament.

Since the publication of the KJV in 1611, so named because it was compiled under the tutelage of James I of England, the adjective gracious has been used to describe a friendly, compassionate, and tender woman. One Proverb (KJV) describes her: "A gracious woman retaineth honour and strong men retain riches" (11:16). The RSV translates this, "A gracious woman gets honor, and violent men get riches," all of which make us know that a gracious woman's very manner, if praiseworthy, is achieved through her own efforts. She never has to seek honors. They come to her because she merits them.

A Good Wife, a Crown to Her Husband

"A virtuous woman," says another Proverb, "is a crown to her husband: but she that maketh ashamed is as rottenness to his bones" (12:4). This method of startling contrast is effective. An evil wife can harm a man as much as a malignancy or some other dreaded disease. Worry and embarrassment over her could bring on disease.

Another Proverb, cited in another chapter, asks, "Who can find a virtuous woman? for her price is far above rubies" (31:10). A man may buy rubies and other jewels but not an excellent wife. She comes only as a result of his good judgment and oftentimes as a special gift from God, because he deserves her.

Another Proverb reads, "Houses and riches are the inheritance of fathers; and a prudent wife is from the Lord" (19:14). A lack of prudence in a woman too often signifies a lack of virtue. A prudent woman is judicious and provident. She conforms to the rules of reason, truth, and decency at all times and in all circumstances. She locks up her motives and allows only those dear to her to have a key to her heart. A woman guided by prudence knows not to talk too much. She learns that silence is oftentimes wise; again, she may need to say what she thinks.

Another caustic Proverb reads "as a jewel of gold in a swine's snout, so is a fair ["beautiful," RSV] woman which is without discretion" (11:22). What a pertinent comparison! Who but a Bible writer in an agricultural civilization would ever think of that? And yet it says so much. What good is a gold ring in a swine's snout? How long can an indiscreet woman retain beauty? If she is imprudent for long, her beauty falls away quickly, and she mourns all too late its passing.

The Noisy, Brawling Woman

And then there is the brawling (contentious, RSV) woman. "It is better to dwell in the corner of the housetop, than with a brawling woman and in a wide house" (25:24). A servant living alone in a garret is better off than the husband who lives in a splendor of a mansion with a peevish, quarrelsome woman. At least the servant is free from vexation while in the garret.

"A continual dropping in a very rainy day and a contentious woman are all alike" (27:15). Everyone knows
that a woman's contentiousness, like the dripping of rain
in the jungle day and night, is difficult to live with. A man
has to learn to bear patiently the affliction of being married to such a woman. Another Proverb states that "it is
better to dwell in the wilderness than with a contentious
and angry woman" (21:19). She can make her husband's
life miserable. He might better be living in the wilderness,
exposed to the elements. At least he could find more
peace.

On Wickedness in Woman

There are many didactic sayings on wickedness in womanhood. One of the most effective appears in Ecclesiastes 7:
26–29, which will be fully delineated in another chapter.
But the most effective of all again appears in the Book of
Proverbs.

"Lust not after her [the wicked woman's] beauty in
thine heart; neither let her take thee with her eyelids. For
by means of a whorish woman a man is brought to a piece
of bread: and the adulteress will hunt for the precious life"
(6:25–26). The picture is even more caustic in a later
Proverb: "Such is the way of an adulterous woman; she
eateth and wipeth her mouth, and saith, I have done no
wickedness" (30:20), quoted in a preceding chapter. And
the wise, unnamed mother of Proverbs implores her son
to watch out for the "strange ["loose," RSV] woman . . .
which flattereth with her words" (7:5); "which forsaketh
the guide of her youth and forgetteth the covenant of her

God" (2:17). She is further pictured in 7:11 as "loud and stubborn" ["wayward," RSV], and is said to be "subtle ["wily," RSV] of heart" (7:10), and as having an "impudent face" (7:13).

THE UNLOVELY AND THE WISE

The Book of Proverbs also describes well the "odious ["unloved," RSV] woman" (30:23). It compares her to "a servant when he reigneth, a fool when he is filled with meat; . . . and an handmaid that is heir to her mistress" (30:22–23). Such a woman is unloved because she is so unlovely. Her ill nature becomes a constant source of annoyance to all around her.

"A foolish woman is clamorous: she is simple and knoweth nothing" (9:13). A part of her foolishness is that she thinks she knows much. "Every wise woman buildeth her house: but the foolish plucketh it down with her hands" (14:1). The RSV merely states, "Wisdom builds her [own] house, but folly with her own hands tears it down."

Blessed is the wise woman. Elsewhere in this book mention is made of the wise woman of Tekoa and the five wise virgins. Other Proverbs accentuate the qualities these wise ones possessed. "The law of the wise is a fountain of life" (13:14), "the lips of the wise disperse knowledge" (15:7), and "How much better it is to get wisdom than gold" (16:16).

As mentioned in a preceding chapter, Judah called Tamar more "righteous than I" (Gen. 38:26), because she had not been promiscuous with him but had only declared her rights to motherhood, according to the levirate law.

RUTH—THE WOMAN OF WORTH

The RSV has a very apt phrase for Ruth, when it calls her "a woman of worth" ("virtuous," KJV) (Ruth 3:11). Before she became the wife of Boaz, a wealthy landowner for whom she worked, he commended Ruth, then a widow, because she had not "gone after young men, whether poor or rich." She had shown herself to be a worthy woman, and because she was, Boaz asked her to be his wife.

The Shunammite is called "a great ["wealthy," RSV] woman" in II Kings 4:8. She was both great in faith and wealthy in position. The woman who is "all glorious within" is referred to in Psalm 45:13. Isaiah (32:9) gives an excellent description of "careless ["complacent," RSV] daughters," who are more fully described later.

In Lamentations 4:10, we read of the tragic fate that came upon the "pitiful" ("compassionate," RSV), but hungry, cannibalistic women during the siege of Zion.

The KJV applies an interesting adjective, "outlandish," (Neh. 13:26) to describe the "foreign" (RSV) women of other nations, who caused King Solomon to sin. The inference is that intermarriage with pagan women was against the laws of Israel, and if too many men in places of power married such women, the nation would be turned away from God. Here Nehemiah is advocating marriage reform for the refugees returning from Babylonia and Egypt. Nehemiah seems to imply that Israel needed the witness of righteous women who remembered their covenant with God, not foreign women, who had neither knowledge nor respect for it.

APOCRYPHAL ADJECTIVES ON WOMEN

While this book is based on the KJV, with additional quotes from the RSV, the following adjectives are from the Douay Version, the official Roman Catholic Bible translated at the English Catholic University at Douay, France, in 1582. This includes the Apocrypha, a collection of fourteen books not included in the canonized Hebrew Scriptures and not compiled until two centuries before Christ and during the century he was born. They are our oldest written record of the period between the Old and New Testaments.

The Apocrypha's Book of Ecclesiasticus (Oxford edition), like Proverbs, mainly proverbial, extols the value of wisdom and has quite a lot to say about women. Among the verses on the evil in women are these:

A grief of heart and sorrow is a woman that is jealous over another woman . . .

An evil wife is a yoke shaken to and fro: he that hath hold of her is as though he held a scorpion.

A drunken woman . . . will not cover her own shame.

The whoredom of a woman may be known in her haughty looks and eyelids.

If thy daughter be shameless, keep her in straitly, lest she abuse herself through overmuch liberty.

A wicked woman is given as a portion to a wicked man . . .

A dishonest woman contemneth shame . . .

A shameless woman shall be counted as a dog . . .

A loud crying woman and a scold shall be sought out to drive away the enemies.

(Eccles. 26:6–10, 23–25, 27)

This same Apocryphal book also has much to say on the good in women, such as:

Blessed is the man that hath a virtuous wife, for the number of his days shall double.

A virtuous woman rejoiceth her husband, and he shall fulfill the years of his life in peace.

A good wife is a good portion, which shall be given in the portion of them that fear the Lord.

The grace of a wife delighteth her husband, and her discretion will fatten his bones.

A silent and loving woman is a gift of the Lord . . .

A shamefaced and faithful woman is a double grace . . .

As the sun when it ariseth in the high heaven; so is the beauty of a good wife in the ordering of her house.

A godly woman is given to him that feareth the Lord.

An honest woman will reverence her husband.

A woman that honoureth her husband shall be judged wise of all.

(Eccles. 26:1–3, 13–14, 15–16, 23–26)

WOMEN MORE POWERFUL THAN KINGS

In Esdras, another Apocryphal book, we find the meaning-ful story of a young Persian who was a bodyguard for King

Darius of Persia, and when asked, "What one force in the world is strongest?" answered, "Women are strongest." A second bodyguard rejoined, "Wine is strongest." A third replied, "The king is strongest." But the first guard, stressing the powerful influence of women, went on to explain:

> Yea, and if men have gathered together gold and silver, or any other goodly thing, do they not love a woman which is comely in favour and beauty?
>
> And letting all those things go, do they not gape, and even with open mouth fix their eyes fast on her; and have not all men more desire unto her than unto silver or gold, or any goodly thing whatsoever? . . .
>
> By this also ye must know that women have dominion over you: do ye not labour and toil, and give and bring all to the woman?   (I Esd. 4:18–20, 22)

The young Persian's listeners realized that women bear men, nurture them, clothe them. Men give up a fortune looking for a "comely" woman, and often lose their heads for her. Men "become servants for their [women's] sakes, and many also have perished, have erred, and sinned for women" (I Esd. 4:26–27). Finally, it was conceded that women are more powerful than either the king or wine.

THE WOMEN OF HIGH PRINCIPLE

The New Testament's finest chapters on womanhood appear in the First Letter of Paul to Timothy and in the Letter of Paul to Titus in his instruction for women in the church. Paul advises that women "must be grave ["serious,"

RSV], not slanderers, [but] sober ["temperate," RSV], faithful in all things" (I Tim. 3:11). The New English Bible has a beautiful translation for this. It says: "Their wives, equally, must be women of high principle, who will not talk scandal, sober and trustworthy in every way." What an inspiring delineation of the best in womanhood. It makes us know that women of high principle wear an invisible armor that is impenetrable.

Paul, who is not always flattering to women, also speaks of "silly ["weak," RSV] women, laden with sins . . . ever learning, and never able to come to the knowledge of the truth" (II Tim. 3:6–7). Silly is probably the more descriptive. Such women are silly because they allow themselves to become so weak.

In the letter Paul wrote, probably from Macedonia, to Titus on the island of Crete, he set up modes of behavior for aged women, and these reach a high point in Christian ethics. He counsels that "they be in behaviour as becometh holiness, not false accusers, not given to much wine, teachers of good things; that they may teach the young women to be sober, to love their husbands, to love their children, to be discreet, chaste, keepers at home, good, obedient to their own husbands, so the word of God be not blasphemed" (Tit. 2:3–5). The RSV says, "Bid the older women likewise to be reverent in behavior, not to be slanderers or slaves to drink; they are to teach what is good, and to train the young women to love their husbands and children, to be sensible, chaste, domestic, kind, and submissive to their husbands, that the word of God may not be discredited."

Although the word lady appears only four times in the Old Testament, Isaiah 47:5, 7; Judges 5:29, and Esther

1:18, the qualities of an elect lady are not fully described until the Letter to the Elect Lady in the Second Epistle of John, which gives an excellent verbal picture of an elect lady, a meaningful metaphor to describe a church and "her children," its members.

Other adjectives signifying the best in womanhood appear elsewhere in the New Testament. When Paul and Barnabas were at Lystra preaching to the Gentiles, who "were glad, and glorified the word of the Lord," (Acts 13:48) "the Jews stirred up the devout and honourable women, and the chief men of the city, and raised persecution against Paul and Barnabas, and expelled them out of their coasts" (v. 50). This should be a warning to all devout and honorable women to show discretion regarding the leaders they follow, for the deceitful and false will try to gain them as cohorts.

Writing of husbands and wives, Peter refers to "the holy women who trusted in God" (I Peter 3:5). Where do we come upon a better definition of a holy woman? Simply one who trusts in God.

"A woman full of good works and almsdeeds" (Acts 9:36) is the way Dorcas's Christian service at Joppa is described. This phrase actually delineates her work more effectively than had the one word charitable been used.

These many descriptive adjectives and phrases on womanhood show that the Bible is a well of information about every facet of womanhood. The writer of fiction, looking for either the good or the bad, can find both types fully delineated. Because the Bible has been called literature's greatest feminine portrait gallery, no doubt it contains more varying and descriptive adjectives on womanhood than any other book ever compiled.

CHAPTER TWELVE

THEIR EMOTIONAL CONFLICTS

The Bible, called the most thorough textbook ever assembled on human behavior, does not throw the spotlight on women when they are ready to pose but when they had rather not be caught in the glare of the spotlight. And so feminine foibles, like pimples on a lovely young girl's face, burst forth amid qualities of excellence. In her mature years, malice and resentment may cloud an older woman's countenance as quickly as romantic love radiated it in her maiden years. Self-centeredness and self-pity declare themselves as unexpectedly as ill temper, deceit, impatience, hatred, envy, and prejudice, and these qualities appear in the strong as well as the weak.

In no other book is there such an astounding collection of psychological types. The pungent phrases, the apt observations, and the drama around their lives give us a sharper understanding of humanity as a whole. Because the Bible projects human nature as it is and not as it ought to be, a study of some of its great women characters suggests an afternoon in a theater in the round with some of its leading heroines. Like the stage, the Bible is made up of a composite of bigness and littleness, beauty and ugliness, love and hate. Were it not for its portrayal of these contrary elements, it would falsify humanity, and we could not identify with it.

Because in the Bible we see some of its great characters not only as being exceptionally human but as understandably fallible and feeble, we glimpse in their frailties some hope for ourselves. Jesus is the one exception. Others, with the exclusion of his mother, Mary, possess a variety of grievous faults. Even the youthful Joseph, often called the most Christlike character in the Old Testament, showed some conceit around his brothers when his father, Jacob, made him "a long robe with sleeves" (Gen. 37:3, RSV) such as the children of a king wore. It is no wonder his brothers were jealous of him.

AN AMBITIOUS MOTHER BUT A DISLOYAL WIFE

Rebekah, wife of Isaac and mother of Jacob, is first depicted in Genesis as courteous, chaste, guileless, and beautiful, but we meet an entirely different woman forty years later. She exercises dominion over her household, challenges the rule of primogeniture, seizes the thread of destiny, twists it in her own way, and is willing to pay the price for her breach of ethics in order to help her favorite son, Jacob. Her blind husband and her pleasure-loving son Esau come out losers.

As the ambitious mother, anxious for her most worthy son to inherit the family blessing, Rebekah faced intense emotional conflicts. She was fearful that Esau would give up his father's blessing as easily as he had given up his birthright to Jacob for a mess of pottage. She did not have the faith to leave this to God. She took the matter into her own hands, and was fair neither to her husband nor to Esau.

Her fall from grace also sheds a different light on the impermanence of girlhood loveliness, such as Abraham's steward recognized in her when he was searching for the loveliest bride he could find for his master's son.

RESENTMENT, DECEIT IN A PATRIARCH'S WIFE

In most of his relationships with others, Joseph reflected the love that his mother, Rachel, and father, Jacob, bore for each other, while his half brothers, by his mother's sister Leah, never seemed to possess as admirable qualities. Although Rachel was Jacob's favorite, she had her shortcomings.

These were polygamous times, and Rachel had had no children by Jacob while Leah had had six sons and a daughter by him. "Rachel envied her sister; and said unto Jacob give me children or else I die" (Gen. 30:1). This was the exclamation of a querulous, self-willed woman, and her impatience angered Jacob, who asked, "Am I in God's stead who hath withheld from thee the fruit of the womb?" (v. 2).

And so she gave Jacob her maid, Bilhah, as a secondary wife, and he had two sons by her. Still perturbed that she had had no children of her own, she became annoyed at her sister Leah, and said to her, "Give me, I pray thee, of thy son's mandrakes" [called the "love apples," sometimes thought to cure barrenness] (v. 14).

The placid Leah spoke the only bitter words recorded about her when she asked Rachel, "Is it a small matter that thou hast taken my husband? and wouldest thou take away my son's mandrakes also?" (v. 15).

No doubt Rachel finally drew closer to God in her distress over her childlessness, because it is recorded, "And God remembered Rachel, and God hearkened to her, and opened her womb" (v. 23). And she conceived and gave birth to her first son, Joseph. Rachel's emotional jealousy and envy are a shocking revelation in the life of a woman so lovely, and so beloved by her husband even long after her death. However, she passed on to her son, Joseph, her best qualities, her unconscious charm and her beauty, so probably her emotional frailties appeared quickly and disappeared almost as suddenly as they came.

Moses's Wife and Her Bad Temper

Zipporah, the wife of Moses, had an ungovernable temper. When Moses was stricken with a sudden illness at their lodging place on the way out of the land of Midian, he was unable to perform his son's circumcision, an instruction that God gave first to Abraham. Believing that God's wrath was upon them because of this neglect, Zipporah hurriedly performed the circumcision herself, speaking harshly to Moses as she did (Ex. 4:25).

One commentator has pointed out that this sudden act on Zipporah's part was to avert the wrath of Yahweh (God). In this primitive crisis, we have no way to judge but we do know that Moses's wife showed neither patience nor love during a family emergency.

Miriam's Prejudice in a Race Matter

Moses's sister Miriam, depicted earlier as a valiant leader of the women of Israel, also had her weaker side. When her brother married a second time, probably after the death of his first wife, Zipporah, both Miriam and her brother Aaron turned against this new wife, who was of another race. Like Aaron, Miriam showed great resentment toward this new wife of her brother. Whether she was of a different skin color and different culture are debatable, but Miriam and Aaron were so angered at the marriage that they jealously asked Moses, "Hath the Lord indeed spoken only by Moses? Hath he not spoken also by us?" And the Lord heard it (Num. 12:2).

Miriam and Aaron may have thought that Moses should relinquish the leadership of his people because of this marriage to a foreigner. But the anger of the Lord, the Bible tells us, was kindled against them because of their resentment, for he was not a God of one race or nation but of all races and nations.

Soon afterward "Miriam became leprous, white as snow. . . . And Aaron said unto Moses, Alas, my lord, I beseech thee, lay not the sin upon us wherein we have done foolishly, and wherein we have sinned. Let her not be as one dead" (Num. 12:10–12).

A meek, forgiving man, Moses held no animosity against his brother and sister, and now prayed, "Heal her now, O God, I beseech thee" (v. 13). In seven days Miriam was well again.

Did Miriam's prejudice trigger her illness? Was she so

overburdened with jealousy and resentment that these negative qualities caused the malfunction of her body?

Sin's Relationship to Bodily, Mental Ills

In Miriam's illness we see that mental hygiene and physical illness may be interconnected, a thesis profoundly delineated in *None of These Diseases*, by a physician, Dr. S. I. McMillen. He bases his study on the Bible: "If thou wilt diligently hearken to the voice of the Lord thy God, and wilt do that which is right in his sight, and wilt give ear to his commandments, and keep all his statutes, I will put none of these diseases upon thee" (Ex. 15:26). Dr. McMillen, focusing his therapy on the Bible, tells that:

> Instead of making frequent, expensive and oftentimes futile trips to a psychiatrist's couch, we are invited by the Lord to make one trip to the cross for crucifixion of the troublemaker. When we drive the spikes into everything in our lives that God has marked for destruction, then God, for Christ's sake, executes that old self which ever breathes out "ego ambition" and licentious, lustful living.
>
> (Pp. 138–39)

This author and these biblical illustrations make us know that we must obey divine regulations in order to be healthy. Many diseases are triggered by emotional turmoil, which can cause debilitating and fatal diseases. The lives of these women, who fell from grace, present an astounding testimony to the potential power of scriptural prescription.

Emotional conflicts may not always cause such specific problems as those outlined here, but in a wife and mother, they may bring endless sorrow and tragedy into her home.

ONE WOMAN WHO TAUNTED ANOTHER

Hannah, the beloved mother of Samuel, mentioned in a previous chapter, had to suffer for the insults inflicted upon her by her husband's other wife, Peninnah. The latter had several sons and daughters by Elkanah, Samuel's father, while Hannah had none.

Glorying in her own good fortune, because she was not childless while Hannah was, Peninnah "provoked her [Hannah] sorely, to irritate her, because the Lord had closed her womb. So it went on year by year; as often as she went up to the house of the Lord, she used to provoke her" (I Sam. 1:6–7, RSV).

While she was so deeply distressed, Hannah prayed for a son, who became one of the great men of Israel. But Hannah's taunter did not produce a child that is even named; nor does the Bible record a good thing about Peninnah or about her children, who were not worthy of the high calling of Hannah's son, Samuel. Except for her insulting sarcasm toward Hannah, who became one of the great mothers in Israel, Peninnah is unknown.

THE IMPATIENCE OF TWO WIVES

Michal, King Saul's daughter, who was David's first wife, had no patience with her husband's religious zeal when she saw him "leaping and dancing before the Lord; and she despised him in her heart" (II Sam. 6:16).

David's enthusiasm centered around the ark of God as he saw it being removed from Philistia to Jerusalem. He and a group of his followers went forth with the ark, a portable shrine, and a symbol of Israel's covenant with God; and as they did so they shouted loudly and danced spiritedly to a trumpet. David was excited because Israel's most treasured religious emblem was on its way to his new capital.

In celebration of the event David wore his priestly ephod, a sleeveless, close-fitting garment. Michal berated her husband before his servants for his manner of dress and his loud actions. Early commentators deride her for taunting David at a moment of happy celebration. But later commentators ask, "Could David's dance have had Baalistic overtones?" If so, Michal's protest may have served a good purpose. At least her protest reveals that wives then as now became emotionally excited about the way their husbands sometimes conduct themselves in public. And when they do, love vanishes for the moment at least.

Amid all of his woes, Job was told by his wife "to curse God and die." Although Job's wife must have had many remarkably fine qualities, they are not recorded. She is remembered for her one shortcoming, impatience in time of trial.

So often it is like that in our own lives. The public only knows about our bad qualities, enlarged upon by tattlers and busybodies, who seldom take time to look for the good qualities.

A Woman's Face, a True Barometer

Amid the drama of these women's lives, where both trials and triumphs, joy and irritation, hope and anxiety are recorded, we find daily wisdom. And we learn that we attain extraordinary knowledge on how to live in the Bible's timeless and timely insight into human beings.

The problems which haunted women in Bible times haunt women now, but in a study of their emotional conflicts we gain a better perspective of how to meet both the trials and triumphs in our own lives. These were living women with faults and passions and virtues. Because they were creatures of flesh and blood, we know that their emotional conflicts were sharply etched in their faces, just as they are in our own. An anonymous poem written several decades ago says this so well.

You don't have to tell how you live each day,
　　You don't have to say if you work or if you play,
Since a tried, true barometer is right in its place,
　　However you live, it shows in your face.

The false, the deceit that you bear in your heart,
　　Will not stay inside where they first got their start
For sinew and blood are a thin veil of lace;
　　Whatever you wear in your heart, you wear it in your
　　face.

If your life is unselfish, if for others you live,
　　Not for what you can get but for how much you can give
If you live close to God, in His Infinite Grace
　　You don't have to say so, it shows in your face.

CHAPTER THIRTEEN

HOW THEY LOOKED
AND WHAT THEY WORE

Our knowledge of what women wore in Bible times is based largely on replicas on ancient monuments, panels, seals, plaques, and the testimony that has been found in graves of civilizations contemporary with them. The thin fabric of a woman's dress and undergarments has not survived the centuries, but the buttons, made of shell or stone, and other ornaments of bronze and silver have survived. From such sources, including a few Bible references on women's apparel and a study of anthropology of Bible times, scholars have pieced together the story of how they looked and what they wore.

THEIR APPEARANCE

Because many of the women, especially those in nomadic times, walked or rode an ass, and also helped in agricultural pursuits, it is natural to suppose they were not overweight. Neither were Hebrew women as tall as women today, even though there probably were exceptions to this rule, for they intermarried with the Hittites, Babylonians, Assyrians, Persians, Romans, Greeks, Philistines, and Egyptians, some of larger stature than the Hebrews.

These primitive women were straight and erect. A part of this was due to their outdoor life. Every day they came home from the well, their full water jugs atop their heads, and they walked proudly and upright. Even the plain women would draw attention because of their beautiful carriage. The maiden in the Song of Songs is complimented because her "stature is like to a palm tree" (7:7). Hebrew women were sturdy too. They usually bore their children easily and quickly, often before the midwife reached them (Ex. 1:19). The Bible, however, does speak of sudden destruction coming as "travail upon a woman with child" (I Thess. 5:3).

"Even though the skin color of the Mediterranean people appears dark to us," says Ludwig Kohler in his book *Hebrew Man*, "we must not be led astray by this. For the basic color is white. It is only pigmentation and sunlight which make it appear dark" (p. 22). Dr. Kohler also points out that "Today a fair skin ranks as beautiful." But the maiden in Song of Songs is depicted as "black but comely." "The color of the skin," continues Dr. Kohler, "depends upon where the person normally lives."

This same author describes women's hair as "black or dark brown, straight, not curly." Even men wore their hair long, though the New Testament says, "if a man have long hair, it is a shame to him. But if a woman have long hair, it is a glory to her: for her hair is given her for a covering" (I Cor. 11:14–15).

Women in Bible times might have been vain creatures but they were never mannish creatures. About one thing the Bible is very specific. And that is, "A woman shall not wear anything that pertains to a man, nor shall a man put on a woman's garment; for whoever does these things is an abomination to the Lord your God" (Deut. 22:5, RSV). This concept was directed against the simulated changes of sex in the Canaanite religion. The motivation came from the Israelite aversion to all that was unnatural. In pagan countries such exchange of garments was generally for immoral purposes.

THEIR MANY COLORS

The women dressed in many vivid colors. The master painters clothed them in carnelian red, madonna blue, sunset gold, a sunny orange, and regal purple. In *The Bible as History*, Werner Keller relates that "they colored their dress, the walls of their houses, and the faces of their women. Even in the days of the patriarchs, their delight in color was apparent" (p. 217). "Ye daughters of Israel, weep over Saul, who clothed you in scarlet, with other delights, who put on ornaments of gold upon your apparel" (II Sam. 1:24), laments David over the death of Saul, whom he succeeded. Of Tamar, the daughter of David by his wife Maacah, it is written that she had a garment of "divers colours" (II Sam. 13:18). Werner Keller explains this love of color:

Nature had given the land of Canaan one of the most wonderful painters' palettes. The children of Israel needed only to stretch out their hands. Pomegranates and saffron yielded a lovely yellow; madder root and safflower, a fiery red; woad, a heavenly blue; there was also ocher and red chalk. The sea donated the queen of all dye merchants, the murex snail. Its soft colorless body turned purple in the sunlight. . . . The Phoenicians were the first to create a proper industry for the extraction of purple in their seaports, but later Palestine, too, devoted itself to the profitable business of snail catching.   (Pp. 217–18)

THEIR FABRICS OF WOOL, SILK, LINEN

Their fabrics, all hand-woven, oftentimes were very beautiful. Especially was this true of the queens, women in harems, and others able to afford them.

As early as Deborah's time, about 1100 B.C., we see the mother of Sisera, the Canaanite chieftain who became general of Jabin's hosts in the war against the Israelites, peering through her latticed window, wondering why her son's chariot was so long in coming. Her son, she knew, would have access to the most valuable spoil. And so this haughty, luxury-loving mother asked herself: "Are they not finding and dividing the spoil?—a maiden or two for every man; spoil of dyed stuffs for Sisera, spoil of dyed stuffs embroidered, two pieces of dyed work embroidered for my neck as spoil?" (Judg. 5:30, RSV). What this luxury-loving mother did not know was that her son had already been killed by Jael, the wife of Heber.

The dress of women varied from these elaborate embroidered and dyed fabrics, such as the mother of a general might wear, to the gold robes worn by the king's daughter in Psalms 45:13. Some of these fabrics were woven by the women on their own looms, but many were brought in by richly laden caravans from Arabia. It is easy to imagine that the Queen of Sheba, in addition to bringing gold in abundance and precious stones, also brought along fine fabrics for Solomon's many wives. King Solomon's ships also made long voyages through the Red Sea to Arabia and no doubt brought back with them many luxurious fabrics from these and other lands. "Ships of the desert" (camels) also trudged toward Israel with a wide range of goods, probably fine fabrics from many places.

But oftentimes the plain homespuns worn by the poorer women were lovely too, for they were all hand-woven, sometimes of wool, the oldest of fabrics, although some contend that linen, which was cultivated in Bible times, goes back to early antiquity. Women of the courts wore luxurious fabrics of linen, silk, and wool. Moses spoke of the fine linen of Egypt and of its superior excellence. Although the linen was usually bleached for summer wear, blue linen threads were used in some of the textile materials found with the Qumran Scrolls. The excellent wife and mother of Proverbs is described as having clothing of silk and purple.

Their Jewelry, Ointments, etc.

Jewelry for those who could afford it was plentiful from early times. When Abraham's steward journeyed to Mesopotamia and selected Rebekah for the bride of his master's son Isaac, he presented as gifts from his master "a golden earring of half a shekel weight" [of gold] (Gen. 24:22), also nose rings. Ezekiel describes precious stones of carnelian, topaz, and jasper, chrysolite, beryl, and onyx, sapphire, carbuncle, and emerald, all wrought in gold (28:13,

RSV). Rubies too were common. The writer of Proverbs compares a virtuous woman's price as "far above rubies." Isaiah, writing of Israel's most affluent period, the Hebrew Monarchy, describes a wide variety of luxuries worn by the women of the court and harems, everything from tinkling ornaments on their feet to signet rings and nose rings. He also tells of their perfume.

Exquisite toilet sets for women have been found in Ur, dating from before the time of Sarah and Abraham. Ivory and bone hairpins have also been found in ruins dating several centuries before Christ, as well as tiny stone mills for grinding eye paint, and cosmetic spoons with skillfully carved handles. The women rouged their faces and traced heavy black lines under their eyes to make them look larger. Even curling rods and ivory combs were found in the Lachish mound at the level of Amenhoptep ruins in 1400 B.C.

The lover of the Song of Songs describes his betrothed as having lips like "a thread of scarlet . . . temples like a piece of pomegranate" (4:3). She probably used rouge to accent these natural colors. Sweet-smelling ointments were also quite common, for again this lover describes the sweet ointments of his betrothed as being lovelier than all spices. She probably wore a bundle of myrrh (1:13). The king's daughter of Psalm 45 is described as having on garments that smelled of myrrh and aloes and cassia.

Botanists investigating the authenticity of these stories have found these fragrances in delicate flowers and herbs and in the sap of shrubs and blossoms. Some came from foreign lands; cassia, for example, from a tree with a cinnamon-like bark, and the aloes from the island of

Socotra in the Arabian Sea. Others still grow in Palestine today.

Cosmetics, such as the eye paint Jezebel wore, were common. An ivory rouge pot found in the grave of Thutmose III, Egyptian king, who ruled from 1479–1447 B.C., indicates that women used a variety of cosmetics. Egyptian cosmetic spoons with handles of skillfully carved nude women have been found, as have sets of toilet instruments, including tweezers, ear picks, stilettos, and paint sticks. Some date as far back as Ur of the twenty-fifth century B.C.

Their Hair, Eyelashes, Sandals

Wigs made of human hair or sheep's wool were not uncommon. The women also dyed their hair with henna, using it also for their toenails and their fingernails. They also decorated their hair with delicate sprays of fresh flowers. As for their headdress, they tied their heads, as did Queen Jezebel, with fine hand-woven fabrics wrapped turban style.

Again like Jezebel, they painted their eyelashes and eyebrows, using both galena and powdered lapis lazuli. They painted their mouths with cochineal, made of dried insects.

From the Nile, they imported curling pins, hair pins, and mirrors of polished bronze. On their dressing tables might also be found tiny bottles of burned clay filled with perfume, or ointments as they were then called. In larger jars were oils (probably from olives) for dry hair and dry skin. There also were ivory ointment boxes as well as mixing jars and rouge pots, all of which have been salvaged from archaeological ruins.

Sandals were simply made of leather the size of the foot, and straps were sewed to hold them onto the ankles. For dressier occasions, the sandals were gilded or decorated with flowers.

This was in the more affluent periods when women thought much about what they wore. But with the coming of Christ, a new era dawned. The Christian radiance in a woman's face brought a glowing light, and so make-up, jewelry, and fine fabrics came to have much less significance.

MEANING OF MODESTY, SIMPLICITY

Tertullian (160–230), the ecclesiastical writer and one of the fathers of the Latin Church, mentions the modest dress of the early Christian women as indicative of the consciousness of their new spiritual wealth and worthiness. They no longer needed outward adornment. On the other hand, they desired to be clothed with the beauty and simplicity of a Christlike character. Jesus had admonished, "Take no thought . . . of what ye shall put on" (Matt. 6:25). Their simplicity was a rebuke to and reaction from the shameless extravagances of the wealthy in the period of both the United Kingdom and the Divided Kingdom.

There are other such references in the New Testament. In writing to Timothy on the position of women in the new church at Ephesus, Paul says that "women should adorn themselves modestly and sensibly in seemly apparel, not with braided hair or gold or pearls or costly attire but by good deeds, as befits women who profess religion" (I Tim. 2:9–10, RSV).

Finally John, who called himself a servant of Christ and brother of the suffering Christians, says that "he that overcometh shall be clothed in white raiment, and I will not blot his name out of the book of life" (Rev. 3:5). White has always had special significance, for it signifies both purity and simplicity, like that worn by a bride then and now.

CHAPTER FOURTEEN

BEAUTY IN WOMANHOOD

A truly beautiful woman in Bible times possessed a quality of mind and heart and spirit that embraced the whole personality, suggesting what Sir James Barrie has called "a sort of bloom on a woman. If you have it, you don't need to have anything else; and if you don't have it, it doesn't matter what else you have."

Beauty took in much then as now, magnetism, a natural dignity, good judgment, courteous manners, tenderness, thoughtfulness, poise, serenity, kindness, love, and an indefinable radiance, like a light within. These qualities seem to proclaim what Washington Irving has called "a divinity within that makes the divinity without." Such a woman enables others who come into her presence to remember that she has a God who is great enough to believe in and rely upon.

The adjective beautiful is used to describe five maidens in the Old Testament and four mature women, revealing to us that beauty then as now had no age and that it took many forms at many ages, but it always implied the ability to choose between right and wrong.

The word beautiful is never used to describe a woman in the New Testament because the qualities of mind and heart seem to transcend any reference to mere physical beauty. Not even Mary, the mother of Christ, is referred to as a woman of beautiful countenance, although the master artists Raphael, Leonardo da Vinci, Angelico, Bellini, Van Eyck, to name but a few, have portrayed her in that light. So luminous is their conception of Mary's spiritual beauty that they oftentimes have surrounded her with a halo that illumines her whole face.

REAL BEAUTIES: FIVE MAIDENS, FOUR WOMEN

The five Bible maidens who are called beautiful, all from different periods of time, lived under dissimilar conditions. They are: Rebekah, Rachel, Tamar (David's daughter), Abishag, and Esther. All five seemed to possess more than mere prettiness, which Shakespeare describes as "a vain and doubtful good." In later years several of these developed unattractive qualities, but all were born lovely and developed into ravishingly beautiful maidens.

Abishag (I Kings 1:1–4) was chosen as a young maiden, because of her beauty, to minister to King David in his declining years. In ancient times it was believed that the life breath of young people, warm and vigorous, could be transferred to an aging person and so prolong his life.

The term for Rebekah, "very fair to look upon" (Gen. 24:16), is immediately followed by the description "a virgin." Rachel, described as "beautiful" (29:17), is also called "well favoured," meaning very lovely in spirit and mind as well as of countenance. The young Tamar is called Absalom's "fair sister" (II Sam. 13:1) in the KJV but "beautiful" in the RSV. She too is described in the next verse in the KJV as "a virgin." Abishag is portrayed as "fair" (KJV) and "beautiful" (RSV) (I Kings 1:4). She too had other graces, for the Bible tells us she was sought for David "throughout all the coasts of Israel" (v. 3), and they found her, a Shunammite, and brought her to David and she "cherished [nursed] the king and ministered to him: but the king knew her not" (v. 4). Esther is depicted as being both "fair and beautiful" (Esther 2:7).

The four mature women called beautiful are Sarah, the wife of Abraham; Abigail, first the wife of Nabal and later one of the wives of King David; Queen Vashti of Persia, the first wife of King Ahasuerus, and Bath-sheba, first the wife of Uriah and afterward one of the wives of King David and the mother of Solomon.

Sarah, One of Beauties of the Ages

As the first of these, Sarah, and her husband, Abraham, were about to enter Egypt in their journey there during a famine in the land of Canaan, he said to Sarah:

> I know that thou art a fair [beautiful] woman to look upon:
>
> Therefore it shall come to pass, when the Egyptians shall see thee, that they shall say, This is his wife: and they will kill me, but they will save thee alive.
>
> Say, I pray thee, thou art my sister: that it may be well with me for thy sake; and my soul shall live because of thee.
>
> And it came to pass, that, when Abram was come into Egypt, the Egyptians beheld the woman that she was very fair.　(Gen. 12:11–14)

Sarah's beauty has been extolled for centuries. G. S. Wegener in his *6000 Years of the Bible* (p. 326) relates that the Genesis Apocryphon, one of the Dead Sea Scrolls, found in the Qumran Cave in 1947, contains a touching description of Sarah's beauty. This ancient manuscript, containing a paraphrase of the first ten chapters of Genesis, was unrolled and deciphered in 1956 by Professor Beiberkraut of the Hebrew University. Sarah must have attained a beauty of mind, heart, and spirit, for her husband, Abraham, loved her so much that he never seemed to see her shortcomings.

REBEKAH AND THE MASTER ARTISTS

Sarah's daughter-in-law, Rebekah, depicted by the master painters as a great beauty, seemed to possess a certain dignity and a grace that bathed her whole being with a purity that imparted an indefinable radiance. Because of her kindness and thoughtfulness to Abraham's aged steward, her physical beauty took on a new dimension in the artists' eyes.

These master painters turned to Rebekah for their highest conception of maidenly beauty. Murillo has caught Rebekah's loveliness as she stands at the well, so have Poussin, Veronese, and Guido Reni.

The first meeting of Isaac and Rebekah is also a subject that has attracted the master artist. This scene has been painted by Julius Schnorr von Karolsfeld, and again by Raphael. Francesco Penni has done a charming courtyard scene of Isaac and Rebekah in fond embrace, in Gerar, while the king of that country, wearing a splendid crown, gazes down on them from a high window, raising his hand in surprise at his discovery that this woman whom he had admired belongs to another man.

THE EVER RADIANT RACHEL, WIFE OF JACOB

When Rebekah's daughter-in-law Rachel, whom she never saw, is described as both "beautiful and well favored," we seem to have the feeling that God had bestowed upon her a beauty of spirit as well as of form and figure. A certain radiance surrounds her as we see her coming down the low-lying, sun-kissed hills of her native Haran, just as Jacob, trudging over the crest of the hill, beholds her for the first time. We can picture her wearing a graceful, loosely fitting, brightly colored dress. She must have dazzled her beholder as she walked with light-footed grace in the warm sunshine, her grazing sheep straying in the foreground. Jacob, born of an emotional people, was so overcome with Rachel's loveliness that he kissed her and "lifted up his voice and wept" (Gen. 29:11).

Suddenly we are confronted with another picture, sharp in its contrast, the introduction of Rachel's less attractive sister, Leah, described as having eyes that were not strong (Gen. 29:17), suggesting it seems that she could have been verging upon blindness. Whatever the condition, we can be sure that Leah's eyes detracted from her personality, and that she was deceitfully passed on by her father, Laban, to Jacob, after he had promised to give seven years of service for the lovely and lovable Rachel. So much did Jacob love

Leah's beautiful sister, Rachel, that the fourteen years he had to serve for her "seemed unto him but a few days" (Gen. 29:20).

One of Raphael's great paintings depicts a pastoral view of Rachel with her father's sheep, their watering trough in the immediate foreground. Andrew Appiani has done another painting of this same scene for the church of Alanzo, near Bergamo, city in northwest Italy. Palma Vecchio has painted a picture of Jacob saluting Rachel; so has Giordano.

The latter depicts Rachel in graceful attire, her neck and arms exposed, as well as her feet and ankles. Rubens also has portrayed Rachel in all of her loveliness, when she prominently figured in the meeting of Jacob and Esau. Rubens used his own wife, as he often did, as his model. Still beautiful in death, Rachel is again portrayed by Giovanni Cignaroli. Jacob bends over her, the image of despairing grief. At her feet is a midwife holding her second son, Benjamin, to whom she had just given birth.

Artists' Acclaim of Patriarchal Wives

Sarah, Rebekah, and Rachel, the three wives of the patriarchs, all favored subjects of the master artists, seem to possess a mysterious beauty that lends both drama and light to the lives of the patriarchs Abraham, Isaac, and Jacob. Again and again these three patriarchal wives are mentioned in the definitive work in its field, *Heroines of the Bible in Art*, by Clara Erskine Clement.

She does not, however, mention Abigail, whom the Bible describes as of "beautiful countenance" as well as "a woman of good understanding" (I Sam. 25:3), suggesting that she had the kind of goodness that heightens beauty. And that is the greatest compliment that can be paid to a woman's beauty. To try to describe inner beauty in a mature woman such as Abigail is like trying to describe a glowing sun on an early June morning. In both a lovely woman and a spring sun, beauty is indescribable.

Beauty of the lasting kind knows no age. It often grows with the years. James M. Barrie said of his lovely mother, Margaret Ogilvy, who died at age seventy-six, that "God sent her into the world to open the minds of all to beautiful thoughts." And he exulted in her beauty, even at the grave. "Her soft face," he says in his biography of her, "came early at the loss of a merry-faced little boy. And other mothers after that found comfort in her when they lost a child."

The lovely women in Bible times seemed to have developed a spiritual beauty that did not fade amid sorrow, trials, hardships, defeats, and disappointments, which come into every woman's life. On the other hand, we can imagine that they gave a woman's face gentleness and warmth, if she accepted whatever came in life, the good and the bad, with grace, and if she remained spiritually aware, physically fit and mentally alert.

A Daughter Who Is All Glorious Within

The wise Socrates, praying that he might be beautiful within, expressed a kinship of thought with the scribe in Psalms who writes of the king's daughter as "all glorious within" (45:13), again signifying that outward loveliness comes only from inward loveliness.

Addressing the king's daughter, she is told, "forget thine own people and thy father's house; and the king will desire thy beauty" (10–11). The king's daughter is then described as joyfully entering the palace of the king, accompanied by her virgin maidens and her escort.

Portraying as it does the marriage of the princess to an ancient king of the line of David, this Psalm has added charm because of this unnamed king's duaghter, who is "all glorious within," one who possessed not only queenly grace but excellence of character.

BATH-SHEBA, BEAUTIFUL OF FORM AND FACE

Bath-sheba, another wife of David, was a very popular subject with the master artists. One of the pictures in Raphael's Bible illustrates the story of King David: "And it came to pass in an eveningtide, that David arose from off his bed, and walked upon the roof of the king's house: and from the roof he saw a woman washing herself; and the woman was very beautiful to look upon" (II Sam. 11:2).

In Raphael's painting, just as David comes onto the balcony of his palace, suddenly he looks out in delight upon Bath-sheba bathing her feet and combing her hair on the roof of a nearby house. Her drapery is thrown over her knees, leaving the upper portion of her figure nude, and David throws up his hands in wonder at her beauty.

In the Dresden Gallery is another picture of Bath-sheba

bathing. This time she is on the balcony of the house of her husband, Uriah, who is asleep nearby. This was painted by Francia Bigio, a friend of Andrea del Sarto, in the sixteenth century.

Rembrandt twice painted Bath-sheba at bath. In the best known of these, she is shown with her attendants, making an elaborate toilet. Here she is a beautiful nude woman, sitting in a golden light on a richly colored rug. A black woman combs her hair, while an old servant wipes her feet. The picture glows with color.

THE BEAUTIFUL VASHTI AND HER COURAGE

Queen Vashti, whom Esther succeeded, is described as one whom the king desired "to shew the people and the princes her beauty: for she was fair to look on" (Esther 1:11). When Vashti learned that the king wanted to show her off to his visiting princes, after they had been drinking for seven days, she refused to go before the king's inebriated guests, and the king divorced her because of her disobedience.

Through the centuries, Vashti has been extravagantly admired as a woman of honorable convictions and one who had the courage to stand up against a demanding husband, the king of a large dominion at that. She was willing to sacrifice everything she had, a palace, her husband the king, and a secure future, in order to do what was right. Modest, serene in time of trial, determined, she later left her palace at her husband's command, rather than to walk into a crowd of drinking guests, who might have looked upon her beauty with lustful eyes.

Artists' Conception of Esther's Loveliness

Queen Esther, the second wife of King Ahasuerus, has been painted more often by the great masters than any of the five young maidens, except Rebekah and Rachel. In Esther we find the dazzling loveliness of a maiden, wife, and queen. Her pulchritude was so cherished by her family that, at the death of her mother and father, her cousin Mordecai brought her up as "his daughter" (Esther 2:15). After it was announced that King Ahasuerus, who reigned over one hundred and twenty-seven provinces from India to Ethiopia, would take as his bride the most beautiful maiden in all the land, Mordecai personally escorted Esther to the palace of the king. There he left her in the custody of Hegai, the king's eunuch in charge of the women's quarters. Every day the solicitous Mordecai walked before the court of the women's house to see how Esther was.

The Bible tells us that "Esther found favor in the eyes of all who saw her" (Esther 2:15, RSV), first Hegai, and then the king, "loved Esther more than all the women" (2:17, RSV), indicating that she possessed a quality of mind and heart that appealed to the king as well as to his lowly helper, Hegai.

In his painting in the Uffizi Gallery in Florence, and in his coronation of Queen Esther in the Church of San Sebastiano in Venice, Paolo Veronese has celebrated the loveliness of Queen Esther. Another portrait extolling her beauty has been painted by Julius Schrader. Tintoretto also has done a magnificent painting of Queen Esther. In all of these masterpieces Esther is depicted as a queen, whose inner as well as outer beauty magnetically attracts all who come into her presence.

New Testament Definition of Beauty

All nine of these, the five maidens and the four mature women in the Old Testament, lend drama and beauty to the Bible. Although the New Testament, as mentioned earlier, does not describe a single woman as beautiful, it does present this, the Bible's best definition of real beauty in womanhood:

> Your beauty should reside not in outward adornment—the braiding of the hair, or jewelry, or dress—but in the inmost center of your being, with its imperishable ornament, a gentle, quiet spirit, which is of high value in the sight of God.   (I Pet. 3:3–5, NEB)

CHAPTER FIFTEEN

ROMANTIC LOVE IN WOMANHOOD

The miracle of romantic love even astounds the writer of Proverbs, who observes, "there be three things which are too wonderful for me . . . the way of an eagle in the air, the way of a serpent upon a rock, the way of a ship in the midst of the sea; and the way of a man with a maid" (30: 18–19).

Romantic love, like a golden thread, is woven all through the Bible, beginning with Genesis and continuing with Revelation, sometimes in allegory and again in metaphor. Early, the narrative attributes to the Lord God a deep sense of gratitude for the wonder of his creation of man and woman. Five times in the second chapter of Genesis, God's part in their creation is set forth. Twice it is related the woman was created as a helpmate for man (vv. 18, 20); a third time it is said that "God . . . made . . . woman, and brought her unto man" (v. 22); a fourth time it is recorded, "she shall be called Woman, because she was taken out of Man" (v. 23). Finally, comes the beautiful and romantic phrase on oneness in marriage, "A man shall leave his father and his mother, and shall cleave unto his wife: and they shall be one flesh" (v. 24). The emphasis in marriage is always upon faithfulness and per-

manence, and on the personal-sexual-spiritual companionship ordained by God.

The marriage of Adam and Eve (Gen. 4:1) becomes
the means by which the image of God is passed on to
succeeding generations. Sexual love emerges as the most
divine and yet the most mysterious of all blessings, the
gift of little children, through whom God speaks to both
mother and father. In marriage man inherits a helpmate
who mothers his children, tends his home, and ministers
to him in other areas of his life, while woman receives
love and protection for herself and her children as well as
a father for her children.

Samuel Rolles Driver, one of the revisers of the English
translation of the Old Testament (1876–84), calls this
conception of the creation of woman "a wonderfully conceived allegory, designed by a most significant figure to
set forth the moral and social relations of the sexes to
each other, the dependence of woman upon man, her
close relationship to him, the foundation existing in nature
for the attachment springing up between them, and the
feelings with which each shall naturally regard the other."

Romance in Patriarchal Times

No modern novel excels in beauty and simplicity the Genesis romances of Isaac and Rebekah, and Jacob and
Rachel. In the betrothal of the former, gifts were presented to Rebekah, and to her brother and mother from
Isaac's father, Abraham. In a few but meaningful words,
the marriage is described as Rebekah and her maids and

their caravan drew near Canaan after a journey from her homeland in Mesopotamia:

> And Isaac went out to meditate in the field at the eventide: and he lifted up his eyes, and saw, and, behold, the camels were coming.
>
> And Rebekah lifted up her eyes, and when she saw Isaac, she lighted off the camel.
>
> For she had said unto the servant, What man is this that walketh in the field to meet us? and the servant had said, It is my master: therefore she took a veil, and covered herself.
>
> And the servant told Isaac all things that he had done.
>
> And Isaac brought her into his mother Sarah's tent, and took Rebekah, and she became his wife: and he loved her: and Isaac was comforted after his mother's death.   (Gen. 24: 63–67)

This union unfolds with subtle simplicity and tender warmth until it comes to that final statement that Isaac loved Rebekah. The romance of their son Jacob and Rachel, the daughter of Rebekah's brother, is even more dramatically depicted from their first meeting in the hills of Mesopotamia until old age. Romantic love seems to have been born at first sight in both of them and there is no delay in the narrative that "Jacob loved Rachel" (Gen. 29:18) and that he was willing to serve her father seven years in labor "for the love he had to her" (v. 20).

Their married happiness was normal and in keeping

with the advice of the writer of Ecclesiastes, "Live joyfully with the wife whom thou lovest all the days of thy
life which he hath given thee under the sun" (9:9).
Their love even had continuity beyond death, for long
after Rachel died, following the birth of their second son,
Benjamin, Jacob mourned for his beloved wife. The Bible
seems to say that romantic love, such as Rachel and Jacob
had for each other, possesses a deathless quality.

Romance in a Second Marriage

Love in a second marriage could be quite romantic too, if
one is to judge by the love that Ruth and Boaz bore for
each other. She had lost her first husband, Mahlon, when
she lived in her homeland of Moab. Boaz, it seemed, had
never been married. Ruth no doubt had happy memories
of her first romance but she was wise enough not to live
in the past. Instead, she went forward with her first husband's mother into a new country and a new romance.

Nothing is written of her grief for her first husband, but
her love for him found expression in her love for his aged
mother, Naomi, and her willingness to accept Naomi's
plans for her marriage to her next of kinsman, Boaz. When
Ruth came into a new life and a new love for Boaz, her
romance found further joy in the birth of a son, Obed.

Her whole story sings of respect for a love that has gone
but complete dedication to a second husband, as if she
were a new person absorbed in romantic love at its best
both times. For Ruth herself represented the noblest and
most loving type of womanhood.

Personal Togetherness in Love

Romantic love is most dramatically depicted in the Song of Solomon (Song of Songs), a collection of marriage poems, which portray the wonder of sexual love but which stress the devotion upon which it is founded. The adjuration in the refrain of the song (2:7; 3:5; 8:4) is that personal togetherness, which comes in love, must not be aroused prematurely but must be given time to unfold.

Called many things, an allegory, an anthology of love poems, a series of secular love songs, and a Syrian wedding ritual—the Song of Songs meets every requirement for what Milton has defined as true poetry depicting romantic and nuptial love. It is both simple and passionate, sensuous but never sensual.

The first verse describes the bride as she awaits her lover singing, "Let him kiss me with the kisses of his mouth! for thy love is better than wine" (1:2). This is followed by their joyous meeting in which he thrice tells her, "Behold, thou art fair, my love" (1:15–16), during which she afterward admits, "I am sick [with] love" (2:5).

She says she dreams of when his "left hand is under my head, and his right hand doth embrace me" (2:6). As she eagerly awaits his arrival, she sees him "leaping upon the mountains, skipping upon the hills" and hurrying to her like a "roe or a young hart." Finally she sees him through the lattice and hears him sing to her this, one of the most beautiful love songs in literature:

Rise up, my love, my fair one, and come away.
For, lo, the winter is past, the rain is over and gone;

The flowers appear on the earth; the time of the singing of birds is come, and the voice of the turtle is heard in our land;

The fig tree putteth forth her green figs, and the vines with the tender grape give a good smell. Arise, my love, my fair one, and come away.

O my dove, thou art in the clefts of the rock, in the secret places of the stairs, let me see thy countenance, let me hear thy voice; for sweet is thy voice, and thy countenance is comely. . . .

My beloved is mine, and I am his. (2:10–14, 16)

IN AN ATMOSPHERE OF LOVE

There is a freshness, naturalness, and purity about the love between this young shepherd, who feeds his flocks among the lilies, and this graceful shepherdess, who goes "forth by the footsteps of the flock" (1:8). Nature sings of beauty everywhere when they are together.

No other book in the Bible has so much to say about the nature lore of Israel, its flowers, trees and vines, all of which lend drama to the youthful romance as it unfolds. The north and south winds waft the fragrance of lilies of the valley, also wild roses and the pungent smell of pine, fir and cedar trees, as well as cinnamon, frankincense, and myrrh. The landscape is dotted with flocks and vineyards, doves and little foxes, young stags and gazelles and hinds of the field. Pictured too are great clefts of rocks, blossoming vineyards, and turtledoves. Even the vine blossoms with fragrance, for the time of joy is at hand.

Youth, too, is at its best. The young man is handsome

and manly. The young maiden is unsophisticated and all the more charming because she regards herself as lowly and insignificant. Her eyes are like "doves," her hair like "a flock of goats," her teeth like "shorn ewes," her lips like a "thread of scarlet," her cheeks like "halves of pomegranates," and her breasts like "two fawns that feed among the lilies."

She dreams of when she actually will become the young shepherd's bride and when he will bring her "into [her] mother's house, and into the chamber of her that conceived me" (3:4).

THE CONSUMMATION OF MARRIED LOVE

After his lavish praise of her and her acceptance of his proposal for marriage, he lovingly says to her, "Thou hast ravished my heart, my sister, my [bride]" . . . how much better is thy love than wine! and the smell of thine ointments than all spices! Thy lips . . . drop as honeycomb . . . the smell of thy garments is like the smell of Lebanon (4:9–11).

Like all lovers, she fears for the security of her love and is disturbed about a dream she has about him. Finally, however, their love for each other is culminated in marriage. This is followed by this final song on the beauty of love, during which the bridegroom begs of his bride:

Set me as a seal upon thine heart, as a seal upon thine arm: for love is strong as death; jealousy is cruel as the grave: the coals . . . are coals of fire, which hath a most vehement flame. Many waters cannot quench love, neither can the floods drown it: if a man would give all the substance of his house for love, it would be utterly contemned.   (8:6–7)

Then we hear her final call, "Make haste, my beloved" (8:14).

Although the New Testament does not depict romantic love so dramatically as this in the Song of Songs, Jesus gave his sanction to married love when he appeared with his mother at the marriage at Cana and multiplied the water into wine. Even John in Revelation describes "the holy city, new Jerusalem, coming down from God out of heaven, prepared as a bride adorned for her husband" (21:2).

Romantic love as portrayed in the Bible brings with it a respect for human beings as male and female and produces lasting companionship, which transcends its physical basis. Woman achieves a wholeness that is never possible except in a godly marriage, and man gains a respect for the sexual sanctity of womanhood, the subject of the next chapter.

CHAPTER SIXTEEN

SEXUAL SANCTITY IN WOMANHOOD

Woman's destiny is to learn the nature of love and seek spiritual rebirth. She cannot fulfill her destiny when she regards the sexual act as a purely biological function rather than as an expression of love between two persons, the kind that can be defined only within the context of marriage. Unless a woman possesses a noble and lofty spirit and is filled with a sense of wonder regarding her body, she is not all that God intended her to be and is unable to bring to marriage and motherhood reverence for her body.

The Bible is the wisest book of the ages regarding the sexual sanctity of womanhood. Sexual relations are based on the Bible thesis that only God created us. We did not come out of a test tube in a laboratory but from God himself. When we see God's wonders in a rose or a tree or a beam of light or even so small a thing as a grain of mustard seed or a drop of water, we realize that our own bodies are his most wondrous creation. They house the soul on its earthly journey into eternity, and the body in this sense takes on new sanctity.

Sex, a Part of the Divine Plan

Because there is a strong relationship between sexual behavior and personal integrity, the act of sex demands the ethics of religion. Sex is a part of the divine plan first introduced in Genesis. In its right use sex becomes a moral and spiritual commitment; in its wrong use it becomes a fleeting physical relationship only. The woman who accepts only the carnal pleasures of the body becomes cynical, callous, shallow.

Sex has a God-given purpose: the regeneration of the human race and the climax of true love within marriage, so that both husband and wife can share with each other what Katherine Anne Porter calls "a mystical state, mystical in the sense that the real experience can not be communicated to others, nor explained even to oneself on rational grounds." In her essay "Marriage Is Belonging," Miss Porter wisely defines "the flesh in real love as one of the many bridges to the spirit" (*The Days Before*, p. 186).

Sexual standards, according to the laws of Israel, were even more binding upon women, the mothers of the race, than upon men. A young maiden must be chaste, for the loss of chastity might bring unprotected motherhood. She must never engage in any sexual deviations such as homosexuality or bestiality. Homosexuality was an "abomination" (Lev. 18:22; 20:13). A married woman must never have intercourse during her menstrual cycle (Lev. 18:19). Marriage must be monogamous. Adultery violates one of the Ten Commandments.

Respect for these laws led to wholeness and wholesomeness among the people of Israel. In periods when they were disobeyed, the nation fell, as in the time of the Hebrew Monarchy, when women probably sank to the lowest standards in Israel's history.

Again let us refer to the wise mother of Proverbs. She

seemed to realize there was a strong relationship between man's respect for the sanctity of woman's sexual self and her own personal integrity. This mother of Proverbs, like the noble mothers of today, taught her son wisely regarding sex.

How Sex Can Bring Reverence for Life

Pearl Buck, the daughter of missionaries and one of the wisest of mothers, makes this provocative statement in her book *To My Daughters, With Love*, quoted earlier:

> I would, if I were a teacher, educate the young male and female first of all in what it means to be born, to struggle for life, and then to find oneself deprived of family and home. Perhaps when this lonely individual becomes a reality for them, they will consider their own bodies, their sexual capacities and functions, and perceive the necessity to understand and to control and to use wisely the strong and significant power of sex.
>
> Am I implying the word SACRED? It is not a fashionable word or one often used in our modern times. It is tarnished by its connection with puritanical religion. Nevertheless I will use it, for I believe that the physical creation is sacred, as art is sacred, and for the same reason. It is creation.   (P. 237)

Mrs. Buck also stresses that sex must bring "joy and ecstasy and triumphant pride, and above all reverence for life."

Safeguarding Woman's Sexual Sanctity

In his book *Hebrew Marriage*, David R. Mace, authority on ancient marriage, highlights the reasons why the sexual sanctity in womanhood must be respected:

> Her (woman's) sexuality represents the means by which she might hope to compass the crowning achievement of her womanhood, and maintain her husband's line by providing him with progeny. It was a precious possession which guaranteed her an honored place in society, and must therefore be jealously safeguarded. To the man, his bride represented the soil in which his seed was to be planted, the means by which he could secure the offspring which represented his immortality. It was therefore imperative that her sexuality should be his and his alone; any idea that he was securing "second-hand goods" would be intolerable to him. (P. 231)

Mace further observes that premarital unchastity on the part of Hebrew girls must have been rare. He says that no specific instance of "fornication in the strict sense" (premarital unchastity) appears in the Old Testament. There is an instance of the forced violation of a maiden's virginity by David's son Amnon, who seduced his half sister Tamar, Absalom's full sister by their mother, Maacah. She begged of him:

> "No, my brother, do not force me; for such a thing is not done in Israel; do not do this wanton folly. As

for me, where could I carry my shame? And as for you, you would be as one of the wanton fools in Israel. Now therefore, I pray you, speak to the king; for he will not withhold me from you." But he would not listen to her; and being stronger than she, he forced her, and lay with her.   (II Sam. 13:12–14, RSV)

As is so often the case in an immoral act like this, afterward "Amnon hated her [his sister] with very great hatred; so that the hatred with which he hated her was greater than the love with which he had loved her: And Amnon said to her, "Arise, be gone" (v. 15). And he called an attendant to come and bolt the door after her, and she went away, crying aloud as she went.

This is the Bible's most tragic instance of a young maiden's heart-rending anguish over being forced into unchastity and incest as well.

"SUCH A THING OUGHT NOT TO BE DONE IN ISRAEL"

Tamar's most meaningful phrase, "No, my brother, do not force me; for such a thing is not done in Israel," encompasses a great deal. In these words, she disclosed the ideal inherent in the chaste young maiden of Israel. Incest ran counter to the inherent decency and good sense of the people of Israel, and violated the covenant of its people.

This same phrase "for such a thing ought not to be done" (Gen. 34:7) appears a second time in the story of the defilement of Dinah, daughter of Jacob and Leah, by Shechem, the uncircumcized son of a Hittite prince. Her brothers were so incensed over the defilement of their only sister that they lost all sense of reason. They murdered Shechem and his father and other young men of the town. They plundered the city, seizing herds, flocks, asses, houses, little children, and wives. Jacob never forgave his sons for the extremes to which they went, not even on his deathbed, but their question "Should he [Shechem] treat our sister as a harlot?" (Gen. 34:31, RSV) is a stirring indictment of the way these brothers in Israel felt about the defilement of a beloved sister. Even its most erratic young men in these primitive times fought to maintain respect for the sexual sanctity of the women in their own family.

The high ideals upheld for Israel's womanhood began to unfold during Israel's patriarchal period. When these ideals were lost, the people rebelled. A third time the phrase "ought not to be done" appears in the Genesis record (20:9) during Abraham's and Sarah's journey into pagan Gerar when King Abimelech seized Sarah for his harem. Sarah was not forced into adultery, but the brief biblical insertion that she was forced into this king's harem throws light on the patriarchs' concern over the sexual relationship of their own wives, especially Sarah, who was destined to become "the Mother of Nations." Through her son, Isaac, Sarah's life was engulfed in the stream of the generations.

The God-loving people of Israel prayed that "our daughters may be corner stones, polished after the similitude of a palace" (Ps. 144:12). The Psalmist further sang, "Happy

is that people" (v. 15) who live by God's law for right conduct. This emphasis on chastity not only set forth high
maidenly ideals but heralded a mystery which embraced
inward as well as outward loveliness.

CHASTITY—ITS SIGNIFICANCE TO CIVILIZATION

When we compare the history of Israel with the history of
other nations who have achieved greatness, we see that
some of their sexual laws were upheld in other early civilizations too, some of which may not even have had the
Bible record to guide them. The sociologist, J. D. Unwin,
published in 1934 a scholarly work, *Sex and Culture*, still
a classic in its field.

He found that when the women of these great early cultures spent their early years in an atmosphere of intense
continence, the energy of the new generation exceeded
that of its preceding polygamous generation. This greater
energy was maintained so long as the mothers of the new
generations were reared in a sterner environment than that
of sanctioned polygamy.

Unwin tells that the history of the Arabs affords the
best example of this. The early Arabs did not compel their
women to be prenuptially chaste. But in the generations
that immediately preceded the birth of Mohammed, ideals
were strengthened. The Arabs believed in the existence of
a God who created the world, and prenuptial chastity was
introduced. Mohammed himself charged his followers to
"reverence the womb" that bore them.

MONOGAMY, THE IDEAL IN MARRIAGE

In his extensive study of different societies in various parts of the earth that flourished and then declined, Unwin says that he does not know of a case in which an absolutely monogamous society has failed to display great energy. His survey included the Sumerians, Babylonians, Hellenes, Romans, Anglo-Saxons, and English.

He tells in detail of the Aztecs, who in the fourteenth and fifteenth centuries, through a sustained series of conquests and alliances, gradually extended their political control. They finally dominated a large area of Mexico and through war, trade, and colonial efforts, a great many of the tribes and nations of Mexico.

Unwin stresses that in this period of progress the Aztecs, like the Hebrews of old, insisted upon tokens of virginity at marriage. This law (Deut. 22:14-21), practiced also by other primitive people, stresses chastity in maidenhood. Unwin's excellent study points out that every civilization attained its highest stage when it experienced the highest degree of monogamy in marriage as well as premarital chastity. His thesis is that as sexual standards weaken, the civilization itself declines and sometimes disappears altogether.

In his survey, Unwin discovered that the nations which observed monogamy as the ideal in marriage advanced rapidly and produced strong characters. He further observes:

In the records of history, indeed there is no example of a society displaying great energy for an appreciable period unless it has been absolutely monogamous.

Moreover, I do not know of a case in which an absolutely monogamous society has failed to display great energy. . . . In every case the society started its historical career in a state of absolute monogamy, manifested great energy while it preserved its austere regulations, and relaxed after a less rigorous tradition had been inherited by a completely new generation. . . .

The existence of a monarchy depends upon two factors: first, the energy of the ruling clan; secondly, the lethargy of the subjects. If a small group displays a greater energy than the remainder, the political organization is aristocratic; and the aristocrats retain both their power and their privileges so long as their energy is greater than that of their subjects. If they relax their sexual regulations, their energy decreases; those who hitherto have been dominated succeed to the domination. This is what happened among the Athenians and English, also the Romans in the time of the Republic. (P. 369)

THE DECLINE OF ENERGY IN LOWER STANDARDS

The loss of energy, due to a relaxation of sexual standards, may not be immediately realized in the generation that first lets down the bars, says Unwin, but it shows up in the second and third generations afterward. Greater energy is maintained, according to his theory, so long as the mothers of new generations are reared in an environment of high ideals. "The Moors of Spain could never have advanced," he says, "had they not mated with women who had been reared in a more rigorous tradition than their own." The quality of their wives helped to create a more rational culture.

The Hebrews were the wisest of all, for they recorded in the Bible their laws regulating sexual standards. Although the rigorous laws in Leviticus and Deuteronomy are too often forgotten in the world today, they demanded then as now that men and women render perfect obedience to all the moral laws of God.

These sexual laws are intermingled in the Bible with ceremonial laws in which there have been vast changes, but those laws dealing with moral behavior never change. Women then as now must be the standard-bearers of the race in sexual matters, which hold the clue to our weakness or our strength as a nation.

In this era of a sexual revolution and the commercialization of sex, when young and even mature women terrify not only their mothers but themselves by their sexual looseness, we can be grateful that we still have the Bible to guide us. Where else can we go for our models in moral and ethical conduct? In what other great literary work is there such a clear conception of the essential goodness of the sexual function as the appointed means of regeneration; also an experience of religious significance and spiritual enrichment? Where else do we find greater emphasis on all that is excellent in womanhood through all the years of a woman's life?

Section Four

HER DENIAL
OF HER LEGACY

CHAPTER SEVENTEEN

THOSE WHO
DO NOT HEAR THE WORD

The ungodly women depicted in the Bible are so out of focus with the godly women that they suggest badly blurred photographs in an old album. Since the Bible has been called literature's most remarkable portrait gallery of womanhood, it would not be true to life were the godly and the godless not depicted side by side.

Among the latter are the murderers and others who for one evil cause or another were murdered. There also were those who committed incest, who were rebellious, jealous, and who possessed other contemptible qualities.

In certain periods of Israel's history, these types seemed to dominate, until some, even the writer of Ecclesiastes (430–400 B.C.), became suspicious of women in general. He makes these caustic comments, in which he deplores the wickedness in womanhood:

And I found more bitter than death the woman whose heart is snares and nets, and whose hands are fetters; he who pleases God escapes her, but the sinner is taken by her. Behold, this is what I found, says the Preacher, adding one thing to another to find the sum, which my mind has sought repeatedly, but I have not found. One man among a thousand I found, but a woman among all these I have not found. Behold, this alone I found, that God made man upright, but they had sought out many devices.

(7:26–29, RSV)

It is easy to see that the author of Ecclesiastes has no faith in woman and believes that the wicked woman, who plays with subtlety to ruin souls, predominates. He thinks she is more deceitful and dangerous than a wicked man, because she is more elusive in her deception. Her hands are like bands with which she holds fast those whom she embraces. Her lustfulness and her heartlessness can encircle a man like "snares and nets" and then finally, like a malignancy, bring a man to his death. It is impossible for a wicked man to escape the wiles of such a woman.

When Woman's Seed Is Bad

Beginning with the first woman, Eve, no effort is made to gloss over the sins of woman. God created Eve in his own image, but early she ate the fruit from the forbidden tree and then gave some of the same fruit to Adam who, in eating it, shared in some of her guilt. The Genesis account of the temptation and the sin of Adam and Eve is the ancient writer's way of telling of the degeneration of the first woman, who not only sinned against God, her Creator, but who counseled her husband in his denial of God.

In Eve's fall we see that the whole family of mankind suffers when woman's seed is bad. Gertrud von le Fort, quoted in another chapter, has made the significant comment that the fall of woman is not that Eve took the apple first, but because she took it as a woman. "Humanity is fallen in the feminine substance, for it fell in the religious sphere. Hence it is with justice that the Bible ascribes the greater guilt to Eve and not to Adam. . . . Just as the fallen angel is more terrible than the fallen mortal, so also is the fallen woman more wretched than the fallen man."

The Chronicler lists several evil queen mothers who produced wicked sons. One of these was Ahinoam, a Jezreelite, the mother of Amnon, who abused Tamar, David's daughter by another marriage. Another evil queen was Hamutal, the mother of two ungodly kings, Jehoahaz and Zedekiah. The first reigned only three months. In the other son's reign of eleven years, the Bible tells that his leaders did not heed the word of God.

Jeremiah, in a few words, wrote this biography of this queen mother. "His mother's name was Hamutal . . . and he did that which was evil in the eyes of the Lord" (52:1–2). What might these sons have been, had their mother's glance been upon God?

Murders Involving Women

Evil became so rampant in the bloody era of the Judges that a murder as ghastly as anything in modern life centered around a woman, identified only as the Ephraim Levite's concubine. She was abused all night by base Benjaminite men, and when her husband found her dead at the door of their house the next morning, he was so angered at the "lewdness and folly" of these degenerate men that he committed a very ghastly deed himself (Judg. 20:6).

This aroused his Israelite brethren to such anger over the wickedness of the Benjaminites that the former assembled at the house of the Lord at Mizpah to counsel together regarding this dastardly murder. They then demanded that these beastly men who had committed the crime be put to death.

The Benjaminites prepared for a mighty battle. The Israelites went up to Bethel to ask the counsel of the Lord. But the war continued. Thousands were killed on both sides. Finally, when the Benjaminites saw that disaster was close upon them, and the Israelites realized that one of the original twelve tribes of Israel was about to be destroyed, they wept bitterly. Another time they sought the counsel of the Lord.

Afterward, the Bible tells us, they "had compassion on Benjamin their brother" (Judg. 21:6, RSV). Finally, they decided to send as wives to the remaining Benjaminites four hundred young virgins from Jabesh-gilead.

The total debasement of the Benjaminites had come about because their tribe had failed to provide enough pure young maidens as wives. This need was partially resolved when the Israelites gave their own young maidens to them.

These pure young women no doubt filled a great need in the lives of the depressed and iniquitous Benjaminites, for after their marriage to them, they "repaired the cities, and dwelt in them" (Judg. 21:23).

It was also in this same period of the Judges, the twelfth century B.C., that another woman, Jael, the wife of the

Kenite Heber, murdered Sisera, the Canaanite general of Jabin's hosts in war against the Israelites, commanded by Deborah and Barak. Weary from battle, Sisera came to the tent of Jael and her husband for rest and thought he was under the protection of friends. But to Jael Sisera was no longer a friend but an enemy now at war against her own people, so while he slept she took a workman's hammer and drove a tent peg into Sisera's temple.

Earlier than the period of the Judges, Cozbi (Num. 25:15), the daughter of the head of the house of Midian, in the northwest Arabian desert, south of Moab, was murdered. Phinehas, the grandson of Aaron, developed such indignation over the whoredoms in Baal worship that he thrust a javelin through Cozbi's stomach.

Earlier Moses, the uncle of Phinehas, had given orders publicly to execute chiefs of those people who committed such whoredoms. Cozbi no doubt had had an immoral influence on many Hebrew men.

From this crude but stirring story we get a glimpse of the high standards that the Israelites demanded of their women. They seemed to understand better than we the evil that overtakes a nation when immoral women gain a foothold.

WICKED WOMEN IN NEW TESTAMENT

In the New Testament are three despicable women, Herodias, Bernice, and Drusilla, who are as wicked as any women in history.

Herodias was evil to the core. She committed incest in her marriage to her half uncle Herod Philip and afterward entered into an incestuous and illicit union with his half brother Herod Antipas, the tetrarch of Galilee.

Because John the Baptist protested her divorce and her incestuous union, she hated him with a passion. A real child of the devil, she first influenced her daughter by her first marriage to tempt her husband with her sensual dancing, and then, when Herod became enraptured with the daughter's dancing, Herodias persuaded her to make a ghastly request of Herod.

The daughter went before Herod and commanded, "I want you to give me at once the head of John the Baptist on a platter" (Mark 6:25, RSV). The request was too lurid to seem real. Herod no doubt was shocked. But he, the mighty tetrarch of Galilee, who now sat in the presence of so many guests, "did not want to break his word to her [Herodias]" (v. 26). What a choice to make, that of taking a man's life to please an evil wife for fear of breaking his word to her?

While his guests waited, Herod sent a soldier of the guard to the place where John the Baptist was imprisoned and ordered that he be immediately beheaded. When the head of the great John the Baptist was presented to Herod on a platter, he promptly turned and gave it to his wife.

When John the Baptist's followers heard of the hideous murder of their beloved leader, they came and took his decapitated body and laid it in a tomb. And the world has been horrified ever since over the ghastly death of this superior man, the noble son of a priestly family, who had devoted himself to religious reform, baptized Jesus, and taught many to pray. Who would ever remember the name of this evil woman, Herodias, except that she had demanded the beheading of one who had publicly denounced her evil?

The sisters Bernice and Drusilla had backgrounds as evil as that of Herodias, for like the latter they too were born of the same wicked Herod line, the daughters of Herod Agrippa I, the first royal prosecutor of the Church, and the great-granddaughters of Herod the Great who, in ordering the massacre of all infants, forced Mary and Joseph to flee into Egypt.

Drusilla was an adulteress, having left her first husband to marry Felix, procurator of Judaea. Bernice, first married to her uncle Herod of Chalcis, had lived openly in Rome for some time with her brother Agrippa II and had now come with him to Caesarea while Paul was under trial there.

Paul, the great apostle of Christ, was defending himself against several accusations made about him. First, that he was an agitator among Jews all over the world, and next, that he was a ringleader of the Nazarenes, and finally, that he had defiled the temple. The last charge was known to be utterly false, but had his enemies not been able to carry out this accusation, he would not have incurred the death penalty.

Both Drusilla and Bernice sat with their husbands in this just man's trial. They heard him give his famous declaration of Christ and the Resurrection. They heard him state that the purpose of his mission was to turn the people "from darkness to light, and from the power of Satan unto God, that they might receive forgiveness of sins, and an inheritance among them which are sanctified by faith that is in me" (Acts 26:18).

These two sisters, powerful forces in the Roman government, listened to Paul say, "I would to God that not only you but also all who hear me this day would become [a Christian] such as I am—except for these chains" (Acts 26:29, RSV). But the wickedness of these sisters ran so deep in their veins that they could not hear the plea of this godly man. And they left the praetorium with their husbands amid the pomp and glory of the occasion. And Paul, this beloved apostle of Jesus, went back in his chains for two years of incarceration in the "Bastille" at Caesarea.

WOMAN'S TRUE DESTINY FOR GOOD, NOT EVIL

These evil women here represent woman's fall from her divine destiny, according to the Creation. When these wicked ones fell into sin of all kinds, lust, greed, prejudice, hate, the fountain of their nation's life was poisoned at its very source. The symbolic significance of womanliness, which had its origin in God, vanished.

All here make us know that woman can never emerge victorious unless she remains true to herself and to what God intended her to be. "God, in his wisdom, has linked the whole human family together," spoke Elizabeth Cady Stanton, the woman's rights leader of the middle nineteenth century, "that any violence done at the end of the chain is felt throughout its length, and here, too, is the law of restoration. As in woman all have fallen, so in her restoration shall the race be recreated." The world cries out for the deep and tender chords of sympathy and love in the hearts of good women, on whose shoulders civilization rests.

In his essay on "Woman," Ralph Waldo Emerson, the nineteenth-century sage of philosophy, says, "Women are [by their conversation] and their social influence, the civilizers of mankind. What is civilization? I answer, the power of good women" (Emerson's *Complete Writings*, p. 1179). We might ask, "What causes a nation's downfall?" The power of evil women in high places, like some of these in Bible times.

CHAPTER EIGHTEEN

THE INFLUENCE OF PAGAN GODDESSES

In God-loving Israel it was hard to believe that the cult of sensuality could even exist. But "the abominations of the heathen," referred to so often by the Chroniclers and Prophets, were as scandalous and common as these writers lead us to believe, and there is every evidence in secular history that the condition was not exaggerated.

Philo Byblius, the first-century Phoenician scholar and author of a work on Phoenician religion, presents abundant material on Phoenician gods and goddesses and mythologies and religious practices. Bishop Eusebius of Caesarea (264–340) discovered Philo's writings and gave a further account of these abominations in his *Historia Ecclestiastica*, in which he said that many of the details seem so shocking that people refused to believe his description of sensual depravity.

In his book *The Bible As History*, Werner Keller relates some of the horrifying situations connected with these sensual cults of the pagan world. He further tells that "men and women prostitutes ranked as 'sacred' to the followers of the religion, and the rewards for their 'services' went into the temple treasuries as 'offerings of the gods'" (p, 272),

Many of the discoveries regarding these sensuality cults

are of fairly recent origin. Since 1929, Claude F. A. Schaeffer has excavated the ancient city of Ras Shamra where important Phoenician texts in great numbers have been uncovered. He and his associates made new discoveries on the religions of Canaan, which early Israel had encountered. They were able to clarify much about these goddesses of fertility, branded in the Bible as "holy whores," and they found them to be exactly as depicted.

THE SENSUAL FERTILITY CULTS

"They forsook the Lord, and served the Baals and Ashtaroth" (Judg. 2:13, RSV). "And the children of Israel did evil again in the sight of the Lord, and served Baalim, and Ashtaroth . . . and forsook the Lord, and served not him" (10:6).

Samuel was one of the first to sound a fervent appeal to the people to protest against this worship of Ashtaroth. "Prepare your hearts unto the Lord, and serve him only: and he will deliver you out of the hands of the Philistines" (I Sam. 7:3), he told them. The people became so fearful of their mighty enemies that they admitted they had sinned because they had forsaken the Lord, and had "served the Baals and the Ashtaroth" (I Sam. 12:10, RSV).

Ashtaroth was the original plural form of Ashtoreth, who was the Canaanite fertility goddess and the one divinity who was found wherever the Semitic race was represented. She was the most ancient of the greater Semitic divinities, and her name makes all the proper phonetic changes from one dialect to another. In South Arabia she appears as Ashtart, in Syria, as Attar, and in Assyria and

Babylonia, as Ishtar. As the consort and counterpart of
Baal, she was known all over the Eastern world as the
personification of the generative principle. As the goddess
of love, "she [Ashtart] was honored by the exercise of
the passion that she inspired, and chastity was sacrificed
in her honor," says Elmer W. K. Mould in his *Essentials
of Bible History*. "The freedom of the sexual relation that
characterized the primitive matriarchal state of society
was continued in the gedeshoth or shrine prostitutes [holy
ones], who were attached to the sanctuaries of ancient
Canaan" (p. 206). It is further related by Mould that:

> Lying behind this practice of sexual relations in
> worship was the idea that just as the male sperm pro-
> duces the child in the mother's womb the rain creates
> life in the ground. This was thought to be accom-
> plished through the marriage of the storm god of rain
> with the goddess of fertility. The sexual activity on
> the part of the worshipers was simply an acting out,
> the dramatic presentation, of the myth of the marriage
> of the gods. This imitative magic, it was believed,
> would induce the continual copulation of the gods,
> without which there could be no escape.
>
> (Pp. 206–7)

From nomadic days, Yahweh was the one and only God,
the transcendent deity, the holy one everywhere present.
How could the God-loving mistake these shrine prostitutes attached to the sanctuary of ancient Canaan as holy
ones? These Semitic divinities so heathenly worshiped
were an insult to the God-loving women of Israel. It is no

wonder that prophets and preachers, beginning in Bible times, have violently denounced this god Baal and his consort Ashtaroth who influenced sensuality of the worst sort.

The worship of pagan goddesses persisted through many centuries, because as Will Durant explains in *The Story of Civilization* (chap. 9, "The Common Culture of Early Greece"), the ancient man's death rate was high and he paid devout homage to the mother goddess. Dr. Durant tells that:

He sees in her the basic fact of nature—that man's greatest enemy, death, is overcome by woman's mysterious power, reproduction; and he identifies this power with a deity. The mother goddess represents for him the sources of all life, in plants and animals as well as in men; if he surrounds her image with fauna and flora it is because these exist through her creative fertility, and therefore serve as her symbols and her emanations.   (Vol. 2, p. 13)

Solomon, First King to Erect Pagan Shrines

King Solomon, who married many foreign women, was the first king of Israel to erect a shrine to a pagan goddess. And it stood until destroyed by King Josiah more than three centuries later. King Solomon was wise and he was wealthy and influential all over the world, but his marriages were his downfall. It is the Chronicler's belief that King Solomon's marriages inflicted an evil influence upon all of Israel. This is well explained here:

Now King Solomon loved many foreign women: the daughter of Pharaoh, and Moabite, Ammonite, Edomite, Sidonian, and Hittite women, from the nations concerning which the Lord had said to the people of Israel, "You shall not enter into marriage with them, neither shall they with you, for surely they will turn away your heart after other gods"; Solomon clung to these in love. He had seven hundred wives, princesses, and three hundred concubines; and his wives turned away his heart. For when Solomon was old his wives turned away his heart after other gods; and his heart was not wholly true to the Lord his God, as was the heart of David his father. For Solomon went after Ashtoreth the goddess of the Sidonians, and after Milcom the abomination of the Ammonites. So Solomon did what was evil in the sight of the Lord, and did not wholly follow the Lord, as David his father had done. Then Solomon built a high place for Chemosh the abomination of Moab, and for Molech the abomination of the Ammonites, on the mountain east of Jerusalem. And so he did for all his foreign wives, who burned incense and sacrificed to their gods.

(I Kings 11:1–8, RSV)

Solomon's many marriages were in flagrant violation of the Deuteronomic Code, which read, "And he shall not multiply wives for himself, lest his heart turn away" (17:17, RSV). And when Solomon's foreign wives turned him away from the God of his fathers, immoral practices and idol worship set in, and the women of Israel were subjected to inferior and degrading disabilities.

The idea of Solomon's harem, as well as the pagan worship, debased Israel's womanhood, and its noble image fell to the lowest level in Israel's history. This was a step backward, and it was worse than the polygamy of patriarchal times.

Immoralities of the worst kind set in. Adultery began to spread, beginning with King David and continuing on through his son Solomon and Solomon's son Rehoboam, the last king of the United Kingdom. Pagan goddesses and the harems had debased much that was excellent in womanhood through the reigns of this son, father, and grandson, a period of about a century.

Solomon's foreign wives, who brought their gods into Israel from their own foreign lands, complicated the people's loyalty to the one God. The shrines of these foreign gods occupied conspicuous places everywhere. On the "Hill of Offense," as it was called, was the shrine of Chemosh, god of the Moabites. Down the valley of Jehoshaphat, amid the pleasant walks and trees of the king's gardens, rose the abhorrent statues of Moloch of Tyre, to whom human sacrifices were offered. These and many other lesser gods stole the king's heart and drew the people away from the simpler and more austere faith of their fathers. Israel never recovered from these idolatrous practices until the Exile wiped out this kind of idolatry once and for all.

QUEENS WHO MALIGNED ISRAEL'S WOMANHOOD

Some queens, like some kings, introduced into Israel revolting customs of worship that maligned all womanhood as well as themselves. One of these was Queen Maacah

(I Kings 15:10, 13), who erected an image to a pagan goddess. After Asa, her son (maybe her grandson), took his place as the third king of Judah (913–873 B.C.), he removed Maacah from her role as queen mother because she had an abominable image made of Asherah, which Asa had burned by the brook Kidron.

Queen Maacah no doubt worshiped this pagan goddess, replicas of which were built "on every high hill and under every green tree." With this pagan worship, sodomy and other "abominations" became prevalent.

The tragedy of it, too, was that some of Israel's women even wove hangings for these pagan worship centers instead of hangings for the Lord's tabernacle, as they had done in the time of Moses.

Jezebel's pagan shrines, which she established beneath her ivory palaces, became centers of worship for the fertility cults. It is recorded that after Israel's King Ahab married Jezebel, the daughter of Ethbaal, king of the Zidonians, that he "went and served Baal, and worshipped him."

"He erected an altar for Baal in the house of Baal, which he built in Samaria. And Ahab made an Asherah. Ahab did more to provoke the Lord, the God of Israel, to anger than all the kings of Israel who were before him" (I Kings 16:32–33, RSV). His wife Jezebel not only cut off the prophets of the Lord, including the great Elijah, but she fed at her table the "four hundred and fifty prophets of Baal and the four hundred prophets of Asherah" (I Kings 18:19, RSV).

There is a good deal of confusion about the exact meaning of an Asherah, as it is translated in the RSV, and a "grove," as it is translated in the KJV. Whether the Asherah was the cult object of the Semitic goddess or a sacred area of worship is not certain, but a fuller discussion of the confusion around the words grove and Asherah may be found in *The Interpreter's Bible* (vol. 1, pp. 250–52).

It is no shock that God-loving Israel hated with a vengeance Jezebel, the Phoenician wife of King Ahab, who popularized these fertility cults beneath her ivory palace. In her native Phoenicia she had worshiped Baal-Moloch and Asherah as personifying the male and female principles in nature. It is no surprise either that the prophet Elijah defied her until the end by violently fighting her and her false gods and goddesses. Nor is it any wonder that with the downfall of her daughter, Athaliah, queen of the Southern Kingdom of Israel, Judah, came the almost immediate destruction of the Baal temple in Jerusalem.

Athaliah was the first ruler of Judah who was not of the Davidic line. Like her mother, she had evil flowing through her veins. She not only worshiped false gods and goddesses, but she achieved everything by brute force.

The Book of Proverbs tells us that "the lamp of the wicked will be put out" (24:20, RSV). Athaliah's lamp was choked out when Joab, rescued by Athaliah's stepdaughter Jehosheba, was made king. Athaliah was slain as she entered the horses' gate by the palace, screaming "Treason! Treason!" (II Chron. 23:13). Not only was Athaliah slain, but the same horses that transported her to the palace in a carriage trampled over her body when she lay dead at the palace gates. When Athaliah's son, the second Ahaziah, succeeded her to the throne, it is recorded that "his mother was his counselor in doing wickedly" (II Chron. 22:3). What a horrible indictment of a mother!

But what more could you expect of one who, it is sup-
posed, had a portion of the Temple of the Lord pulled
down and used to build a temple of Baal (II Chron. 24:7)?
It was not until nearly two centuries later, during the reforms of King Josiah (640–609 B.C.), that these images of
Baal were tossed into the Kidron, burned and sent as
ashes to Bethel.

BAALISM'S DESTRUCTION OF WOMANLY IDEALS

"Where morality reigns they [women] reign, and where
licentiousness reigns, they are as nothing," says Goethe,
the German poet and dramatist in his play *Torquato
Tasso*, which deals with his conflict with the world. Baalism wrenched apart much that was fine in the ideals set
forth for Israel's womanhood in the Decalogue and Holiness Code.

From the time of Solomon on through Jezebel and
Athaliah, the standards of womanhood were lowered im-
measurably. It took Israel's women many centuries to overcome the harm done by them, because the evils they
introduced into Israel spread like the bubonic plague, cast-
ing down many who would never rise again.

Too few women had the strength to withstand such evil
influences, especially when they were perpetrated by those
in power. And few tabernacles could endure as powerful
forces for good when they had to compete against state-
controlled shrines, where the godless worshiped.

Womanhood did not recover its full sense of righteousness as a way of life until the appearance of Christ many
centuries later, and then it still had to combat godless
women like Herodias, the wife of Herod Antipas.

CHAPTER NINETEEN

THE HARLOT (PROSTITUTE) AND THE ADULTERER

The promiscuous man and woman "move from one bed to another, yet all beds are only beds, unless love attends—not casual love but faithful, mutual love, deeply rooted in all of life. The sex act is the most intimate communication possible between two human beings, the one man, the other woman," says Pearl S. Buck in her profound book of the relations of men and women, *To My Daughters, With Love.* When the sex act "is carelessly and casually bestowed, the degradation is profound. I have not seen a promiscuous man or woman who did not show the effects of this degradation," continues Mrs. Buck. His-her spiritual quality is gone; he-she is animal, this human being created after some divine image whose beginning we still do not know!

"The chief commandment of the new morality, therefore, is that this closest and most intimate relationship between man and woman is not to be misused as mere physical relaxation or sport. For if it is so misused, the effects are harmful to the personality. There is loss," concludes Mrs. Buck in her book (p. 247), dedicated to women of all ages everywhere, but written specifically to her own seven daughters.

Adultery, a Violation of Commandment

The Bible teaches that the adulterer who voluntarily enters into sexual relations with a married person and one not the lawful spouse violates one of the Ten Commandments, "Thou shalt not commit adultery" (Ex. 20:14). This commandment immediately precedes "Thou shalt not steal." Adultery is itself a form of stealing. The adulterer not only violates one of the sacred laws of the Bible but denies a husband the assurance that his children are his own. Most of all, he denies God's image in himself.

The prostitute, or harlot, as she is called in the KJV, sold her body, as if it were a worthless penny, for the lusts of the flesh. In doing so she defied the law of Israel (Deut. 23:17), which prohibited its daughters from becoming harlots (Lev. 19:29) and forbade a priest to marry a harlot (Lev. 21:14). Although these rigid laws, further stating that the girl found to be guilty of harlotry was to be stoned to death (Deut. 22:21) or the priest's daughter who acted as a harlot was to be burned to death (Lev. 21:9), do not reflect consistent practice, they denote that the Israelites were deadly in earnest about eliminating sexual looseness among their daughters, for whom the highest laws of chastity are set forth in another law (Deut. 22: 13–20).

Harlotry, a Denial of Love

Harlotry promoted intercourse from which ensued no enduring relationship. It was emotionally empty and violated the sanctity in marriage, which is an act of affirmation and deep commitment, not just to the man or woman, but to life itself and most of all to the children born of the union, as explained in an earlier chapter.

The common harlot is first portrayed in Genesis as one who sits by the side of the road, wrapped in a veil, presumably of a brilliant color. Twice widowed by two husbands, Er and Onan, Tamar plays the part of a common harlot, although she is not one herself. But she waits with other harlots until her father-in-law, Judah, passes by. Earlier he had refused her levirate law rites to motherhood, according to the custom of these ancient times, both with his last remaining son and himself. She now prepared to demand this right, although she pursued her course deceitfully.

When Judah came upon the veiled Tamar he did not recognize her as his daughter-in-law, but made his way to her in preference to several harlots with whom she sat. "Go . . . let me come in unto thee" (Gen. 38:16), he said to her.

Tamar was wise. She did not demand a harlot's price from Judah but a pledge, his signet, his bracelet, and his staff. "And he gave it [the pledge] to her, and came in unto her, and she conceived by him. And she arose, and went away, and laid by her veil from her, and put on the garments of her widowhood" (Gen. 38:18–19). From this union twins were born.

When Judah, her father-in law, learned that the woman, whom he thought to be a harlot, was Tamar, the widow of his sons Er and Onan, and that she had demanded her rights to a son according to the law (Deut. 25:5–9), in order to carry forward the family name, Judah declared,

"She hath been more righteous than I . . . And he knew her again no more" (Gen. 38:26).

Tamar's experience is cited here only because it is the Bible's best description of how a harlot dressed and how she engaged in harlotry in a public place.

A Mother's Warning Against Both

The most indignant protest against harlotry comes from the wise mother of Proverbs, who warns her son against both harlots and adulterers. This mother symbolizes the wise and loving mother of the ages, who seeks to guide her son in what is morally right. Sitting beside her window and looking through her casement at passers-by, among whom is a foolish youth on his way to a prostitute, this mother's passionate disapproval represents the eternal concern of godly mothers everywhere. In speaking of a young man's senselessness in yielding to a harlot, this mother describes a harlot as one who dresses gaudily, who waits at every corner, and who says to a young man as he passes by, "I have decked my bed with coverings of tapestry, with carved works, with fine linen of Egypt. I have perfumed my bed with myrrh, aloes, and cinnamon. Come, let us take our fill of love until the morning: let us solace ourselves with love" (Prov. 7:16–18).

The harlot enticingly induced the young man to yield, "with the flattering of her lips she forced him. He goeth after her straightway, as an ox goeth to the slaughter, or as a fool to the correction of the stocks; Till a dart strike through his liver; as a bird hasteth to the snare, and knoweth not that it is for his life" (vv. 21–23).

It is no wonder that this wise mother cried out to her son, "Keep my words, and lay up my commandments with thee. Keep my commandments, and live . . . Bind them upon thy fingers, write them upon the table of thine heart. Say unto wisdom, Thou art my sister; and call understanding thy kinswoman" (7:1–4).

This ancient mother had the wisdom to know that the harlot not only defaced God's image of womanhood but destroyed God's concept of all that is fine in young manhood. This mother had lived long enough to see that many strong men can be slain by the harlot, that "her house is the way to hell" (v. 27).

THE GUILTY ADULTERER

In Bible times the adulterer was as guilty of wrongdoing as the harlot. The Egyptian wife of Potiphar, the chief of Pharaoh's bodyguard, attempted adultery with the noble Joseph, head of her husband's entire household, but was unsuccessful. Potiphar had trusted all he had to Joseph's care, even his wife, but she quickly betrayed that trust when she cast her eyes upon Joseph and said to him, "Lie with me." But he answered, "My master has no concern about anything in the house, and he has put everything that he has in my hand . . . nor has he kept back anything from me except yourself, because you are his wife; how then can I do this great wickedness, and sin against God?" (Gen. 39:7–9, RSV).

This last phrase states clearly why high-minded Israelites in patriarchal times vehemently denounced adultery.

In the time of Moses sacred and immutable laws were enacted against it.

Day after day Potiphar's wife tried to taunt Joseph, but when she could not induce him to commit adultery, she made her husband believe that Joseph had committed adultery with her. Potiphar was so angered that he cast Joseph into prison.

Potiphar's Egyptian wife probably had had many adulterous unions, for it seems that she accepted adultery as a way of life. But Joseph, an Israelite, knew that adultery was a shameful sin against God.

David and Bath-sheba's Adultery

The Bible gives no record of Bath-sheba's emotional reaction to her adultery with King David. She probably had no choice since David was the king and could make his own demands.

David's vantage point from his own roof gave him the opportunity to observe Bath-sheba at what was doubtless her private bath. Her husband was away, serving in David's army, and David immediately became enamored with the beautiful Bath-sheba. In a few words the Bible says that "David sent messengers and took her, and she came in unto him, and he lay with her" (II Sam. 11:4). Afterward she sent word to David, "I am with child" (II Sam. 11:5).

In order to avoid a court scandal, David perpetrated much deceit against Uriah and finally placed him in the forefront of battle, where he was killed. Afterward, David sent for Bath-sheba and made her his wife. The son born of this adulterous union soon died, after which David spoke his famous lament, "I shall go to him, but he shall not return to me" (II Sam. 12:23). David's true greatness comes forth in Psalm 51, in which he is saddened and repentant over what he had done, and he begs God to have mercy on him.

David, like other great characters in the Bible, had stars to guide him, principles that were fixed, goals that were reachable, and he went back to them.

Another adulterous situation, quite different from David's, was that of Hosea's wife, an acknowledged whore. Only one of her three children was born of Hosea, a great prophet, who suffered much grief over his wife's sin, for he loved her devotedly. Hosea's account of Gomer, his wife, often thought to be the prophet's allegory over God's sorrow at his wayward people, ends with tolerance toward Gomer (Israel's) sins.

God's Forgiving Grace

Hosea's attitude, one of forgiveness, suggests that of Jesus toward the woman taken in adultery and brought to him by the scribes and Pharisees. God's mercy for those who sin is simply illustrated in the story of Michelangelo, who was walking one day through the streets of Florence. Behind an ugly board fence he saw a block of fine white marble that had been spoiled by an amateur in sculpture. Michelangelo asked the man who owned it what he intended to do with it.

"Nothing," replied the man. "What could anybody do with that?"

In words that have become immortal, Michelangelo answered him, "It is not so bad as that, not useless. Send it over to my studio. There is an angel imprisoned within that stone, and I must set him free." Out of the badly cut stone Michelangelo carved a masterpiece, an angel with wings that gave him an inward lift. God, like the master sculptor Michelangelo, can carve new lives too out of ill-spent ones, and, like the artist, can sculpture a new being, even an angel with wings.

CHAPTER TWENTY

AMOS—THOSE WHO NEVER HAVE ENOUGH

Amos, the prophet of justice, who thought in pictures, has some vivid imagery and striking metaphors based on the lives of the luxury-living, pampered women of his time. Although the Book of Amos is the seventh book printed in the Bible after the Book of Isaiah, Amos prophesied before the first half of the eighth century B.C., while Isaiah began his ministry in 742 B.C., and is the first of the "major" prophets and the book in which his prophecies appear comes first in the Bible. But here we shall list Amos, although a minor prophet, according to the chronology of the time.

A plain man of the people, Amos lived at Tekoa, in the wild, rock-strewn Judean wilderness, six miles southeast of Bethlehem. Although his desolate hill country was in the Southern Kingdom, his prophecies were directed largely against the unrighteousness and social injustices in the Northern Kingdom.

In his trade as a herdsman and a tree pruner, he had much time to be alone with God. All the year round he tended the flocks, and just before spring approached, he pruned the sycamore trees, which produced a fruit that was a cross between the mulberry and fig, and provided a staple food for the poor in his area.

Early in his life, Amos began to receive information concerning the economic, social, moral, political, and religious life in the urban centers, and he had grave concern because of the spiritual decadence in them and its effect upon the land he loved. His timeless messages to the women of these centers were directed largely at their greediness for material possessions. The more they received the more they wanted. But as in most periods of history, with the possession of too many material things, came moral decay.

Amos was among the first to realize that Israel, whom God had led out of exile in Egypt, must now face the necessity and certainty of punishment for its evils, which probably meant the loss of all that the people of Israel held dear.

We can see Amos setting forth from his bleak hills, wearing a sheepskin coat, which he probably had made himself, and riding a donkey to the royal shrine at Bethel, where materialism prevailed. And we can hear him blazing forth in his impassioned address as he pronounced judgment on the surrounding countries: Damascus (Syria), Gaza (Philistia), Tyre (Phoenicia), Teman and Bozrah (Edom), Rabbah (Ammon), and Kerioth (Moab). He predicted that Jerusalem also would suffer.

In Bethel, where he preached on the street corners, the people worshiped the golden calf. In these other areas, many evils were prevalent, and the richer the people became the less time they had for God.

THOSE IN IVORY HOUSES

In order to have everything for themselves, the rich men and their wives callously disregarded the rights of the common man. Some of the wealthy merchant class had both summer houses and ivory-trimmed town houses. The latter were handsomely furnished, some with ivory inlaid couches, on which the women leisurely lounged, while hosts of servants waited on them. These houses were enclosed within walled courts, inside which were patios with glazed fountains made of costly ceramics. The cool spray over these well-landscaped gardens suggested a cool oasis in hot weather.

These women dressed in finery in keeping with their houses: in expensive silks and linens and fine jewels, many of them imported by their merchant husbands.

Amos, this plain man of the people, had no patience with these selfish, indulgent women, so he thundered out at them this prophecy in the name of the Lord: "And I will smite the winter house with the summer house; and the houses of ivory shall perish, and the great houses shall have an end" (3:15).

THOSE IN LARGE HAREMS

Amos had less patience with the women who lived in the large harems, begun in the time of King David and continued on through the reign of his son Solomon, his grandson Rehoboam, and other kings. Using the imagery of his own cattle country, Amos thundered out at these harems: "Listen to this, you cows of Bashan, you women in high Samaria, you who defraud the poor and are hard on the needy, who tell your husbands, 'Let us have wine to drink!'" (4:1, Moffatt).

Amos's vitriolic but effective words give a vivid picture of the pampered women of the harems, who gorged them-

selves on rich foods and grew fatter and fatter. It is no
wonder they reminded Amos of the fat cows from the fertile grain-producing country of Bashan, the land east of the
Sea of Galilee.

"As sure as I am God, the Lord Eternal swears, your
day is coming," said Amos, "when you will be dragged
out with prongs, the last of you with fish-hooks: out
you go through breaches [gaps] in the walls, each of you
headlong, chased to mount Hermon—by order of the
Eternal" (4:2–4, Moffatt).

Amos was right in his prophecy. In about thirty years
the Assyrians gained control of the Mediterranean trade
routes and overran Samaria. The enemy was merciless in
its treatment of the captives. The luxury-loving women in
the big houses actually were led out by hooks and thrown
through the openings in the city walls, just as Amos had
said they would be.

His Plea for Justice and Righteousness

But before this disaster came to Samaria, Amos had told
the people how they might avert it. He pleaded with them
not to go to Bethel and transgress; and also to Gilgal, an
important town in southwest Samaria, to multiply their
transgressions. In plaintive words Amos finally told all of
the people,

Seek good, and not evil, that ye may live: and so
the Lord, the God of hosts, shall be with you, as ye

have spoken. Hate the evil, and love the good, and establish judgment in the gate. It may be that the Lord God of hosts will be gracious unto the remnant of Joseph. (5:14–15)

Afterward Amos called upon the people to "let judgment run down as waters, and righteousness as a mighty stream" (5:24). In this, the key verse of the Book of Amos, justice and righteousness take on new meaning in the life of Israel. Since righteousness is nothing more than a right relationship with God, Amos tried to make the people see that unless God became first in their lives, Israel could not go forward as it had in earlier centuries when they had made a covenant with God.

These passages, which immediately follow Amos's denunciation of the pampered women of Samaria, leave the impression that Amos spoke specifically to them. Why? Because he seems to say that women have the greatest influence for either good or evil over men. Good women carry the torch, as it were, that sends light across civilization. Evil women spread only darkness. The arrogant women of Samaria, Amos makes us know, had betrayed a divine trust. They had forgotten that through their children, at least, they had a holy link with the future.

THE LUXURIES OF THE GREEDY

Amos could not tolerate the greedy women at all. He knew better than others that their luxuries often were bought at the expense of the poor. Amos, who lived among the poor, was familiar with all of their problems: the plagues of locusts in the fields, the lions roaring at night after their prey, the droughts and the famines, during which the poor could barely exist. So great were the needs of some of them that they had to sell their daughters into slavery. Such a sale, said Amos, might buy a rich man or woman only another pair of shoes (2:6).

Amos reminded his listeners that the men practiced dishonesty and merciless cruelty toward the poor, in order to give the women all of these luxuries. He told how the men falsified weights by adding dust to the wheat so that it would weigh more (8:5–6), how they consumed wine by the bowlful (6:6). Some of the wine, of which they drank so heavily, had been unjustly extorted from the condemned (2:8). Their immoralities, too, he said, were open and shameless (2:7).

Amos also denounced their prophets and priests who, because of the revenues they had received from the rich, would not condemn their iniquities. As Amos observed too how the nation's leaders had perverted justice and oppressed the poor, he reminded them of Israel's long-time relationship with God, of how they, of all the families of the earth, had been honored by their covenant with him (5:2).

God's choice of Israel as his family, Amos stressed, involved both privilege and responsibility, yet Israel's rich, greedy class regarded this as the nonsense of a man who did not know what he was talking about. Who was this plain herdsman from the hills to prophesy that they would be punished for all of their iniquities? They went on oppressing the needy and indulging themselves in more expensive luxuries. They went on stretching themselves upon their beds of ease inlaid with ivory. They never learned what it meant, as Amos said, to seek him "that maketh the seven stars and Orion, and turneth the shadow of death into the morning, and maketh the day dark with night: that calleth for the waters of the sea and poureth them out upon the face of the earth" (5:8).

Many of the leaders in fact were hostile toward this fiery preacher from the bleak hills. One of these was Amaziah, a priest at the Bethel sanctuary, who tried to thwart Amos in his prophetic ministry. "I was no prophet," Amos told Amaziah, "neither was I a prophet's son, but I was an herdsman, and a gatherer of sycamore fruit; and the Lord took me as I followed the flock, and the Lord said unto me, 'Go, prophesy unto my people Israel'" (7:14–15).

Like these priests and the political leaders, the greedy, spoiled, and sophisticated women of Samaria probably never even heard of Amos, this humble sheepherder and tree pruner. Many never knew that he existed, much less that he had spoken of God in all his majesty. The names of these women, so prominent among the rich of Samaria, were soon forgotten, but this humble prophet, Amos, from the bleak hills of Tekoa, became one of the towering figures of all time.

He started a new epoch in spiritual history, and his message continues to embody all of our cherished ideals, none of which we can either disregard or forget. Most of all, he gave the world a knowledge of a God in whose presence there is no triviality.

Amos's Influence on History

Through his special allusions to greedy, pampered women, Amos verbally has walked into many periods of history. His words may be applied to the luxury-loving women of Plato's time, to the pampered women of Nero's time, to the sophisticated women of the French Court before the Revolution.

But many of these never heard of this great prophet, either. Probably if they had, they thought of him only as a country yokel who knew nothing. They had no understanding of his revolutionary phrases teaching that God is righteous and that he demands righteousness of men. If they had heard of his penetrating message, they did not want to listen, for they had no desire to seek good.

If Amos were to walk into one of our large metropolitan centers today, he again would come upon gay, carefree, arrogant women who, like the women of Samaria and the women in other periods of history, are too absorbed in their trivia to have time for God. Behind the magnificence of their palatial homes, Amos would find emptiness. Behind all of their personal luxuries, he would discover their love for more. Behind their arrogance, he would see they had little or no compassion for the less fortunate. In their purposeless lives, he might have to search a long time before he came upon one woman who understood his primary call, a return to God.

CHAPTER TWENTY-ONE

ISAIAH—THE FASHIONABLE AND FRIVOLOUS

Although many centuries divide us and the prophets who wrote of the period of the Hebrew Monarchy (1000–586 B.C.), suddenly we realize they kindled a fire that cannot be put out, and that they are fearfully modern and strangely relevant. Four of them, Amos of the preceding chapter, and Isaiah, Jeremiah, and Ezekiel in this and the two succeeding chapters, in desperation over the condition of their country, addressed the women specifically.

The prophets were makers of "a new and higher ideal," but "they had not one word of progress" in regard to women, says Charles Ryder Smith in his book, *The Bible Doctrine of Womanhood* (p. 50). That is a startling statement, but this eminent scholar goes on to explain that "It is perhaps more surprising that the prophets did not apply the principle of righteousness to the subject of womanhood. Indeed, on this subject they added almost nothing to the idea of the preceding period. This was their chief omission. The new phenomenon of the Hebrew Monarchy in relation to womanhood was the coming of the harem. This was a step backwards" (p. 18).

Strangely enough, no great heroines of Israel belong to the Hebrew Monarchy, about which the prophets write. It is almost ironic that the two ablest women under the Monarchy were Jezebel, queen of Samaria, the Northern Kingdom, and her daughter, Athaliah, queen of Judah, the Southern Kingdom. With these two women as the chief examples, it is no wonder that the prophets denounced the evils they saw in womanhood.

State of Samaria, Judah

Although the country seemed stable and prosperous economically, Isaiah foresaw that calamity was brooding. Assyria had overcome Samaria and now threatened Judah. A religious reformation had been under way but it had done little good, for the wrongs of the preceding decades could not be righted overnight.

Peasants had been evicted from their farms to make way for the large estates and fine manor houses of the rich. The land was full of silver and gold. Luxuries from abroad were plentiful. Fast-stepping horses and expensive chariots, probably imported from Egypt for the armies, clattered along the narrow streets of Jerusalem night and day. Banqueting lasted until dawn, and then many of the revelers went home in their chariots, drowsy from too much food and drink.

Pride in material wealth and military strength filled the hearts of those in power. Many of the priests, caught up in affluence of the times, no longer counseled wisely. Because bribery flourished, judges could also be bought easily. The people had unclean lips and called "evil good and good evil" said Isaiah (5:20). The trade of soothsayers and diviners flourished because the people of Judah had forgotten the God of Israel.

Isaiah, who belonged to a family of rank, as may be inferred from his easy access to the king and his close intimacy with the priest, probably knew conditions in these wealthy circles at first hand. Also as the court preacher, he was keenly aware of the many decaying signs in Judah. He also had no illusions about the obduracy of his people.

The Proud, Pampered Women

After denouncing the many evils, Isaiah thundered out at the vain, luxury-loving women of Jerusalem, who were so immersed in their own gay, carefree pursuits that for them this was the only world that existed. Because he seemed to feel that their loose morals were hastening the nation's decay, Isaiah pronounced judgment on their arrogance and pride. He called their immoralities "the filth of the daughters of Zion" (4:4). He did not mince words when he spoke.

> The Lord said: Because the daughters of Zion are haughty and walk with outstretched necks, glancing wantonly with their eyes, mincing along as they go, tinkling with their feet; the Lord will smite with a scab the heads of the daughters of Zion, and the Lord will lay bare their secret parts.   (3:16-17, RSV)

In his dramatic portrayal of these snobbish, frivolous women, walking with heads high and eyes flirting, you can almost hear their silver bells tinkling on their ankles as they go mincing along.

The stern realist that he was, Isaiah did not soften his words when he boldly told them that their way of life would change so fast that they would wonder if it had been an unreal dream. In a desperate attempt to arouse them from their lethargy, Isaiah reminded them that they were not immune to leprosy, a disease which would leave them with loathsome scabs. Further warning them, Isaiah, this spokesman for God, predicted that,

> In that day the Lord will take away the finery of the anklets, the headbands, and the crescents; the pendants, the bracelets, and the scarfs; the headdresses, the armlets, the sashes, the perfume boxes, and the amulets; the signet rings and nose rings; the festal robes, the mantles, the cloaks, and the handbags; the garments of gauze, the linen garments, the turbans, and the veils.   (3:18–23, RSV)

Here we have the Bible's most detailed picture of how the rich women of the Hebrew Monarchy dressed. The many parts of their wardrobe, cited here, sound like the inventory of a fashionable woman's wardrobe today. Not a pin or bracelet escaped his notice. Isaiah went further in his prediction of the fearful tragedy that awaited such women in Judah and Samaria. War was certain to envelop Jerusalem, he said, and when it did, their ostentatious way of life, once so seemingly secure, would go with the wind. The great prophet further projected this picture to come:

Instead of perfume there will be rottenness; and instead of a girdle, a rope; and instead of well-set hair, baldness; and instead of a rich robe, a girding of sackcloth; instead of beauty, shame. Your men shall fall by the sword and your mighty men in battle. And her [Zion's] gates shall lament and mourn; ravaged, she shall sit upon the ground. (3:24–26, RSV)

His Warnings Unheeded

These favored women had no time for Isaiah's prophecies. They probably could not conceive that any fashionable woman's head would be shaven or that she would have to don common sackcloth, a black badge of slavery. Neither could they believe that their luxuries and their beauty would pass too, or that they could know shame because of the evils they now perpetrated but refused either to admit or correct. And certainly they didn't dare to think of the time when their fine houses would vanish and all of their frivolous pleasures would become only a fleeting memory.

It was hard for them to believe that death and destruction would be so common in the war to follow that "seven women shall take hold of one man, in that day, saying, 'We will eat our own bread and wear our own clothes, only let us be called by your name; take away our reproach'" (4:1, RSV).

Isaiah's message is as timeless as the condition. Women in war and destruction long to have the protection of the few men left, weak and maimed though they may be. That is one of the qualities of greatness in Isaiah. He writes not only for then but for all time.

A Call to Women to Rise Up

After this, Isaiah turned his criticism on the rural women, who danced at harvest festivals with a careless gaiety. In the following year, he said, those who had once been so merry would wake up, not to a harvest of plenty but to a harvest of destruction, unlike anything they had ever imagined. Isaiah lashed out once more at all the women of Zion, those in the city and those in the country.

> Rise up, you women who are at ease, hear my voice;
>   you complacent daughters, give ear to my speech.
> In a little more than a year
>   you will shudder, you complacent women:
> for the vintage will fail,
>   the fruit harvest will not come.
> Tremble, you women who are at ease,
>   shudder, you complacent ones;
> strip, and make yourselves bare,
>   and gird sackcloth upon your loins.
> Beat upon your breasts for the pleasant fields,
>   for the fruitful vine,
> for the soil of my people
>   growing up in thorns and briers;
> yea, for all the joyous houses
>   in the joyful city.
> For the palace will be forsaken,
>   the populous city deserted;

the hill and the watchtower
  will become dens for ever,
a joy of wild asses,
  a pasture of flocks.   (32:9–14, RSV)

Isaiah's cry, "Rise up, you women who are at ease," has rung through the centuries too. Sometimes it has been heard. Most often it has not. For it is much more pleasant to continue in the easy paths, until calamity forces one to do otherwise. However, Isaiah expressed hope for those who would listen. Like sunshine dispelling the darkness, he finally shifts from a threat of calamity to this promise of restoration:

> Until the spirit be poured upon us from on high, and the wilderness be a fruitful field, and the fruitful field be counted for a forest.
> Then judgment shall dwell in the wilderness, and righteousness remain in the fruitful field.
> And the work of righteousness shall be peace; and the effect of righteousness, quietness and assurance for ever.
> And my people shall dwell in a peaceable habitation, and in sure dwellings, and in quiet resting places.
> (32:15–18)

MORAL DECAY, SPIRITUAL DECADENCE

In assuring his listeners that God is "wonderful in counsel and excellent in wisdom," Isaiah upheld the ideal of that remnant of good men and women who, then as now, love

God. He solemnly promised that God continues to pour out his spirit, if they will seek righteousness. Then will come peace, quietness, and assurance of God's goodness.

Although Isaiah, this great spokesman for God, is not addressing our generation specifically, he is speaking to it, for we, too, live in a critical era of war, riots, moral decay, and spiritual decadence. And we, too, face a kind of spiritual starvation.

Although many crises and calamities are all about us, we allow ourselves to become entirely absorbed in our own selfish pursuits and trivia: our bridge scores, our fashions, our own battle of the bulge, our illnesses, our hates, and our fears.

While centuries of pampered, frivolous, complacent women come and go and will soon be as consigned to oblivion as if they had never lived at all, Isaiah's clarion call will continue to ring forth. His doctrine of God is so vast that we have not yet, not in these many centuries, caught up with what he tried to say to our world as well as to his own little country:

> He that walketh righteously, and speaketh uprightly; he that despiseth the gain of oppressions, that shaketh his hands from holding of bribes, that stoppeth his ears from hearing of blood, and shutteth his eyes from seeing evil;
>
> He shall dwell on high; his place of defence shall be the munitions of rocks; bread shall be given him; his waters shall be sure.   (33:15–16)

CHAPTER TWENTY-TWO

JEREMIAH—THOSE WHO WORSHIP FALSE GODS

Jeremiah, who was by nature gentle, tender, sympathetic, and pure of heart, seemed to have such a sympathetic bond with women that he employed feminine imagery in his sermons and prophecies. Because he had neither wife, sons, nor daughters to love, he turned his love on his little country of Judah and spoke of it in the most poignant terms, such as, "When I would comfort myself against sorrow, my heart is faint in me. . . . For the hurt of the daughter of my people am I hurt" (8:18, 21).

His own grief was unavailing because his people had turned away from Yahweh, God of their fathers, and because they worshiped graven images of other nations instead of the Holy One everywhere present.

His Feminine Imagery

Haunted by the premonition of doom for Judah, Jeremiah applied the feminine imagery again and asked, "Hast thou seen that which backsliding Israel hath done? she is gone up upon every high mountain and under every green tree, and there hath played the harlot" (3:6). Sometimes, as in this case, Jeremiah was critical of the womanhood of his time. Again he would express great sadness because he said he seemed to hear the wild cry of his people and the mighty sobs of one of Israel's ancient mothers, Rachel, "weeping for her children." Once more, like a mother talking to her children, Jeremiah spoke of his stupid children skilled only in doing evil.

The catastrophe that was approaching Israel nearly broke Jeremiah's heart. He could not understand why it had turned from the God of their fathers, whom Jeremiah loved with all of his heart. More than seven hundred times Jeremiah chants the word of the Lord. No other prophet— and all were spokesmen for God—calls on his name so often.

Jeremiah lived by faith in his God, whom he said, "giveth the sun for light by day and the fixed order of the moon and stars for light by night." A man of mystical religious experiences, Jeremiah came by them naturally, for he was of religious descent, possibly from the priesthood of the shrine at Shiloh, which explains Jeremiah's profound feeling for Israel's covenant with God. He was born at Anathoth, four miles northeast of Jerusalem, and began his career, while still a lad, five years before the lawbook was found in the Temple.

As a boy, Jeremiah lived close to the beauties of nature in his own pleasant little village, where he drew ever closer to God and nature, never forgetting that God gave the rain in the appointed season, that he reserved and designated the weeks of the harvest, that he determined the time of the coming of the stork, the turtle dove, the swallow and the crane, that he even made the almond to blossom in the spring.

As Jeremiah grew older and saw his people stealing, murdering, swearing falsely, and committing adultery, he knew they would be defeated by their more powerful neighbors, the Chaldeans, who had already conquered Assyria and Egypt. In a dialogical encounter with God, Jeremiah deplored the actions of some of the men, whom he described as being like "well-fed, lusty stallions, each neighing for his neighbor's wife" (5:8, RSV).

A Call for Mourning Women

So desperate was Jeremiah over the condition of his dying nation that he finally called for the mourning women, whose task it was to lament the passing of the dead. In his stirring Temple Sermon at Jerusalem, Jeremiah made this impassioned plea for them to lament the passing of his country:

> Call for the mourning women, that they may come; and send for cunning [skilful, RSV] women, that they may come.
>
> And let them make haste, and take up a wailing for us, that our eyes may run down with tears, and our eyelids gush out with waters. . . .
>
> O ye women . . . let your ear receive the word of his mouth, and teach your daughters wailing, and every one her neighbour lamentation.
>
> For death is come up into our windows, and is entered into our palaces, to cut off the children from without, and the young men from the streets.
>
> (9:17–18, 20, 21)

In times of grief it was the duty of these mourning women to console the mourners as well as to eulogize the dead. Some of these professional mourners played musical instruments. Others performed on the flute, while others sang mournful dirges. The "skilful" ones, to whom Jeremiah referred, led off with metrical phrases and rhymes of sympathetic appeal.

Several such funeral dirges sung for the dead may be found in the Old Testament. In one of these, David, grieving for Saul and Jonathan, calls for the weeping daughters of Israel (II Sam. 1:24).

As late as in Christ's time, it was customary for mourning women to go to the grave early in the day to anoint the corpse with sweet spices. Their audible grief at the tomb for the dead has been described as sounding like the far-off wailing of many owls, first shrill, then swelling to a loud pitch, and finally dying away. The mourning voices of these women might again become soft and plaintive, like the moaning of the wind at sea. These who made a business of mourning used such various techniques effectively.

In one of two visions, Jeremiah told the people that the Lord would roar from on high, his clamor would resound to the end of the earth, and that he would put an end to Israel's wickedness (25:30–31). It was lamentable, but these mourning women had no influence on the people of dying Judah.

Prophet's Suffering Over Evils

Jeremiah's activity spanned four decades before the Chaldean conquest of 587 B.C. He spoke fervently to the people, trying to arouse them to the disasters that awaited his nation. He lived close to the activities of Manasseh's long reign of fifty-five years, beginning in 687 B.C., through the reign of his son Amon (642–640 B.C.), and the reigns of five other kings, Josiah (640–609 B.C.), Jehoahaz II (609 B.C.), Jehoiakim (609–598 B.C.), Jehoiachin (598 B.C.), and Zedekiah (598–587 B.C.).

Because of Jeremiah's predictions of the approaching destruction of Judah, the irreligious and tyrannical King Jehoiakim hated Jeremiah with a vengeance. Jeremiah had the utmost contempt for the king, because he squandered funds to build a finer palace than his father had had and made his laborers work for nothing. Jeremiah lashed out violently against King Jehoiakim. The angered king demanded that Jeremiah's prophetic scrolls be sent to his winter palace, where they were read to the king as he sat before a fire burning in the brazier of his palace. When the reader had finished the text, the king took his penknife, cut the papyrus on which the prophecies were written, tossed them, piece by piece, into the fire and watched the flames consume them. Then the king ordered Jeremiah and his scribe Baruch to the palace. But they were able to elude the king's messenger and to remain in hiding for several years, during which time Jeremiah dictated again the words of the burned scrolls, chapters 1–25 of the Book of Jeremiah. Baruch afterward added other chapters. This time he included a condensed biography of Jeremiah, who he says was flogged, cast in dungeon cells, put in stocks, thrown into a muddy cistern, left there without food, and afterward lifted out by ropes made of old rags. All of this generated among the evildoers greater hate against the aging prophet.

Just as Jeremiah had predicted, Jerusalem was destroyed in 587 B.C. He ministered to the small remnant left in Jerusalem for a while and then finally was taken by the Chaldeans in 586 B.C. to Egypt, where he died, probably a martyr's death, but before his passing he ministered tenderly to other exiles there.

Again Jeremiah was brought face to face with idolatry and immorality, and he was grief-stricken that his exiled people, lacking confidence in the Lord's all-sufficient power, thought it expedient to propitiate other gods and goddesses. One was the Queen of Heaven, an ancient Semitic goddess, to whom the women made cakes and the men poured drink offerings for their ritual worship to her.

HIS CRIES TO ALL THE WOMEN

Jeremiah, manifesting an intense preoccupation with this problem, asked these idolaters if they had forgotten the wickedness that existed while they lived in Jerusalem. He made a special appeal to "all the women that stood by" (44:15). Their defiant reply was:

> As for the word that thou hast spoken unto us in the name of the Lord, we will not hearken unto thee.
> But we will certainly . . . burn incense unto the queen of heaven, and pour out drink offerings unto her, as we have done. . . .
> But since we left off to burn incense to the queen of heaven, and to pour out drink offerings unto her, we have wanted all things, and have been consumed by the sword and by the famine.   (44:16–18)

A second time "Jeremiah said unto all the people, and to all the women . . . Ye and your wives have both spoken . . . We will surely perform our vows that we have vowed, to burn incense to the queen of heaven, and to pour out drink offerings unto her: ye will surely accomplish your vows" (44:24-25). But he warned them that no longer could any man in Judah say, "The Lord liveth," for they had permitted him to die in their hearts. This wise old prophet prophesied also that the king of Egypt, where they were now exiled, would be taken by Nebuchadnezzar, king of Babylon. Because of the impending doom, even in the land of their exile, they need no longer seek goodness for themselves. No queen of heaven could achieve that for them.

Jeremiah's admonition has not lost any of its effectiveness for us today. We do not have a queen of heaven to bow down to, but we do worship in her place, in the same manner, our material possessions. Our obstinacy about a return to God, like theirs, is painfully evident. Vanity instead of sanity rules us. We strive harder to be sophisticated in the ways of the world than we do to achieve humility in the presence of the Lord. Fleeting pleasures call us away from the church and other spiritual endeavors.

Only a small remnant then as now understands Jeremiah's plaintive cry in time of distress: "O Lord, the hope of Israel, all that forsake thee shall be ashamed, and they that depart from me shall be written in the earth, because they have forsaken the Lord, the fountain of living waters" (17:13).

CHAPTER TWENTY-THREE

EZEKIEL—THE LEWD AND THE WORSHIPERS OF FALSE CULTS

Like the three other prophets in the preceding chapters, Ezekiel zealously denounced woman's desertion of good moral and ethical principles. With great frankness he spoke out against the instability and immorality of those in Jerusalem as well as those in exile in Babylon. He was compelled to do so, because as he said, "the hand of the Lord was strong" upon him.

One whose main burden was judgment, Ezekiel, like the other prophets, used oratory and logic but largely allegory when he presented his views regarding the loss of values among the women. Each allusion to them suggests that these women of his time were purveyors to the world of the superfluities of life, and nothing else seemed to matter to them.

A youth in his teens when Jeremiah was a mature man, Ezekiel continued what Jeremiah had begun but in a different spirit and under altered and more favorable circumstances. He lived as a youth in Jerusalem and then went into Babylon with some ten thousand other exiles, among whom were King Jehoiachin and the king's mother, wives, smiths, craftsmen, and "men of might." Because he had survived the crisis in Jerusalem that led to exile in Babylon, Ezekiel developed a faith that he was able to pass on to others. Like a good watchman, who had heard the sound of the trumpet, he tried to warn others that the word of the Lord had come unto him saying,

> For I will lay the land most desolate, and the pomp of her strength shall cease; and the mountains of Israel shall be desolate, that none shall pass through.
> Then shall they know that I am the Lord, when I have laid the land most desolate because of all their abominations which they have committed. . . .
> And when this cometh to pass, (lo, it will come), then shall they know that a prophet hath been among them.   (33:28–29, 33)

Ezekiel had settled among a colony of exiles at Telabib on the Cheba, an important canal in the Euphrates irrigation system. There he preached to a small, remote congregation, and through them addressed the exiles from Israel, trying to keep alive in them a sense of hopefulness in the mercy of God.

THE UNSTABLE WOMEN

The unstable women who were members of cults, based largely on superstition, and who told fortunes for a liveli-hood, received his first attention. Instead of trying to save souls, as God-loving people should do, these women, said Ezekiel, tried to sell souls for profit. After first speaking to the false prophets who, he said, acted like the "foxes in the deserts," he then vigorously denounced these false prophetesses:

> Likewise, thou son of man, set thy face against the daughters of thy people, which prophesy out of their own heart; and prophesy thou against them,
>
> And say, Thus saith the Lord God; Woe to the women that sew pillows to all armholes, and make kerchiefs upon the head of every statue to hunt souls! . . .
>
> Will ye pollute me among my people for handfuls of barley and for pieces of bread, to slay the souls that should not die . . . by your lying?   (13:17–19)

This text leaves us a little uncertain about whether these women fortunetellers either wore veils and arm bands themselves or put them on their clients. It is probable that they disguised themselves in veils, so as to attract attention, and that they sewed the bands on their clients' wrists, making them believe that the bands brought luck.

Usually of the ill-fed, lower classes, these fortunetellers probably received no coins for such services but only a few handfuls of barley and a piece of bread. Like the modern gypsy, they went about hunting their clients. Ezekiel, however, is more accurate in saying they hunted souls for profit. He warned the people that only God can breathe life into the human soul; that only those who seek God can actually know him.

It is probable that these fortunetellers learned their

trade from the Babylonians. Although sorcery had been practiced in early Israel, the people enacted laws against such idolatrous practices, common among the Canaanites.

Conspicuously attired in bright Babylonian colors, these women fortunetellers lay in wait for those who were silly enough to listen to them profane the name of the Lord with their deliberate lies about the future. Their clients evidently were women, who sought to humor their own sins and had rather hear pleasant lies than unpleasant truths.

Ezekiel was confident that these ignorant and superstitious women fortunetellers knew nothing of God, from whom all power comes. He was sure they grieved the hearts of good people who venerated God's word, and that they provided the godless with arguments against God.

Many such false cults, which slur over the distinction between right and wrong, compete with Christianity today. Often their membership is made up of either the blissfully ignorant or the intellectually elite. The woman who is active in such cults, either as a mind reader or a faith healer, defies God's laws. In her own irresponsibility and instability she denies God, the giver of all good.

Ezekiel would remind woman that holiness is the very heart of religion, and that it is always available to those who search diligently to know God. Ezekiel's words ring as true today as when they were written, "A new heart also will I give you, and a new spirit will I put within you and cause you to walk in my statutes, and ye shall keep my judgments, and do them" (36:26–27).

THE FOUNDLING GIRL AND THE UNFAITHFUL WIFE

Ezekiel's first most famous feminine allegory was that of the foundling girl (16:1–14), who represented the Israel of his time. He describes quite eloquently how the rescued foundling became a child of light, but when she arrived at full maidenhood and grew exceedingly beautiful and prosperous, she prostituted her beauty and became a child of darkness.

Ezekiel depicts her as dressed in fine linens and silks and wearing bracelets on her arms, an elaborate chain on her neck, a jewel on her forehead, dangling earrings, and a crown upon her head.

Israel, like this foundling girl, said Ezekiel, was greatly blessed by God with both natural beauties and riches. But this maiden (Israel again) played the harlot and offered herself to every passerby. From some of her jewels she made images of men with whom she engaged in sensual practices, as had those women in Jezebel's time who sensually worshiped false gods in the Baal temples.

This maiden grew bolder in her harlotries as she matured, said Ezekiel. She forgot the days of her youth when she had been both naked and bare, and became an "adulterous wife, who receives strangers instead of her husband! Men give gifts to all harlots; but you gave your gifts to all your lovers, bribing them to come to you from every side for your harlotries. So you were different from other women in your harlotries" (16:32–34, RSV).

Ezekiel prophesied that judgment would be executed upon this unfaithful wife in the sight of many women. In this part of the allegory appears the famous passage, "As is the mother, so is her daughter" (v. 44). Her (Israel's) mother was a pagan-worshiping Hittite, whose desertion of principles had caused her downfall.

Though born as a foundling, Israel, like the foundling girl, became a child of light (opportunity). Again drawing the same parallel, Ezekiel said she developed into a child of darkness (evil).

Ezekiel's timeless allegory suggests how easy it is for beautiful and affluent maidens to prostitute God's blessings, and like Israel, discover their sin too late.

THE HARLOTRIES OF TWO SISTERS

In a second feminine allegory, Ezekiel refers to the whoredoms of this foundling's two sisters, Aholah, representing Samaria (the Northern Kingdom of Israel), and Aholibah, typifying Jerusalem, the capital of the Southern Kingdom. Ezekiel, who never covers up reality, tells how Aholah "doted" on her lovers, the Assyrians, "all of them desirable young men," and then committed whoredoms with them. "Her sister Aholibah," he said, "was more corrupt in her inordinate love than she [Aholah]" (23:11), with both the Assyrians and the Babylonians, who "came to her into the bed of love . . . and she was polluted with them" (v. 17).

The great prophet predicted that both of these sisters of darkness would be laughed to scorn. Because they had forgotten God with their adulteries and idolatries, he was certain their punishment was at hand.

Finally, Ezekiel concludes with this dramatic and horrifying allegorical prediction on the two lewd sisters:

Thus will I cause lewdness to cease out of the land, that all women may be taught not to do after your lewdness.

And they shall recompense your lewdness upon you, and ye shall bear the sins of your idols: and ye shall know that I am the Lord God. (23:48–49)

HIS OWN GOD-LOVING WIFE

Unlike Jeremiah who never married, Ezekiel was blessed with a God-loving wife, who is referred to as "the desire of his eyes." Near the end of his ministry, on the day that the siege of Jerusalem began, his wife, who no doubt had lovingly walked beside him in his ministry, died of a stroke. The suddenness of her death makes the tragedy all the more poignant.

But Ezekiel tells us that the words of the Lord came upon him, saying, "neither shall thou mourn nor weep, neither shall thy tears run down." And so Ezekiel's own courageous words are a record to his people of his own discipline, "So I spake unto the people in the morning: and at even my wife died; and I did in the morning what I was commanded" (24:18).

Bearing his own sorrow ever so quietly, he addressed his listeners without any display of emotion. He seemed to be preparing them to face more valiantly impending sorrows in their own lives and when they did, they would not forget the courage of their own pastor, prophet, and watchman, who had resolutely carried on his mission of lifting their hearts, even on the day his own much beloved wife died.

Her high quality of character no doubt was Ezekiel's

gauge for judging other women, many of whom he found so unstable and immoral in this period of iniquity. But he was still convinced that despite their many evils God would call his people, as he had in the days of Moses, and that he would make a new covenant with them, inscribing its laws upon their hearts.

How Woman Achieves Moral, Spiritual Rebirth

Like the other prophets, Isaiah, Jeremiah, and Amos, Ezekiel left some valuable lessons for all women. His world was not our world, but spiritual truths do not change, nor does our dependence upon God.

Always exceedingly practical in his approach, Ezekiel spoke out against some serious faults in womanhood. For example, in denouncing those who worship false cults, he turns the mirror on us too and lets us see our own spurious religions as uncertain anchors in which we try to take refuge from reality. Many such false cults, which slur over the distinction between right and wrong, compete with Christianity today.

Like the other prophets, Ezekiel was an extraordinary man, able to reflect upon human life and to see deeply into human nature. Their truth is true always, and their words are unassailable and never wear out. Their spirit of unshaken confidence in the ultimate strength of good gives us strength also. Although their world is not our world, spiritually, the prophets are still our teachers.

They make us know, as they did, of God's unutterable excellence and glory. Their sense of right and wrong was sure, and they make us surer. They make us see the good, and we cannot let it go. What they wanted for the world still carries this strange compulsion like that of a magnet we cannot let go.

They make us surer that if we cease to stand up for excellence and goodness in our own lives, these qualities would cease to be, for apart from us they have no existence on this earth planet of ours. But even then, God would still be immeasurable, inconceivable, above his creation, infinite, and eternal, bounded neither by space nor time. The prophets not only bring us near him but make us feel the awe of his infinite perfection and our own sense of weakness and unworthiness. As the spokesmen for humanity then and now, we realize the permanence of their vision for the good, the continuity of human life, and the underlying unity of all human beings.

CHAPTER TWENTY-FOUR

WOMAN'S INESCAPABLE MAN-MADE DISABILITIES

The rights and privileges of Hebrew women set forth during Israel's birth vanished in periods of powerful pagan influences. Especially was this true during the long decades in Egypt, the years of the United Kingdom, beginning with King Saul in 1020 B.C. and continuing through the division into the Southern and Northern kingdoms, also during the Babylonian captivity, and in the period immediately preceding Christ's birth.

Women's disabilities multiplied as the Hebrew people began to mingle with people in godless nations. Subjection became a way of life, and women soon found that where there is subordination neither order nor co-ordination exist, for order comes into being only among equals in an atmosphere of helpfulness and service.

The excellencies of moral and spiritual living are of first concern in biblical laws. God is ever the supreme governing force, and therefore holiness, truth, and justice are foremost. Consequently these laws set up by Moses and strengthened by Jesus engendered standards that exalted men and women alike.

Attitude of Pagan Cultures Toward Women

Unlike the eminent religious leaders of Israel, the great men of nations contemporary with the Bible considered women as inferior creatures. Aristotle (384–322 B.C.) placed women between freemen and slaves. Socrates (470?–399 B.C.) and Demosthenes (385?–322 B.C.) looked down on women. Plato (427–347 B.C.) advocated a community of wives. The elder Cato of Rome (234–149 B.C.) stated smugly:

"If you should find your wife in adultery, you may with impunity put her to death without trial. If you commit adultery or indecency yourself, she dare not lay a finger on you. And she has no legal right to do so."

In his book *Caesar and Christ*, Will Durant tells us that a woman in Stoic Rome (508–202 B.C.) was not "allowed to appear in court, even as a witness. Widowed, she could not claim any dower rights in her husband's estate; he might if he wished, leave her nothing. At every age of her life she was under the tutelage of man—her father, her brother, her husband, her son, or a guardian—without whose consent she could not marry or dispose of property." (*The Story of Civilization*, vol. III, pp. 57–58.)

In an oration in Rome on the increasing birth rate, Caesar Augustus (63 B.C.–A.D. 14) spoke such grandiose sentiments as this:

"If it was possible to live without wives, gentlemen, we should all save ourselves that bother. But nature has ordained that, while life with them is not easy, life without them is quite impossible, and so we act with a view to our lasting well-being, not to the pleasure of the moment."

The courtesan in this early period of Rome was shown more honor than the wife. If a Roman husband desired to cater to a friend, he might give his wife to that friend. Such a transfer was not considered dishonorable, but an act of accommodation to the friend.

Early Greece was no different from Rome. Although the Greeks excelled in architecture, sculpture, philosophy, poetry, and the theater, there is hardly any great society in the world's history where the status of woman was so low as it was in Athens after 500 B.C. No education was thought necessary for girls. The whole structure of Athenian social life was for man's benefit, and never were morals lower. The Greeks honored the shameless Phyrne, the Athenian courtesan, and lifted their hands to public prostitutes when they prayed in their temples.

Among the other ancient civilizations that have left laws degrading women are the Hittites, the Babylonians, and the Assyrians. In the *Ancient Near Eastern Texts,* a scholarly work edited by James B. Pritchard, appear the legal texts from Collections of Laws from Mesopotamia and Asia Minor (pp. 157–220), and there is a vast difference from the biblical laws in their treatment of women. Except in a few rare instances, the pagan laws are degrading to women. Viewed in retrospect, it is easy to see that a nation's treatment of its women often determines the course of its civilization.

BIBLICAL LAWS SAFEGUARDING WOMEN

Biblical laws had their beginning with Moses's experience on Mount Sinai between 1300 and 1200 B.C. But an older set of laws appears in the Code of Hammurabi, the sixth

king of the first dynasty of Babylon (1792–1750 B.C.).
There is one great difference in the origin of these laws.
Hammurabi took personal credit for his laws, while Moses
gave God the credit. And so we find the religious element
written into all of the laws of Moses, to whom God
"made known his ways . . . and his acts unto the people of
Israel" (Ps. 103:7). But when ancient man ceased to worship God and wrote his laws to what best suited his own
egotistical needs, woman sank to the level of crouching
slave, with man her lord and master.

The first of the Hebrew laws appears in the Book of
the Covenant (Ex. 20–23; 34:12–27). The second is the
Deuteronomic Code, the second law, or repetition of the
law (Deut. 4:44; 5:1–21), in which Moses urges the people
to walk according to the will of God. The third is the Holiness Code (Lev. 17–26), composed in the sixth century.
Finally, we have the Priestly Code, produced in the fifth
century and incorporated in parts of Exodus, Leviticus,
and Numbers. These laws lift the quality of life and provide a kindly consideration for all creatures, men and
women alike.

Although many of the latter laws were set up specifically for the needs of a primitive people, the laws on sexual
relations, holiness, and personal conduct (Lev. 18:1–30;
19:1–35), are introduced as follows;

And the Lord said to Moses, "Say to the people of
Israel, I am the Lord your God. You shall not do as
they do in the land of Egypt, where you dwelt, and
you shall not do as they do in the land of Canaan,
to which I am bringing you. You shall not walk in

their statutes. You shall do my ordinances and keep my statutes, and walk in them, I am the Lord your God." (Lev. 18:1–4, RSV)

No Religious Influence in Babylonian Laws

The laws of Hammurabi (Codicils 130 and 156) involve the violation of betrothed virgins, and are in a general way parallel to Deuteronomy 22:23–26. These Babylonian laws have received close scrutiny in the last decades since they were found, written on ancient clay tablets, in 1937 at Mari, a flourishing city in the middle Euphrates.

The Bible contains two laws concerning the violation of unbetrothed virgins (Ex. 22:16–17; Deut. 22:28–29). These are not in the Babylonian laws, and impose penalties for the defilement of virgins. In both of the Hammurabi laws, the loss of a girl's honor was to be compensated for by money, and this was foremost. But the Deuteronomic law places a value on a young maiden's honor that money cannot buy. Should her honor be violated, the man was required to marry her.

The laws against incest in the Bible (Lev. 18:16–18; 20: 11–12, 19–21) are very comprehensive, while the laws of Hammurabi (Codicils 155–58) touch on the subject in a limited way. Leviticus deals with the whole problem in a broad, comprehensive, and righteous manner.

But in all fairness to the Code of Hammurabi, the laws on divorce, Codicils 138–41, are in advance of the one biblical law (Deut. 24:1–4). The Code of Hammurabi provides a marriage portion to the woman from her husband and her return to her father's house, while the law in Deuteronomy makes no mention of alimony. Codicil 129 of Hammurabi imposes the death penalty upon a man who commits adultery with another man's wife. This finds an exact parallel in Leviticus 20:10 and Deuteronomy 22:22.

The Hittite Code of Laws, dating from about 1350 B.C.(?), the period of the great Hittite dynasty, is much briefer than either the Babylonian or the Hebrew regulations. The underlying principles of justice in the Hittite laws are not far different, but they are based on civil needs and offer no religious insight. Again the stricter laws against incest in the Hebrew Code guard the purity of the family much better than do the Hittite edicts. The latter, Codicils 199 and 200, recognize and legitimatize bestiality in a repulsive manner.

The Assyrian Code, compiled about the time of the Hittite laws, sets up more special regulations concerning woman than are found in either the laws of Moses or the Babylonian or Hittite codes. In adultery, the Assyrian law commits the wife to the mercy of her husband, and even then provides for mutilation of the face and hands of the guilty woman.

While civil dictates of these other nations made concessions to the customs of surrounding nations, as in granting the father power to sell a daughter into bondage, Israel went one step further in giving her all of the protection possible (Deut. 22:16), as cited in an earlier chapter. Nehemiah decried this law of bondaged daughters and lamented that it is not in our power to redeem "for other men to have our lands and our vineyards" (5:5). This was when Nehemiah's reforms were just initiated in Jerusalem, following the captivity in Babylonia.

A daughter also could be sold for debt by her father (Ex. 21:7) and could be made a prostitute by her father (Judg. 19:24). But these early laws reflect the influence of the pagan civilizations, and Israel did not honor them during the later periods of her history.

WOMAN'S RIGHTS UNDER OLD HEBREW LAWS

Christ reiterated the old Hebrew laws in Deuteronomy and Leviticus when he said:

> The Lord our God is one Lord:
> And thou shalt love the Lord thy God with all thy heart, and with all thy soul, and with all thy mind, and with all thy strength: this is the first commandment.
> And the second is like, namely this, Thou shalt love thy neighbour as thyself. There is none other commandment greater than these.   (Mark 12:29–31)

When one obeys this there is no inequality, unfairness, or injustice. Based on the spiritual ideal of love, this law takes both man and woman to their greatest heights.

Christ's mother, Mary, set the example in her own life of the eternal truth of the equality of men and women before God. She stands at the pivotal point in history where all women were persons in their own right. Paul was to declare later "when the fulness of the time was come, God sent forth his Son, made of a woman, made under the law, to redeem them that were under the law, that we might receive the adoption of sons" (Gal. 4:4–5).

God, the creator of the universe and arbiter of the destinies of all men and nations, had sent his son, born of woman, who freed men from slavery to sin and law and adopted them as his sons. They might fall far from his image in themselves, but he was still their father by creation. In Christ, all men and women were summoned to clothe themselves with his righteousness and to declare themselves as sons and daughters of God. As will be shown in the next section, women received from Christ an entirely new conception of their priceless legacy.

Section Five

WOMAN'S LEGACY FROM CHRIST
AND HIS CHURCH

CHAPTER TWENTY-FIVE

HIS MOTHER, A TRUE HANDMAID
OF THE LORD

Christ's mother, Mary, never faltered as a humble hand-maid of the Lord, a connotation first used by Hannah, mother of Samuel, having evolved earlier from the word slave, then to domestic servant.

Hagar, Abraham's concubine, was a slave to his wife, Sarah, when they brought her back with them from Egypt. So was the little maid in Naaman's household in Damascus. He had taken her in a raid into Israelite territory, and she served his wife faithfully and lovingly.

In later times, the woman of status in the community, who achieved real humility, referred to herself as a hand-maid. When Abigail, the great lady of a rich household, referred to before, called herself David's handmaid, she showed profound humility to David and his men. David was won over immediately by Abigail because she was meek, thoughtful, and generous, all attributes of a humble servant of God.

David knew a true handmaid of the Lord, because of his own mother. In two of the Psalms attributed to him, he makes intercession to God as "the son of his handmaid" (86:16; 116:16). We know little otherwise about David's mother, but this is a fitting memorial to the unassuming mother of a notable son.

SERVANTHOOD AKIN TO PRIESTHOOD

Isaiah's splendid songs about the servant of the Lord (42:1–4; 49:1–6; 50:4–9; 52:13–15; 53:1–12; 61:1–4) recount in depth the meaning of servanthood. Although Isaiah's references apply largely to God's servant Israel, they may be addressed to the individual as well.

From them we learn that a servant of the Lord works quietly and unobtrusively. He accepts hardships and suffering without bitterness, and finds that they purify the soul. Servanthood for him becomes akin to priesthood in that it requires a special kind of dedication.

MARY'S UNDERSTANDING OF SERVANTHOOD

Better than any of her forerunners mentioned above or her contemporaries, Mary understood what the servanthood of God implied. Naturally, as a true daughter of Israel, she was familiar with Isaiah's servant songs, and in her own approaching motherhood, she seemed to give new meaning to this Psalm:

> Behold, as the eyes of servants look unto the hand of their masters, and as the eyes of a maiden unto the hand of her mistress, so our eyes wait upon the Lord our God; until that he have mercy upon us.   (123:2)

Mary, as already noted, had been brought up on the vow of Samuel's mother, Hannah, who in her humble, prayerful supplication before her son's birth (I Sam. 1:11) bequeathed to all mothers the example of what a handmaid of the Lord should be.

Mary's own words in the Annunciation, "Behold the handmaid of the Lord: be it unto me according to thy word" (Luke 1:38) give us our loftiest conception of the servanthood of God. After that, in the Magnificat, Mary thanked God for regarding "the low estate of his handmaiden" (1:48). She did not dwell upon self at all but upon her relationship to God.

In this spiritual analysis of the servanthood of herself and her people, which followed (1:49–55), we sense Mary's quietness of spirit, her admirable self-control, her devout and gracious gift of oneness with God, and her understanding of his promises to Israel.

Never for one moment did Mary falter in her obedience to God, even when she knew that she must suffer the pain of criticism from those who did not understand the wonder of her approaching pregnancy. She alone understood that the Holy Spirit had come upon her and that the child to be born to her would be the Son of God.

After her son grew to manhood and entered upon his healing and preaching ministry, she never sought to be known as the mother of the great Messiah but only as the handmaid of the Lord. She understood that she, like her son, was sent to do the will of her Father.

As she witnessed the exemplary life that Jesus set before his disciples and his followers, she was prepared for the tremendous sacrifices that he made as he went among the poor and needy, as he healed the sick, as he carried his cross to Golgotha. She understood better than others no doubt why he never thought of self, why he never accumulated possessions, why he never had a family of his own or owned a house, and why he was content to live a solitary life. Christ's own words highlight this: "The servant is not greater than his lord; neither he that is sent greater than he that sent him" (John 13:16). Mary understood to the fullest too what her son meant when he spoke:

> And that servant, which knew his lord's will, and prepared not himself, neither did according to his will, shall be beaten with many stripes. But he that knew not, and did commit things worthy of stripes, shall be beaten with few stripes. For unto whomsoever much is given, of him shall be much required; and to whom men have committed much, of him they will ask the more.   (Luke 12:47–48)

Mary was being forewarned of what was to come when she heard her son say that as a servant of God he must be willing to suffer many things, even death on the Cross. She had been fully prepared as she walked all the way to the Cross with him and afterward saw him hung between two criminals. She murmured not a word because she had already become what Paul later called "a servant of Christ, doing the will of God from the heart" (Eph. 6:6).

It is no wonder that Mary, this true handmaid of the Lord, has made such a significant contribution to the history of women, and that she stands at the pivotal point in history, where noble women of early Israel had paved the way for her, and where she in turn would inspire many who would follow.

Her Influence on Other Women

Her earliest influence was on the women of the early church, who "labored much in the Lord." Furthermore, she has actuated others in the church through the more than nineteen centuries of Christian history.

Mary's example teaches that a handmaid of God walks not in darkness but in light. She knows how to sustain with a word those who are weary. She brings good tidings to the afflicted and binds the wounds of the brokenhearted. She comforts those who mourn and bestows praise upon the fainthearted. She keeps her tongue from evil and her lips from speaking guile. She worships God in the beauty of holiness, never doubting his faithfulness. She cannot be discouraged, because she is confident that God holds her by the hand, that his spirit is upon her, and that she has been called to righteousness.

Other Noble Handmaids in History

The pages of Christian history glow with the impact such handmaids have made on the world. They are the symbols of love and truth and take their places beside man as his equal in goodness. Some of history's noblest women live on largely because they regarded themselves as God's meek servants sent to do his work.

Joan of Arc, who gave her life at the stake for her beloved France, was one. Isabella of Spain was another. When she married Ferdinand in 1469, she left the wedding ceremony, walked immediately to the cathedral and prostrated herself before the high altar, calling herself a handmaid of the Lord as she did so. Isabella's first thought now was not that she was queen of Spain but that she was God's servant who must ask him to help her rule Spain with wisdom and justice.

Berthé de Chardin, the mother of Pierre Teilhard de Chardin, revered throughout the world as a philosopher, priest, paleontologist, and scientist, was one of this century's most worthy servants of the Lord, doing the will of Christ. Her son has illuminated our generation with his books, among which are *The Phenomenon of Man* and *The Future of Man*. Like Mary and Hannah of old, Berthé de Chardin sought God with a deep hunger. Her worshipful way of life provided a spiritual testament to her son during his formative years and sustained him through the fruitful years of his productive career.

He could remember how she had left at dawn, before her children awoke, and how she had walked two miles to the earliest Mass in her little French village church, rain or shine, even during her pregnancies. Later in the day she would retire frequently to her home altar to pray.

Madame de Chardin was a woman of such faith in God's goodness that when a priest tried to comfort her at the deathbed of one of her children, she consoled the priest with the thought that there was no need to grieve. "He's in heaven before us," this twentieth-century handmaid of God calmly told the priest. In later years her distinguished son Pierre declared:

I owe the best in my soul to my mother. It gives me strength to know that the whole effort of evolution is reducible to the justification and development of the love of God. That is what my mother used to tell me long ago.

THOSE WHO STILL SUFFER FOR CHRIST

We live in an affluent culture that sometimes seems too busy with material pursuits to care about the habitually sick, the destitute dying, the desperately needy, and the seriously handicapped. In our urban society where charitable organizations perform so many of the kind services that once were done by individuals, we seem to have lost the personal touch of Christ.

However, if we look far and long we still come upon a few handmaids who continue to suffer for Christ and who see him in the slums and the broken bodies of forgotten people. One of these is Teresa of India, whom Curtis Bill Pepper calls "a white angel in a sari," in the March 4, 1969, Look magazine. He tells how she denies herself rest, "sleeping in the baggage racks of third-class trains as she shuttles about India establishing homes to help the sick and the poor. The pain of thousands has cut into her gaunt face, white as the mountain stones in Yugoslavia where she once played as a girl."

She has established a home for dying destitutes, and she and her sisters have picked up twenty-one thousand dying from the streets and trash dumps of India. Many are like the old man dying of cancer, the stench from whose body was so strong that other patients protested. As Mother Teresa stood ministering to him, the old man asked,

"How can you stand my stench?"

"It's nothing compared to the pain you must feel," she replied.

As the old man lay dying later, it is further related, he looked up at her and said, "Glory be to you." "No," she answered, "glory be to you who are suffering for Christ." This handmaid, Teresa of India, sees that all suffering is a link to God through Christ. Even the lepers who suffer, she says, find in their own children the only smiles they will ever know, and this enables them to get better.

This modern handmaid also has worked and lived among the three thousand needy people who live beneath the old Roman aqueducts. In conclusion, Curtis Bill Pepper says in *Look* that Teresa, "a saint now or a saint-to-be is a woman with that kind of total faith that has given others like her the strength to raise armies, to humble kings—and to generate in people a wonder and warmth many believe to be a love for God."

Handmaids of the Lord are all about us. Often they are little recognized because they tread such an unobtrusive path and are lost in the sophistication and confusion of our times.

When Neil A. Armstrong first set foot on the moon, and the heavens became a part of man's world, his mother, Mrs. Viola Armstrong, rose forth as a true handmaiden of the Lord as she spoke to a waiting world, "Praise God from whom all blessings flow."

Other handmaidens about us may be the woman pathologist who labors long in her laboratory, searching out disease from its hiding place. The teacher who sacrifices her own pleasure to serve the retarded and sightless. The young maiden who gives her life to a religious order, sacrificing friends and family in order to do so. The nurse who goes to poverty-ridden homes to minister to the aged and dying. The mother who patiently serves her large family, often receiving not so much as a word of appreciation. The wife of the alcoholic, who quietly aids her husband in time of direst need.

These handmaids of the Lord, the true servants of humanity, deserve the accolade Isaiah gives them when he says that they "shall be named the priests of the lord . . . the ministers of our God" (61:6).

In his Pentecostal sermon Peter gives greater spiritual depth to the duties of menservants and maidservants when he reminds his listeners of what the prophet Joel said, "Yes, I will endue even my slaves, both men and women, with a portion of my spirit" (Acts 2:18, NEB). What a great promise! But we must remember that such assurances come only to the humble in heart, like Mary and these others, who exemplify the true servanthood of God.

CHAPTER TWENTY-SIX

HIS EXAMPLE OF PRAYER AND WORSHIP

Although prayer and worship are closely related, they cannot be treated as synonymous. Worship is an offering to God. Prayer is a deliberate attempt to communicate with God. When we worship we come before God as a member of a great family, a part of the communion of saints, both living and dead. When we pray we beseech the Creator for basic blessings, which are being asked by millions of others all over the world.

Christ's communion with the Father was handed down to him from his own people, who as nomads worshiped on desert wastes with a mound of earth for an altar. No doubt Jesus as a lad sang Psalms such as "O Come, let us worship and bow down; let us kneel before the Lord our maker" (Ps. 95:6). And he soon learned that those who truly love God and do his work can accomplish the miraculous.

A Reverent Belief in God

As Jesus grew to manhood and gathered about him his followers, he demonstrated by his own example how to worship God in beauty and holiness. His most faithful disciples became so grateful for his new leadership in prayer and worship that they thought not so much about where they worshiped as how devoutly they worshiped.

Jesus made his most pertinent statements regarding worship to the Woman of Samaria. The Jews and Samaritans disagreed on whether the divinely appointed site for central worship should be on Mount Gerizim, where ancient Canaanites had worshiped, or on Mount Zion, where stood the temple of Jerusalem. Jesus lifted the conception of true worship above the rival claims of cults and showed this woman there was a higher order of worship than the national rites on either Mount Gerizim or Mount Zion. Because God represents a universal fatherhood, it matters little whether he is worshiped on one mountain or another.

Settling this for all time, Jesus told the Woman of Samaria that "the hour cometh, and now is, when the true worshippers shall worship the Father in Spirit and in truth: for the Father seeketh such to worship him" (John 4:23). This has become the Bible's most profound definition of true worship.

THE PRAYING WOMEN ABOUT HIM

Jesus was born into an environment of praying women who moved unobtrusively, serving wherever they could. One of these was Anna, who was in the temple at Jerusalem where his parents brought him when they came for Mary's purification rites forty days after his birth. Of Anna it is said:

And she was a widow of about fourscore and four years, which departed not from the temple, but served God with fastings and prayer night and day.

> And she coming in that instant gave thanks likewise
> unto the Lord, and spake of him [the Christ Child]
> to all them that looked for redemption in Jerusalem.
>
> (Luke 2:37–38)

What an extraordinary tribute to a praying woman! Anna "departed not from the temple." Here she lived, praying and waiting patiently for the Redeemer, for Anna was a woman who expected great things from God. It is no wonder that Anna's name, flashed across Christian history almost twenty centuries ago, has burned brightly every time the name of those looking for redemption is mentioned.

Another of these praying women was his mother's cousin Elisabeth, wife of the priest Zacharias, who served a little group in the hill country of Judaea, in a desert tract west of the Dead Sea, a few miles from Jerusalem. Luke relates that before the birth of her son, John the Baptist, Elisabeth knew that he would "be great in the sight of the Lord . . . and that he would be filled with the Holy Ghost" (1:15).

When Mary came from Nazareth to visit Elisabeth before her son's birth, Elisabeth greeted Mary with the remarkable words, "Blessed art thou among women and blessed is the fruit of thy womb" (Luke 1:42). Mary's answer set the theme for how her soul magnified the Lord. We can imagine that both mothers-to-be prayed long together, for each carried in her womb a child of much promise.

When Mary returned to Nazareth, and Elisabeth gave birth to her son, she inspired her husband in the famous

Benedictus (Luke 1:67–80), just as she had inspired Mary in the Magnificat. The Benedictus celebrates the raising up of a leader out of the house of David and portrays John the Baptist as the forerunner of Christ, the "Prophet of the Highest," sent ahead to prepare the way. As the inspirer of two of the most fervent prayers on record, Elisabeth takes her place among prayerful women, who tower in Christian history.

Into this atmosphere of praying and worshiping women where Jesus was conceived and born and nurtured, the right tempo was set for his own prayer life.

HIS PRAYER FELLOWSHIP WITH GOD

Prayer to Christ meant fellowship with the Father. And so we find him praying in the solitude of the wilderness, on the Mount of Transfiguration, in the Garden of Gethsemane, in the temple at Jerusalem, in the circle of his friends, even on the Cross as he was dying.

Sometimes Jesus continued all night in prayer, never for once asking for his own comfort or his own wishes but only to accept God's will in his life. And he always knelt or stood while praying to his King of Kings. In his Sermon on the Mount Jesus said to the people gathered about him,

> When thou prayest, thou shalt not be as the hypocrites are: for they love to pray standing in the synagogues and in the corners of the streets, that they may be seen of men . . .
>
> But thou, when thou prayest, enter into thy closet, and when thou hast shut thy door, pray to thy Father

which is in secret; and thy Father which seeth in secret shall reward thee openly.

But when ye pray, use not vain repetitions, as the heathen do: for they think that they shall be heard for their much speaking.

Be not therefore like unto them: for your Father knoweth what things ye have need of, before ye ask him.   (Matt. 6:5–8)

Christ followed this with the Lord's Prayer (Matt. 6:9–13), the most widely used of his prayers. Fervently he began, "Our Father, who art in Heaven." People in Christ's time believed there were many heavens, one atop the other and extending into infinity. Isaiah, Job, Paul, and St. John the Divine (in Revelation) express this same concept. Isaiah told that God "created many heavens and stretched them out."

Paul, the most eloquent of all in this regard, said he knew "a man in Christ . . . who was caught up to the third heaven—whether in the body or out of the body I do not know, God knows. And I know that this man was caught up into Paradise—whether in the body or out of the body I do not know, God knows—and he heard things that cannot be told, which man may not utter" (II Cor. 12:2–4, RSV). Paul was probably the man to whom this happened. He lost all consciousness of his own physical existence as he was caught up in a moment of ecstasy. Whether he rose, body and all, and ascended skyward, or whether he left his body behind and went forward in spirit, he did not know, and we do not know the miraculous things he heard.

To Paul as to Jesus, heaven was the highest concept of man and God. In the Lord's Prayer we conceive of a heaven and a God so infinite that both are beyond our finite comprehension.

The women who touched Christ's life closely, especially Mary Magdalene in the moment of his Ascension, perhaps understood better than anyone what his Resurrection signified, for it was far more than a simple resuscitation. Such wonders are incomprehensible and unexplainable but at the very heart of the Christian gospel.

His Prayers for and in the Home

Many of Jesus's other prayers, such as grace at meals (Matt. 14:19) and his blessing of little children (Matt. 19:13), improved the environment of home life for women. The family became a praying unit and the home a worship center.

Jesus made us know that failure to give thanks for every blessing in the home is simply the outcome of a thoughtless, if not a base, ingratitude, and that the family must discipline itself to prayer. Like Samuel before him, Jesus was a prayer-gift child, and therefore born to a divine destiny. In his book *The Prayer Life of Jesus*, M. E. Dodd tells this story to illustrate the importance of prayer in the home:

In a remote district of Wales a baby boy lay dangerously ill. The widowed mother walked five miles through the night in a drenching rain to get a doctor. He hesitated about making the unpleasant trip. Was it really necessary and would it pay? He knew he would receive no money for his services, and besides the child, if his life was saved, would probably be nothing more than an ordinary laborer. But love for humanity and a sense of professional duty controlled him, and the child was saved. Years afterward when this child, David Lloyd George, became Chancellor of the Exchequer, the old doctor said: "I never dreamed that in saving the life of the child I was saving the life of a national leader." (Pp. 63–64)

THE POWER OF PRAYER

Prayer has been likened to electronic power that we can increase by the mere touch of the hand. Dr. W. F. G. Swann, director of the Bartol Research Foundation of the Franklin Institute of Swarthmore, Pennsylvania, writes:

> Just as an electronic apparatus can, by feedback mechanism, when it has a desire for more power, trigger something that has more power, it is not unthinkable that this mechanism, which we call prayer, may be a real kind of physical reactor in the universe as a whole so that the expression of its desire puts us in unity with the forces of the universe to bring into play very much greater forces than we ourselves can operate.

When we pray we link ourselves with that inexhaustible power of the universe and come into communion with God himself. Prayer and meditation can make all the difference in a woman's life, for in such communion she can touch the inner resources of her being where God dwells.

Paul tells us that "the Spirit comes to the aid of our weakness." We do not even know how we ought to pray, but through our inarticulate groans the spirit itself is pleading for us, and God who searches our inmost being knows what the spirit means, because he pleads for God's own people in his own way, and in everything, as we know, he co-operates for good. Prayer often brings very different results from what we expect.

In the conversion of the erring Saul (Paul) on the Damascus road, he saw a flash of light about him and he heard Jesus speak, "Saul, Saul, why persecutest thou me? . . . And he [Paul] trembling and astonished said, 'Lord, what wilt thou have me to do?'" (Acts 9:4, 6). After Paul was healed of a three-day blindness in Damascus by Ananias, an ardent disciple of Jesus, Paul learned that he, like other followers of Christ, must be willing to serve and suffer for his sake. Paul had received not only his sight again but, more important still, he had been filled with the Holy Spirit, all through the intercessory prayers of Ananias.

Paul's experience teaches us that no matter how long we sin or suffer, no matter how long we wait for the coming of the Holy Spirit into our lives, the impossible can be achieved through prayer. Great lives and miraculous events in Bible history make us know that we can never doubt the effectuality of prayer. One of the most earnest prayer poems ever written was this one by Ethel Romig Fuller:

> If the radio's slim fingers
> Can pluck a melody from night

And toss it over continent and sea;
If the petaled white notes of a violin
Are blown across the mountains or
    the city's din;
If songs, like crimson roses, are
    culled from thin blue air—
Why should mortals wonder if God
    hears prayer?*

* From *Masterpieces of Religious Verse*, reprinted by permission of Harper & Row, Publishers, page 407.

CHAPTER TWENTY-SEVEN

HIS EXAMPLE OF STEWARDSHIP AND WITNESS

Good stewards, says Jesus, are both "faithful and wise" (Luke 12:42). Because women serve the family in so many small and large ways, they are well fitted by nature and training to embrace all that steadfast stewardship implies.

Stewardship and witness are closely allied in the Christian faith. One activates the other. To serve well and to witness nobly are the true test of obedience and discipleship. No portion of one's time or money is his alone. Nor are one's friends, honors, talents, opportunities, or material possessions, not even one's children. As Kahlil Gibran says in *The Prophet*, "your children come through you but not from you. And though they are with you they belong not to you. You may give them your love but not your thoughts. For they have their thoughts. You may house their bodies but not their souls." They, like everything else we possess, were lent to us by God.

Stewardship in the literal sense had its birth in Genesis with Eliezer of Damascus, Abraham's steward, who oversaw his large household. Eliezer was actually an heir to all Abraham had, had his only son, Isaac, not survived him. Eliezer could have given an excellent account of his stewardship, for he never coveted what his master or his master's son possessed. He only desired to serve both well. It could never be said of Eliezer that he grew rich while his master grew poor or that he failed his master in even so personal a test as the selection of his son Isaac's bride, Rebekah.

Loyal and Disloyal Stewards

Stewardship evolved into all of its fullness in the New Testament when it came to signify that all Christians must be stewards of the manifold grace of God (I Pet. 4:10). Paul later defined "a bishop as God's steward," one who "must be blameless: he must not be arrogant or quick-tempered or a drunkard or violent or greedy for gain, but hospitable, a lover of goodness, master of himself, upright, holy, and self-controlled" (Tit. 1:7–8, RSV).

This kind of stewardship was broadened to include all Christians, who were commissioned to carry the spirit of Christ into life's everyday tasks, and thus make his gospel more meaningful, so that they who witnessed as faithful stewards would inspire others to become better stewards themselves.

One of the most faithful of these in Christ's time was the widow with the two mites (Mark 12:41–44; Luke 21: 1–4). She cast into the treasury of the temple at Jerusalem all that she had. The rich had cast in more, but only a small part of what they had. Her two mites were hardly enough to notice, but she regarded the little that she had not for her needs but for the greater needs of Christ's ministries. He saw not the smallness of her gift but her devotion in giving all that she had.

The gift of this poor widow so appealed to Jesus that he preserved the story of her sacrificial giving in the safe-keeping of his praise. She might have been a cleaning woman in the great temple at Jerusalem, or a reaper in the fields, or a nurse, or she could have been trying to live off the small earnings of a little acreage left by her husband. These details are not related, but her magnanimous deed is memorialized for all time.

After the formation of the New Church, its followers were so filled with the Holy Spirit, that they saw to it that none among them lacked. Those who had houses and lands sold these and brought the full amount into a common purse for the good of all. "And distribution was made unto every man according as he had need" (Acts 4:35).

One woman, Sapphira, failed miserably in her stewardship. She and her husband, Ananias, kept back for themselves part of the proceeds of the land they sold. It was not required that they give all, but like the others in this early fellowship they had publicly agreed to do this. But when they came before Peter they lied about what they had kept for themselves. It turned out that Sapphira and her husband were more concerned about what they had than what they were. Not only had they forgotten their pledged responsibility to the church but that the truth was one of its guiding principles. When Peter asked Sapphira, "How is it that ye have agreed together to tempt the Spirit of the Lord?" (Acts 5:9), she fell dead at Peter's feet, just as her husband had, when he too told the same lie about what they had and what they had given.

It is no wonder that "great fear came upon all the church, and upon as many as heard these things" (Acts 5:11), about these two unfaithful stewards, who tried to serve both God and mammon.

ELOQUENT AND EFFECTIVE WITNESSING

Pilate's wife became a significant witness to Christ's innocence when she sent word to her husband, the Roman governor of Judaea, to "have nothing to do with that just man: for I have suffered many things this day in a dream because of him" (Matt. 27:19). At this moment Pilate was sitting on the judgment seat in Jerusalem and no doubt could have saved Jesus from death, but the cries of the mob were stronger. When he asked them what to do with Jesus, they all called back, "Let him be crucified." Then when Pilate asked what evil Jesus had done, they repeated the same demand. Washing his hands, Pilate said that he was innocent of the blood of this just person. And the mob hollered back, "his blood be on us, and on our children."

Watching from her Herodian Palace balcony, Pilate's wife probably saw the mobs release Barabbas, scourge Jesus, and deliver him to be crucified. Although her woman's voice could not delay his crucifixion, she became an unforgettable witness to his innocence during his trial and crucifixion. Her strong conviction of what was right and wrong has given other Christian women the courage to speak for justice, even when the mighty speak for what is evil.

The great fourteenth-century saint Catherine of Siena spoke out against the papacy and was instrumental in revitalizing the Catholic Church and having it returned from Avignon, France, to Rome.

Margaret and her daughter, Jeanne d'Albret, devout queens of Navarre, pioneered in the religious freedom of France because they were not afraid to champion the Christian faith. They and Jeanne's son, King Henry IV (Henry of Navarre), became faithful witnesses to the Christianity of Christ and the Apostles. Both mother and daughter had prepared their son and grandson for his famous Edict of Nantes in 1598 favoring the Huguenots (French Protestants) in the exercise of religion, civil equality, and fair administration of justice.

The Quaker woman Elizabeth Fry had the courage to speak out against prison injustices in her eighteenth-century England. Her voice was afterward heard all over Europe, and she accomplished greater prison reform than any woman in history.

These four eminent Christian women received power from God and became what Christ prophesied his true servants should be, "witnesses unto me both in Jerusalem and in all Judaea, and in Samaria, and unto the uttermost parts of the earth" (Acts 1:8).

A Twentieth-century Witness

Without realizing it herself, Madame Marie Curie became one of the most unselfish women witnesses of the twentieth century. With her husband, Pierre, she discovered radium, a substance used in the fight against cancer and other diseases. She was only thirty-two at the time. Not too long afterward, her husband, when crossing a Paris street, was knocked down by a dray and killed instantly. They had worked side by side and had known much happiness together.

Madame Curie continued with her work, constantly denying herself for her two little girls, her laboratory, and her research. During World War I, she helped in the hospitals with various forms of radium treatment and drove as near the firing lines as she could, often administering to the sick and dying. The world soon acclaimed her as one of the zealous servants of humanity.

In 1921, American clubwomen invited her to this country so that they might eulogize her. The story is told that when she arrived at their luncheon in her honor at a New York hotel, she was wearing an old threadbare dress, a much-used shawl, and an odd-looking hat.

Finally, as a token of their esteem, the clubwomen gave her a tube of radium worth more than fifty thousand dollars. When Madame Curie arose to receive the gift, she inquired, "Is this really mine?" And when they told her it was, she asked, "May I do with it as I please?" "Yes," they answered, noting her old hat and dress and supposing she would indulge herself and ensure her old age.

"If it is mine to do with as I please," she told them, "I will give it to my native Poland where there is a hospital that needs it very much."

In her unselfish act Madame Curie set an example of unpremeditated witnessing and stewardship, even in her later years after she became critically ill. She accepted her suffering with such quiet fortitude that scarcely anyone knew of the seriousness of her illness until a day or two before her death.

Madame Curie did not expect to write great deeds across the pages of time. She and her husband toiled together in a cheerless laboratory. Her health failed because she had overworked. Her radium experiments were dangerous and expensive, but she denied herself natural pleasures. Long after her husband's death in 1911, Madame Curie continued to witness in such an effective manner that now, several decades later, she stands forth as one of this century's most valiant witnesses to Christ's teachings. And yet she never strived to be one at all. Like him, she merely denied herself and gave her life for others.

CHAPTER TWENTY-EIGHT

ON BRINGING THE VISIBLE FROM THE INVISIBLE

The New Testament's women of faith live on as stout-hearted soldiers enduring sickness and bereavement, antagonism and affliction, hate and harassment, poverty and persecution. They must have wondered why they had to suffer so grievously, and yet we have no record that they complained. Although their souls often were tempered with fire, they went forth nobly, never allowing adversity or suffering to crush or embitter them, or to make them cynical or hopeless.

They had learned that the faith, such as Christ demonstrated, represents confidence in God's goodness, and so they learned to trust themselves and their loved ones to his providential care, and discovered that if they had sufficient faith they could bring "the visible from the invisible," and hope from hopelessness. They came to realize too that through faith "the worlds were framed by the word of God, so that things which are seen were not made of things which do appear" (Heb. 11:3).

THE HONORED HEROINES OF FAITH

Like Jesus, these women of New Testament times were brought up on the faith of their fathers handed down for generations. Several women in the Old Testament are honored in Hebrews 11, the Bible's most inspiring chapter on faith. Of the first it says, "Through faith Sarah herself received strength to conceive seed, and was delivered of a child when she was past age, because she judged him faithful who had promised" (v. 11). By faith Sarah's son, Isaac, "blessed Jacob and Esau concerning things to come" (v. 20). And by faith her grandson Jacob "when he was a-dying, blessed the sons of Joseph; and worshipped, leaning upon the top of his staff" (v. 21). And by faith her great-grandson Joseph "when he died, made mention of the departing children of Israel; and gave commandment concerning his bones" (v. 22). So it was that the faith of Sarah and the greater faith of her husband, Abraham, was handed down. Their loyalty to unseen reality gives solid dimension to their faith, and concrete examples of the evidence of things they did not live to see.

It is difficult to connect faith in a woman identified as a harlot, as is Rahab, in these heroines of faith. But her good acts reveal that faith redeems even the disreputable. Rahab "perished not with them that believed not, when she had received the spies with peace" (v. 31).

Her house built on the walls of Jericho served as a stronghold for the men of Israel as they prepared to march on her city, which commanded entrance to Palestine from the east. Rahab's faith in the God of Israel came alive when she told the spies, "the lord your God is he who is God in heaven above and on earth beneath" (Josh. 2:11, RSV).

The same faith chapter also acclaims that "By faith, Moses, when he was born, was hid for three months by his parents, because they saw that he was a proper child; and they were not afraid of the king's commandment" (Heb. 11:23) that all Hebrew babies be slain at birth.

And so his mother, Jochebed, built a water cradle and hid him along the banks of the Nile River until the Pharaoh's daughter and her maids came by. And the Pharaoh's daughter, hearing the baby's murmurs, took him into the palace and adopted him, and Miriam, Moses's young sister standing by, watching over the child Moses, obligingly told Pharaoh's daughter that she knew a nurse who would care for the babe in her palace. And Moses's own mother, unidentified to Pharaoh's daughter, became the child's nurse from the time he was found at age three months until he was probably seven years of age.

This mother, Jochebed, had the faith to build her child's water cradle, the faith to let him float in it on the banks of the Nile River, the faith to leave him there alone, knowing that God would protect him. Her active belief in a God who cares brought the evidence of even a greater protection to her child than she had hoped for in the beginning.

From such as these in early Israel, Jesus spoke of a faith that sustains, and is made larger through his Father, who sent him into the world.

THE HEALING LIGHT OF JESUS

Christ's teachings on faith awakened many, even those who were not thought to be receptive. And they make more eloquent his statement, "If ye have faith as a grain of mustard seed, ye shall say unto this mountain, Remove hence to yonder place, and it shall remove; and nothing shall be impossible unto you" (Matt. 17:20). Through his demonstrations of faith, it is easy to understand why Jesus was acclaimed the "author and finisher of our faith" (Heb. 12:2).

The healing light that he brought into the world fell upon two sick women in particular. One of these was the woman who had had a hemorrhage for twelve years, and to whom he spoke confidently, "Daughter, be of good comfort: thy faith hath made thee whole" (Luke 8:48). She had believed that if she could only touch his garment, she would be healed; so eagerly she made her way through the crowds to him, and he healed her. A long illness had left her weak and weary, but now she could walk with vigor, for her step carried with it the assurance that she would be whole again. This woman's healing by Jesus strengthens our belief that God has built a natural recuperative energy and a marvelous wholeness within, which might be likened to a divine radiation, as real as the radiation from the sun.

The miracle of faith also illuminated the life of the woman who was crippled for eighteen years. She was so bent in body that she could not straighten herself up, and yet she had the faith to walk to the place where Jesus was teaching in one of the synagogues on the Sabbath. And when Jesus saw her, he called her to him, and said, "Woman, thou art loosed from thine infirmity. And he laid his hands on her, and immediately she was made straight, and glorified God" (Luke 13:12–13). A God-loving woman, who had traveled the path of faith, she was quick to praise God for her healing.

The faith of these two women healed by Jesus make more explicit his words to the father of the demoniac boy, "All things are possible to him that believeth. And straightway the father of the child cried out and said with tears, Lord, I believe; help mine unbelief" (Mark 9:23–24).

The nameless Syro-Phoenician woman, also called the Canaanite, experienced the miraculous healing by Jesus of her daughter, who was handicapped by what the Bible calls a demon (probably mental retardation). Though she appeared to be a woman devoid of faith, Jesus acclaimed her as one with the power to prove the meaning of faith.

Her daughter was healed instantly when Jesus said to her, "Woman, what faith you have! Be it as you wish" (Matt. 15:28, NEB). Faith for this woman became more than mere words from the lips of the Master. She began to understand better the supreme faithfulness of God, whose spirit can breathe new life into the sickest body.

Another Blessed Recipient

The nameless widow of Nain, whose only son died, received one of Christ's greatest gifts of faith, the raising of her son from the dead. Her story is told with depth of feeling in only four verses.

> Now when he came nigh to the gate of the city, behold, there was a dead man carried out, the only son of his mother, and she was a widow: and much people of the city was with her.
>
> And when the Lord saw her, he had compassion on her, and said unto her, Weep not.
>
> And he came and touched the bier: and they that

bare him stood still. And he said, Young man, I say
unto thee, Arise.

And he that was dead sat up, and began to speak.
And he delivered him to his mother.   (Luke 7:12–15)

Nothing else is known about this nameless widow,
whose only son was raised by Jesus from the dead. But for
some two thousand years she has typified the mother of an
only son, of whom there have been millions since she
walked beside her son's casket through the streets of
Nain. Legions of sorrowing mothers have received new
strength in the miraculous power of Jesus, and in the
knowledge that although he may not walk by and touch
the biers of their dead sons, his miracles forever inspire
them.

This nameless widow perhaps was among Christ's many
benefactors, who afterward "glorified God," as stated in
the passage that follows her son's resurrection. Had not
this widow manifested faith during her poignant grief, she
would not have understood what it means to glorify God.

Others of Great Faith

Several women in the Old Testament either made such
remarkable demonstrations of faith or were such central
figures in the exemplification of faith that Jesus paid recognition to them when he said,

There were many widows in Israel in the days of
Elijah, when the heaven was shut up three years and
six months, when there came a great famine over the
land: and Elijah was sent to none of them but only

to Zarephath, in the land of Sidon to a woman who
was a widow.   (Luke 4:25–26, RSV)

Jesus was also familiar with the miracles of Elijah's
protégé, Elisha, who raised the son of the Shunammite
from the dead and who multiplied the widow's oil when
her creditors, at the death of her husband, demanded that
her sons be sold into slavery in payment of his debts.

Faith in the Old Testament meant trust in God's power,
but in the New Testament it took on the aspect of trust in
God as manifested in Christ. With him nothing was impossible. Once he speaks of removing mountains and afterward of removing a sycamine (black mulberry) tree and
planting it in the sea (Luke 17:6). Literally it would be
impossible for a tree to grow in the sea, but Jesus used the
illustration to show that with faith even nature's processes
of growth can be completely reversed.

The heroes and heroines of old "through faith subdued
kingdoms, wrought righteousness, obtained promises,
stopped the mouths of lions, quenched the violence of
fire, escaped the edge of the sword, out of weakness were
made strong, waxed valiant in fight, turned to flight the
armies of the alien" (Heb. 11:33–34). Such faith as this, in
deeds not words, was what Jesus demonstrated to his followers, who learned how to live not only in the stream of
God's power and wisdom but in the same current of
Christ's miracles. These typify a faith about which Nathaniel Hawthorne wrote so eloquently, "Christian faith
is a grand cathedral, with divinely pictured windows.
Standing without, you can see no glory, nor imagine any,
but standing within every ray of light reveals a harmony of
unspeakable splendors."

CHAPTER TWENTY-NINE

HIS SPIRITUAL REVELATIONS TO WOMEN

Jesus recognized that women possess remarkable spiritual sensitivity but that it needs to be nurtured. They in turn demonstrated to him that they had a passionate eagerness to learn more about the things of the spirit, but that such hunger could be satisfied only by Jesus, the Master Teacher.

To three women, the Woman of Samaria, Martha of Bethany, and Mary Magdalene (of Magdala), he gave some of his most astonishing revelations, and because he did, all occupy an immortal place in Christian history. All appear in the Book of John, the most spiritual of the four gospels.

The first, the Woman of Samaria, had had five husbands and was now living with one to whom she was not married. The second, Martha, was a practical homemaker. The third, Mary Magdalene, had once possessed seven demons, which could have been a nervous breakdown, of which Christ healed her.

His own followers would have picked none of these three as recipients of his most profound spiritual truths, but he showed them that renewal, healing, and reconciliation are possible for all. Those, like the Woman of Samaria, who have fallen into degradation. Those, like Martha, who are busy with many material pursuits. Those, like Mary Magdalene, who have suffered much, both mentally and physically. To all three Jesus brought a new sense of freedom.

THE WOMAN OF SAMARIA—"GOD IS A SPIRIT"

To prepare the Woman of Samaria, of whom we read in John 4, for the spiritual truths he was about to reveal to her, as they stood together at the well at Sychar, both famished for water, Jesus explained that "whosoever drinketh of the water that I shall give him shall never thirst; but the water that I shall give him shall be in him a well of water springing up into everlasting life."

This presupposes the infusion of the Holy Spirit in this woman. The fresh water from the spring that he described is symbolic of nourishment for the thirsty soul, and none was thirstier spiritually than this woman who had lived so long without respectable status. This water from the spring of life, like the "bread of God" or the "bread from Heaven," about which he later discoursed to his followers, instantly nourished her spiritual being.

In the second revelation of what God is, a spirit, Jesus taught this woman how to develop a unique fellowship with God. What is spirit? It has been called an "essence springing from the Spirit of God and imparted to the Spirit of Man." This also presupposes the infusion of the Holy Spirit to quicken and inform, and to develop the spiritual self. This woman, who had lived only for her carnal self, had to learn that the spiritual self was a new creation from God, who is a spirit. Paul afterward clarified this battle between the flesh and the spirit when he explained:

> To be carnally minded is death; but to be spiritually minded is life and peace.
> Because the carnal mind is enmity against God: for it is not subject to the law of God, neither indeed can be.
> So then they that are in the flesh cannot please God.
> But ye are not in the flesh, but in the Spirit, if so be that the Spirit of God dwell in you. Now if any man have not the spirit of Christ, he is none of his.
> And if Christ be in you, the body is dead because of sin; but the Spirit is life because of righteousness.
>
> (Rom. 8:6–10)

After the first two revelations, the woman said to him, "I know that Messiah cometh, which is called Christ." Then it was that he revealed to her that he was the expected Messiah. Daniel earlier had spoken of the Messiah who would come, and a few like Anna, mentioned earlier, had recognized him as the Redeemer. But in this statement alone Christ gives witness, "I that speak unto thee am he." The woman then rushed back to Samaria to say that she had found Christ, the Savior of the world.

MARTHA—"I AM THE RESURRECTION AND THE LIFE"

Jesus often went to Bethany to visit Martha and her sister, Mary. We learn from John 11 that their home had become a place of refuge to him. They urged him to come there when their brother, Lazarus, first was stricken ill, but Jesus was on a mission beyond the Jordan, and he delayed two days in returning to Bethany. After he had the premonition that his friend Lazarus was dead, he returned hurriedly to awaken Lazarus, as he explained, from his sleep.

Martha, ever up and doing, was the first to go forth to meet Jesus, while Mary, the more pensive of the two, "sat still in the house" in an attitude of grief. The plain-spoken Martha murmured quietly to Jesus, "Lord, if thou hadst been here, my brother would not have died." Martha, however, was a believing woman and declared earnestly, "I know that even now, whatsoever thou wilt ask of God, God will give it to thee." When Jesus promised her that her brother would rise again, she told him that she was sure he would in the resurrection at the last day. Then Jesus answered her with that great spiritual truth: "I am the resurrection, and the life: he that believeth in me, though he were dead, yet shall he live: And whosoever liveth and believeth in me shall never die."

Jesus seemed to say to Martha that the death of the body is only a physical incident, like that of falling asleep, but the life which he revealed is the divine life, a life analogous to the life in man, a life of a higher order, spiritual instead of earthly.

When Martha, this practical homemaker, first a doubter but now a believer, saw her brother, Lazarus, rise from the tomb in his graveclothes, she became for all time the channel from which one of Christ's most profound teachings emanated. How could it be explained? Martha must have pondered this as have others of us in the passing of loved ones.

Yet if we search deeply enough, we catch a faint glimpse of this in nature itself. We find its counterpart in the seed, for example, which when planted in the ground disappears in form and substance but does not die. It springs up to new form and substance just as the acorn becomes a stately oak and a bird egg is transformed into a flying creature of a thousand radiant colors.

Cannot man, in like manner, undergo changes equally as impressive in his body? Cannot God who raises the seed to new life, the acorn to the mighty oak, the tiny egg to a flying bird, transform man into newness of life?

We cannot explain the mystery of what Jesus told Martha any better than we can explain the birth of a child, but neither can we doubt, either. The child in the womb possesses life and motion long before it begins to breathe and long before it begins to reason.

In this Space Age, when astronauts physically break the bonds of earth and push back the limits of the universe, who are we to doubt the resurrection of our own loved ones? When we do we distrust the Supreme Mind which makes all of these miracles possible.

Negative answers lead to a finite universe and positive answers to an infinite one. In an age when space has seemingly opened up as limitless, who are we ever to question?

In the raising of Lazarus, Jesus was being prepared for his own death. When Lazarus came forth from the tomb after lying there dead for four days, the chief priests and Pharisees "from that day forth took counsel together to put him to death." His miraculous raising of Lazarus had

been too wondrous for them to behold. Not long afterward
Jesus was on his way to the Crucifixion.

MARY MAGDALENE—"I ASCEND UNTO MY FATHER"

When Christ arose from the tomb, where he was laid after
being nailed to the Cross, and Mary Magdalene stood
alone, weeping, that first morning at his sepulcher (John
20), she saw his body changing from its old form into a
new form fitted to the dimensions and demands of the
spirit in an ethereal world. To see him for only a moment
was her reward for her constancy to him.

Later on, Paul would explain to the Church at Corinth
Christ's Transfiguration. "There are also celestial bodies,
and bodies terrestrial," he told them, "but the glory of the
celestial is one, and the glory of the terrestrial is another"
(I Cor. 15:40). Jesus would now give up "the image of
the earthy" and "bear the image of the heavenly" (v. 49).

And Mary Magdalene had the spiritual perception to
understand. She was so transported in thought that she
forgot herself as she stood to ponder his words. "Tell them
that I must shortly ascend," he said to her. Now she and
others must look higher than his bodily presence and further than the present moment.

Finally conscious of what a change had come over
Christ, Mary Magdalene rushed forth to tell his disciples
that she had seen him arise. Then that same evening he
came and stood in the midst of his disciples. He showed
them his hands and his side where he had been nailed to
the Cross. Eight days later, even the doubting Thomas,
when he saw Christ's fingers and hands, believed that he

now bore a celestial body. All of his disciples began to realize that those who would deny his Resurrection would deny his Divinity and his redemptive work.

"And if Christ be not risen, then is our preaching vain," spoke Paul, "and your faith is also vain, yea, and we are found false witnesses of God" (I Cor. 15:14–15).

The Benefits to Womanhood

Jesus had prepared each of these three women for what it means to be spirit filled and spirit guided. Master teacher that Christ was, he wanted each of them to become new creatures in him, generated, enlightened, imbued, empowered.

He had brought the emotional nature of the Woman of Samaria under the regulating and redeeming sway of the Holy Spirit. He had found Martha's grief a fertile soil for the spiritual life. And he had made Mary Magdalene feel in every fiber of her being and in all the activities of her soul that he was in direct communication with God and that he could in turn make others alive in God, his Father.

He had succeeded in focusing the mind, heart, and energy of all three reverently and affectionately upon a God-centered life that would be an inspiration to others throughout Christian history. Each went forth with new power, ready to impart it to others.

And all three live on as immortal women, the Woman of Samaria as his witness and first missionary; Martha as a communicant of what the Life and the Resurrection mean; and Mary Magdalene, a witness to his Resurrection, the most remarkable event in Christian history.

What a challenge their lives are to each of us. We may not recognize or admit it to ourselves, but we are just as handicapped, emotionally, physically, and spiritually, as were these three women. If we could only be as aroused as they were by Christ's spiritual revelations, we could press on to a new humanity and be better prepared for the unfoldments that await us in this Space Age, many of whose signs and wonders have already appeared on the horizon.

We too must have eyes and hearts open and ears attuned to the new wonders that are now all about us. For we live on the edge of the unknown. What of the new sounds from the vastness of space that astronomers cannot explain, these "pulsing signals," they have been called, coming out of the sky? Astronomers feel confident that their source lies beyond our solar system, and many scientists believe that as man ventures deeper into space, he will encounter intelligent life on planets farther away from the earth than the moon. Mystery piles on mystery about intelligent beings on these other planets, about the new gravitational waves impinging upon and passing through the earth, about other wonders such as pulsars and quasars, the two recently discovered classes of celestial objects, both of which generate powerful radio and light emissions.

With space ships traveling into the unknown, with computers humming and blinking miraculous reports, with organ transplants and all the other new wonders, we must be spiritually as well as scientifically attuned to comprehend them.

Some of these are as inexplicable as Christ's spiritual revelations to these women on the nature of God, the

meaning of the Resurrection, and his own announcement
of his approaching ascent into the unknown.

One astronomer has asked, "Is something crying out to
man without his having heard it yet? Has something been
calling life steadily since its beginning?" Eric Hoffer, the
self-educated longshoreman and philosopher, who has suddenly risen to fame, makes this profound comment:

"I like to play with the fancy that some contagion from
outer space has been the seed of man. Our passionate
preoccupation with heaven, the stars, and a God some-
where in outer space is a homing impulse. We are drawn
back to where we came from. Hence to me the exploration
of space has an inner logic."

Only can those who are spirit filled, as were these three
women cited above, be thoroughly attuned to the wonders
in the heavens and the earth, wonders that Christ made
more real. When the consciousness of God and his son
Christ dwell within us, mental illumination and spiritual
powers can be ours too.

CHAPTER THIRTY

HIS OTHER GIFTS

In Christ, woman attained many transcendent gifts, for he saw all women, the good and the bad, as children of God. He had confidence in their power to apprehend his message, and since his standards of perfection encompassed both men and women, he never excluded woman in his demands, nor did he omit her in his promises. His legacy to womanhood is even greater than in the Creation, for he made more vital her intellectual, as well as her spiritual, capacity.

Consequently, a new era dawned for women in the years of his leadership. Their spiritual wealth and worthiness gained new anchors from him, just as their maternal love, devotion, and fidelity gave him new safeguards in his great mission. Beginning with his mother, Mary, in whose religious thoughts, prophetic hopes, and moral values his band of followers gained a new image of woman at her best, woman was elevated to new heights. Because he learned from her as a child, and she learned even more from him during his ministry, she was able to touch other lives in depth, as he had touched hers after he grew to manhood.

His Discourses on Their Daily Lives

Jesus took insignificant things in a woman's daily life such as a bit of leaven or a lost coin or a grinding mill or a lamp and developed some of his most definitive parables.

In the one of the leaven (Luke 13:20–21), he made every woman conscious that she must become for her family, friends, and community the leavening force by which Christ and his Spirit completely permeate the earth. Like the bread she leavens in her kitchen, a noble-minded woman can permeate life with a leavening force.

In his parable of the woman who lost the coin, lighted a candle, swept her floor, and searched diligently for it (Luke 15:8–10), Christ was saying that every single soul, like the small, mislaid coin, is worth retrieving. And just as the woman rejoiced in finding the coin that was lost, so God rejoices in those who are lost from salvation and then seek peace and reconciliation with God.

In another parable, he told of the two women grinding at the mill, both seemingly well and strong, but one was suddenly taken in death and the other was left. His warning was, "Watch therefore: for ye know not what hour your Lord doth come" (Matt. 24:42).

In these and other discourses, including the one on the wise and unwise virgins cited in an earlier chapter, Jesus withheld from women nothing of the truths that he gave to men. All of these based on the lives of women have become precious parts of their religious legacy. Because Jesus spoke directly to women's hearts and minds in a language they could understand, they drew closer to him in spirit and in truth.

WOMAN, NOT SUBORDINATE TO MAN

Through Christ, woman received full human rights as man's companion and helpmate. As moral personalities neither was subordinate but each perfected the other. If a wife served her husband, so must a husband serve his wife. And this necessitated a ministry of love.

Husband and wife through him learned that each possessed spiritual qualities they could never mutually exchange, but through which they could supplement and perfect each other in God's love. Therefore, neither took pride in dominating the other.

As in Priscilla and Aquila of Paul's time, this ministry of love between a husband and wife was also exemplified by Catherine Booth, mother of the Salvation Army, and her husband, William Booth, the founder. Each shared in the hopes and aspirations of the other and each went forward as a team in the building of one of the noblest movements in Christian history. Their success was based upon their Christian togetherness, he providing the qualities of masculine energy and foresight, and she, feminine tenderness and spiritual sensitivity. And both gave to the world eight children who went forth to all parts of the world, a strong army of Christian soldiers lifting burdens and righting wrongs of the poor and the downtrodden.

Christ's definition of service also opened new vistas for womankind. When he asked, "For whether is greater, he that sitteth at meat, or he that serveth?" woman became his munificent benefactor. And when he answered, "Is not he that sitteth at meat? But I am among you as he that serveth" (Luke 22:27). In his own example of service, woman again benefited because her life has its roots in ministry to her family.

HIS RESTORATION OF OUTCAST WOMEN

Women who had been ostracized from society not only were deferred to by him but restored to purposeful lives. He taught each one that, no matter what her sins had been, she was made "after the likeness of God," and he helped her to see that this likeness was not merely accidental or transitory but a legacy that no one could take from her. She might denounce God in her life by her evil actions, but she could again become what he desired her to be, and when she did, she would be renewed in body and soul. It is doubtful if ever before or since, such women as these met such treatment as this.

One of these was the Sinful Woman, whom the scribes and Pharisees brought before Jesus, after they had found her in the act of adultery. They wanted to have her stoned, as had been commanded in the Law of Moses, but Jesus rebuked them saying, "He that is without sin among you, let him first cast a stone at her" (John 8:7). Her accusers then left one by one. Jesus was left alone with the woman. He looked up at her and said, "Woman, where are those thine accusers? Hath no man condemned thee?" (v. 10). She answered, "No man, Lord." And Jesus said, "Neither do I condemn thee; go, and sin no more" (v. 11).

The men, who probably had committed many sins,

probably worse than the woman's, had meant to trap Jesus. But in his rebuke of them and in his pardon of this woman, guilty of unchastity, she was restored to a new life.

The Woman with Alabaster, who came to wash Christ's feet while he sat at meat in the home of Simon, the Pharisee, also experienced the Master's compassion. When Simon saw her humbly wash the Master's feet with her long hair, then kiss and anoint them, he said to himself: "If this man were a prophet, he would have known who and what sort of woman this is who is touching him, for she is a sinner." And Jesus answered him saying:

> "Simon, I have something to say to you." And he answered, "What is it, Teacher?" "A certain creditor had two debtors; one owed five hundred denarii, and the other fifty. When they could not pay, he forgave them both. Now which of them will love him more?" Simon answered, "The one, I suppose, to whom he forgave more." And he said to him, "You have judged rightly." Then turning toward the woman, he said to Simon, "Do you see this woman? I entered your house, you gave me no water for my feet, but she has wet my feet with her tears and wiped them with her hair. You gave me no kiss, but from the time I came in she has not ceased to kiss my feet. You did not anoint my head with oil, but she has anointed my feet with ointment. Therefore I tell you, her sins, which are many, are forgiven, for she loved much; but he who is forgiven little, loves little." And he said to her, "Your sins are forgiven."   (Luke 7:40–48, RSV)

Christ's experiences set him against the hypocritical piety of the Pharisees. He declared to the chief priest and elders that "the tax collectors and the harlots go into the kingdom of God before you. For John came to you in the way of righteousness, and you did not believe him, but the tax collectors and the harlots believed him; and even when you saw it, you did not afterward repent and believe him" (Matt. 21:31–32, RSV). Jesus had no patience with these hypocrites who only posed moral righteousness.

His Thoughtful Concern for Widows

Next to outcast women, there is no group that has been so desolate in many countries as those women who have lost their husbands in death. In addition to the sorrow of losing their husbands, such widows suffer much. In one moment a woman is deprived of her husband's affection and companionship, of his co-operation in the rearing of their children, of his financial support as the breadwinner. Lonely and oftentimes unprepared to meet life outside her own family circle, her role is difficult at best.

Sometimes, because of her inexperience, others take advantage of her in legal and industrial transactions. Some widows endure flagrant wrongs rather than go to court, where delays eat up their time and money, and technicalities can stifle justice. The widow with no money or influence, and sometimes hungry children, may be driven to desperation, just as was the importunate widow who time and again went before the unjust judge. To illustrate his teaching on the need for persistent prayer, Jesus told this incident of this earnestly solicitous widow in a certain city: "there was a widow in that city who kept coming to him [the judge] and saying, 'Vindicate me against my adversary.' For a while he refused; but afterward he said to himself, 'Though I neither fear God nor regard man, yet because this widow bothers me, I will vindicate her, or she will wear me out by her continually coming'" (Luke 18:3–5, RSV).

The judge at least did from exasperation what he would not do from motives of either justice or mercy. He granted the widow's request in order not to be further irritated by her. In Christ's day the scribes were jurists, and the widows were usually at the mercy of the judges.

It is no wonder that Jesus, hearing of many of the injustices, said, "Beware of the scribes, which desire to walk in long robes, and love greetings in the markets, and the highest seats in the synagogues, and the chief rooms at feasts; which devour widows' houses and for a show make long prayers; these shall receive greater damnation" (Luke 20:46–47). Here, once and for all, Jesus speaks in defense of widows, who are unjustly treated by so-called pious ones with evil intent.

His Ageless Morality

In an era when the new morality seems to signify immorality, women are the heaviest losers; Christ's example and his messages to women become more pertinent than ever, for he raised woman to her true moral dignity. Her womanly rights took on new dimension when he said, "Whosoever looketh on a woman to lust after her hath committed adultery with her already in his heart" (Matt.

5:28). In forbidding not only the adulterous act but also the adultery of the heart, the mind, and lustful glance toward women, Christ brought a new sense of moral being to women, helping them to know that a woman's true worth lies in the quality of her personality, her moral character, and the service she renders to others.

In his ageless morality, Christ did not frame laws for the statute book, as had Moses in the Ten Commandments. He only stated principles and made others feel God's purity and majesty in his inmost soul. The whole law, he concluded, is a love of God, and this for him became the great moral dynamo. He alone had a positive identification with these principles, and he alone made others aware that this is a moral universe, where all must share alike.

In helping women to realize more fully that it is up to them to set high moral standards, to touch the deep and tender chords of sympathy, and to serve as examples of all that is pure, unselfish, honest, and heroic, Christ set into motion a new moral place for woman in the life of the world. Only as woman follows Christ's example and doctrines does she emerge victorious and remain true to the high destiny God intended for her in the beginning. Only then can she claim and administer her inexhaustible legacy from the Bible.

CHAPTER THIRTY-ONE

THE MINISTERING WOMEN ABOUT HIM

Although many of the women who ministered to Christ are unnamed, they take their place among the noblest figures in history. Fatefully interlocked as they are with his ministry, his Cross, and his Resurrection, they add grandeur to Christianity's beginnings.

No adjectives are used to describe them, but if we are to judge by their deeds, some of the loftiest words in the English language may be applied to them. For they served him as he healed and preached. They gave of their substance to his work. They stood off, bewailing and lamenting his early suffering. They knew how he had patiently endured disgraces and revilings, ingratitude for his benefits, even some of his healings, and reproofs for heavenly doctrines. These women also beheld from afar as he trudged wearily carrying his Cross and then saw him nailed to it between two criminals.

The Many Who Served Him

It is noteworthy that the term "ministering" (KJV) to him or "serving" (RSV) him is confined to angels (Matt. 4:11) and to women (Matt. 27:55–56; Mark 15:40–41; Luke 8:1–3). Matthew lists Mary Magdalene and Mary, the mother of James and Joses, as does Mark, although he

calls the mother of James and Joses by her other name of
Salome. Luke cites Joanna, wife of Chuza, thought to be
the nobleman of Capernaum, and Susanna, whom Jesus
healed. Half of Christ's twelve disciples we know nothing
about, but when we add Martha and her sister, Mary, to
the other five, we find mentioned by name more than half
as many of his women associates as his men companions.
However, in addition to these seven there were "many
others" who ministered to him.

Luke's Gospel, aptly referred to as the Gospel of Womanhood, most vividly portrays these ministering women.
Matthew and Mark add as a kind of footnote that many
groups of women went all the way with Jesus.

Like Luke, John presents more vivid pictures of the individual women. He records that after Jesus raised Lazarus
from the dead that this Bethany family composed of Mary,
Martha, and their brother, Lazarus, honored Jesus with a
supper which Martha prepared. Because of Mary's service
to Jesus in his last hours, that of anointing his feet with
costly ointment, Jesus predicted that "Wheresoever this
gospel shall be preached throughout the whole world, this
also that she hath done shall be spoken as a memorial to
her" (Mark 14:9).

John tells also that "there stood by the cross of Jesus his
mother, and his mother's sister, Mary, the wife of Cleophas, and Mary Magdalene" (19:25). Some scholars believe that this Mary, also called Salome, and the mother
of James and Joses, was a sister of Mary, the mother of
Jesus, and these would be his cousins, but other scholars
do not accept this relationship. John also says Mary Magdalene was the first to see that the stone had been taken

away. She it was, too, he says, who ran to Simon Peter, John, and "to the other disciples" and told them that she had seen the Lord.

A WOMANLY SPIRIT ALL THE WAY

Christ's manner of dealing with these ministering women singles him out from all other teachers in history. He not only allowed them to accompany him on his journeys when he went through the cities and countryside, preaching and healing, but his teachings were given as freely to the women as to the men, with the exception of that inner circle of twelve disciples. Many times in the Gospels, though no mention is made of the women specifically, it is presumed they were among his faithful followers. Some of these women tower above the crowds, many of whom were there for curiosity or to mock and to curse him, but these women were there because they understood the greatness of his life and work.

In his book *Woman in the Apostolic Church*, T. B. Allworthy makes this explanation of the vital role women played in communicating the record of Jesus's last days:

> It would seem not improbable that Luke derived from Joanna the detailed account of the trial of our Lord before Herod as recorded in Chapter 23:8. And it may have been she who supplied to him also the story of the visit of the women to the tomb on the resurrection morning. Possibly we owe to her a still greater debt. It is natural to suppose that the stories contained in the first two chapters of Luke's Gospel

came directly or indirectly from the mother of the Lord. William Mitchell Ramsay (the Scottish historian and archaeologist), who thinks that the narrative is founded upon an oral communication, suggests that if it were not told to Luke by Mary herself, "the intermediary is more likely to have been a woman than a man." There is, he says, "a womanly spirit in the whole narrative, which seems inconsistent with the transmission from man to man." (Pp. 10–11)

The "Certain" Women with Him

Early Luke prepares us for the faithfulness of these women disciples when he tells us that, in addition to the twelve who were with him, there also were "certain women, which had been healed of evil spirits and infirmities, Mary called Magdalene, out of whom went seven devils" (8:2), also Joanna, mentioned above. It is thought that her husband, Chuza, was healed by Jesus. John says that Chuza and his whole house believed. In that case it is probable that Joanna, along with members of her household, served Christ joyfully, and that she even gave generously to his work, as did Mary Magdalene.

Immediately following Luke's record that the women gave of their means, Luke relates two of Christ's parables, one of the Sower of the Seed, some of which "fell by the wayside; and it was trodden down, and the fowls of the air devoured it. And some fell upon a rock; and as soon as it was sprung up, it withered away, because it lacked moisture. And some fell among thorns; and the thorns sprang up with it, and choked it. And others fell on good ground, and sprang up, and bare fruit an hundredfold" (8:5–8). Let us imagine these ministering women represented the good soil that grew a hundredfold, also that they fully comprehended what Jesus meant when he said, "The seed is the word of God" (v. 11).

In the other parable, that of the Lighted Lamp, Jesus said, "No man, when he hath lighted a candle, covereth it with a vessel, or putteth it under a bed; but setteth it on a candlestick, that they which enter in may see the light. For nothing is secret, that shall not be made manifest; neither any thing hid, that shall not be known and come abroad" (Luke 8:16–17). These women who so often lighted candles in their own homes understood well that he had brought spiritual light into their lives, so much that their small service to him was meager compared to his lasting gifts to them.

"A GREAT COMPANY OF WOMEN"

When Christ was led to Pilate, "a great company of women" were in the crowds there also. They heard the Judaean mobs cry out, "Crucify him, crucify him." They were there when the mob released the insurrectionist Barabbas, and Jesus said, "Father, forgive them; for they know not what they do" (Luke 23:34).

Although they had great compassion for him it could never equal his compassion for them. And now that his life was coming to an end, and they sought to comfort him in his suffering, he tried to prepare them for the cares, wars, famine, and desolation that awaited their children, but which they probably would not live to see. When Jerusalem was beseiged by Titus thirty-seven years later, all that Jesus had foretold them came to pass.

THOSE "BEHOLDING AFAR OFF"

Of those at the burial, Matthew says, "many women were there beholding afar off, which followed Jesus from Galilee, ministering unto him" (27:55). These women had endured not only the scorn of unruly crowds but the hardship of rugged roads. When it seemed he might falter because of the weight of his Cross, they tried to give back to him some of the strength and understanding that he had so generously shared with them. Of these, John Cunningham Geike in *The Life and Words of Christ* says, "His purity of soul, his reverent courtesy to the sex, his championship of their equal dignity with men before God, and his demand for supreme zeal, in all in the spread of the New Kingdom, drew them after him" (vol. II, p. 127).

Luke more briefly records that "And all his acquaintances, and the women that followed him from Galilee, stood afar off, beholding these things" (23:49)—the Crucifixion, the railing criminals at his side, the darkened sun, and his final cry, "Father, into thy hands I commit my spirit" (23:46). Earlier they had seen the throngs deride him, they had heard his divinity challenged, and viewed the superscription in Greek, Latin, and Hebrew, "This is the King of the Jews."

Because the centurion stood so near, they could no longer be close to Jesus, but now they stood at a distance, lamenting his suffering and no doubt praying it would not be for long. The curious had gone but these faithful women, who had followed him all the way from Galilee, did not desert him, but stood beside him in his dying moments.

Afterward, they walked all the way to the sepulcher. Luke states once more, "And the women also, which came with him from Galilee, followed after, and beheld the sepulchre, and how his body was laid. And they returned, and prepared spices and ointments; and rested the sabbath day according to the commandment" (23:55–56).

Nicodemus brought one hundred pounds of spices to Christ's tomb. The influential Joseph of Arimathea asked Pilate for permission to wrap Jesus's body, and then laid it in the sepulcher. But after both had left, only the women remained on through the hours of dusk. And then, after observing the Sabbath, according to the commandment, early the next morning, taking the spices and ointment with them, they made their way in the pink and gray dawn, through the narrow, deserted streets, and finally into the neighborhood of the "Garden Tomb," where he lay.

The Evidence of Those at the Tomb

Luke dramatically records that they found the stone rolled away from the tomb and saw two men standing by in shining garments who said, "He is not here, but is risen; remember how he spake unto you when he was yet in Galilee, saying, the Son of man must be delivered into the hands of sinful men, and be crucified, and the third day rise again" (Luke 24:6–7).

Matthew, the only Gospel writer to tell of Christ's encounter with several of the women after he had arisen, presents one of the Bible's most remarkable passages regarding women. An angel said to them,

> Fear not ye: for I know that ye seek Jesus, which was crucified.
>
> He is not here: for he is risen, as he said. Come, see the place where the Lord lay.
>
> And go quickly, and tell his disciples that he is risen from the dead; and, behold, he goeth before you into Galilee; there shall ye see him, lo, I have told you.
>
> And they departed quickly from the sepulchre with fear and great joy; and did run to bring his disciples word.
>
> And as they went to tell his disciples, behold, Jesus met them, saying, All hail. And they came and held him by the feet, and worshipped him.
>
> Then said Jesus unto them, Be not afraid: go tell my brethren that they go into Galilee, and there shall they see me.   (28:5–10)

The evidence of these women was not "the idle tale" they first thought. After he appeared to the eleven as they sat at meat, he "upbraided them with their unbelief and hardness of heart, because they believed not them which had seen him after he was risen" (Mark 16:14). The apostles went and saw for themselves, Peter first of all. Then Christ appeared that same day to Peter and Cleophas at a village called Emmaus.

These devoted women had paved the way for the Risen Christ to reveal himself to others. Now that the disciples had seen Christ, they were ready to go forth and say to others, "The Lord is risen indeed" (Luke 24:34).

The honorable place accorded to them in the narrative of the evangelists suggests the high position assigned to them in the New Testament Church. As the first commissioned messengers of the risen Christ, it is natural that they should also be among the first to serve his Church, as will be explained in a succeeding chapter.

CHAPTER THIRTY-TWO

THEIR HARVEST FROM BEARING
HIS CROSSES

"And he bearing his cross went forth . . . to Golgotha, where they crucified him" (John 19:17–18).

At the heart of the Christian gospel is this godly man crowned with thorns, nailed to the Cross, with a spear wound in his side. At the center of those who anguished over his suffering was that band of ministering women, who as already related, followed him all the way to the cross and afterward to the sepulcher, and who now fully comprehended his words, "And whosoever doth not bear his cross, and come after me, cannot be my disciple" (Luke 14:27).

THOSE WHO EMBRACED HIS CROSS

We never understand suffering until we have embraced the cross. These women who ministered to him and who took part in the formation of Christ's church carried many crosses: opposition within their own ranks, imprisonment and martyrdom by the Roman Tribunal, the hate and criticism of unbelievers, the untruths about Christ and his gospel, and the little with which to do and so much to do, in order that his life and message might illuminate the centuries. They did not seek the crosses, but those crosses found them, and in their acceptance of whatever crosses were theirs, they discovered how enduring was their own Christian fortitude.

Bishop Fulton J. Sheen asks, "Which stands up better in a crisis—man or woman?" He answers, "One can discuss this in a series of historical crises, but without arriving at any decision. The best way to arrive at a conclusion is to go to the greatest crisis the world ever faced, namely, the Crucifixion of our Divine Lord. When we come to this great drama of Calvary, there is one fact that stands out very clearly. Men failed . . . on the other hand, there is not one single instance of a woman's failing him" (*The Quotable Fulton J. Sheen*).

Many women embraced his Cross, but none understood it better than three of the Marys, Mary of Bethany, Mary Magdalene, and his mother, Mary. When Mary of Bethany poured the costly ointment on his feet before he was to trudge to the Cross, she spoke to him in actions, not words. In this, her last loving act to Jesus, she seemed to say that his own great beliefs and principles were worth dying for, even if his evil accusers demanded death. She no doubt understood also that one learns to go to the Cross not only for his own transgressions but also for those of others.

His mother, Mary, bore his pain and heartache as she walked with him all the way to Calvary. And yet we hear not a murmur from her. She seemed to perceive to the fullest his great mission and why his accusers demanded death. Mary Magdalene's own poignant cry has echoed down the centuries in her answer to the angel's question of why she wept at the empty tomb, "Because they have taken away my Lord, and I know not where they have laid him" (John 20:13). Without such an anguishing experience, Mary Magdalene could not have gone forth afterward, as if on winged feet, to exclaim, "See, he is risen."

These and other women around him teach us that Christian renewal comes when we accept suffering as a part of our Christian heritage, "For unto you it is given in the behalf of Christ," said Paul, "not only to believe on him, but also to suffer for his sake" (Phil. 1:29). The rewards of suffering also are expressed by Peter, who said, "But even if you do suffer for righteousness' sake, you will be blessed" (I Pet. 3:14, RSV).

Like Peter and Paul, these great women near Christ knew they could not be counted "worthy of the Kingdom of God," unless they were willing to suffer, but if they were, they would learn to "reign with him."

Saints Who Endured for Him

The twelfth-century St. Francis of Assisi, who probably carried Christ's Cross for others more joyously than any saint in history, was born to wealth, the son of a merchant in Italy. As a young man he equipped himself with elegant apparel and fine armory, and rode forth to the countryside. On the way he met a shabbily clad knight and was so filled with compassion at his poverty that he exchanged clothes with him.

That night St. Francis dreamed he saw his father's house transformed into a castle, its walls hung with armor, all marked with the sign of the cross. He heard a voice saying that the armor belonged to St. Francis and his soldiers.

Suddenly he felt contempt for a life wasted on trivial and transitory things. Later, as he prayed in the humble little Church of St. Damian outside Assisi, he saw the eyes of Christ on the crucifix gazing at him and he heard a voice speak three times, "Francis, go and repair my house, which you see is falling down." St. Francis's life was transformed. Suddenly he realized that he could touch Christ only by helping his needy ones. After this, nothing was too hard for St. Francis, and he came to love all natural phenomena, sun, moon, air, water, fire, flowers, birds, beasts, and all of God's creatures. It is no wonder that his great prayer "Lord Make Me an Instrument of Thy Peace" has spanned the centuries:

> Where there is hatred let me sow love
> where there is injury, pardon,
> where there is doubt, faith,
> where there is despair, hope,
> where there is darkness, light,
> where there is sadness, joy.
> O Divine Master, grant that I
> may not so much seek to be consoled
> as to console; to be understood as to
> understand, to be loved as to love;
> for it is in giving that we receive; it
> is in pardoning that we are pardoned
> and it is in dying that we are born to eternal life.

Other great saints, like St. Francis, learned to rejoice in suffering. St. Teresa of Avila (1515–1582) accepted with a glad heart both her physical ailments and her warfare of the soul. She complained not, but remembered what Paul said when he sought God thrice about the thorn in his flesh. "My grace is sufficient for thee; for my strength is made perfect in weakness. Most gladly therefore will I rather glory in my infirmities, that the power of Christ may rest upon me. Therefore I take pleasure in infirmities, in reproaches, in necessities, in persecutions, in distresses for Christ's sake; for when I am weak, then am I strong" (II Cor. 12:9–10).

William Thomas Walsh, probably the best known of St. Teresa's many biographers, says St. Teresa learned this in her suffering:

> When God invites a soul to follow him in the heights of love, and that soul acquiesces, it does not become transformed in an instant from a human being, with all its frailties and passions of the flesh, into an angel of perfection. On the contrary, it sometimes begins to encounter staggering difficulties and temptations. To reach the glory of a resurrection which brings a delightful foretaste even in this world of the eternal heaven, the soul must know hunger and want, neglect and misunderstanding, the sorrow and loneliness of a Gethsemane even God seems to have forsaken, and a more or less protracted crucifixion of fleshly desires, ambitions and vanities.
>
> (Saint Teresa of Avila, pp. 65–66)

Teresa learned that the more she suffered the closer she drew to Christ in his infirmities. And she was comforted in her suffering.

St. Catherine of Siena (1347–1380), another who wel-
comed suffering, said,

> We should rejoice in nothing but in bearing re-
> proaches and sufferings. Crucify thyself with Christ
> the Crucified. Follow him in the way of the Cross,
> conform thyself to him, rejoice in reproaches, suffer-
> ings, contempt, mockery and evil words. Persevere to
> the end and do not fortify thyself with anything but
> the blood flowing down from the Cross. When suffer-
> ing comes, do not shrink from it, but accept it with a
> joyful face. . . . Then bitterness will become sweet
> and consoling and thou shalt end thy life, resting
> softly on the Cross with Christ the Crucified.
>
> Like the child feeding at its mother's breast, so
> feeds the soul that loves God, on Christ, the Cruci-
> fied, and walks always in his steps, following him on
> the path of reproaches and suffering and mockery, and
> not rejoicing in aught else. . . .
>
> She (Catherine) would live the life of Christ. She
> would carry the Cross of Christ. This is the bridge
> over the roaring torrent of the world, the only bridge.
> This is the gate, the narrow gate. There is no choice;
> one must walk either to Golgotha or to Gehenna.
>
> (*Saint Catherine of Siena,*
> by Johannes Jörgensen, pp. 92–93)

THE BLESSINGS OF SUFFERING

Elizabeth Leseur (1866–1914), the saintly wife of a Pa-
risian businessman, said that "Our suffering works mysteri-

ously, first in ourselves by a kind of renewal and also in others who are perhaps far away, without ever knowing what we are accomplishing. Christ on the Cross has perhaps done more for humanity than Christ speaking and acting in Galilee or Jerusalem. Suffering creates life. It transforms everything it touches."

In her noble portrayal of the saintly Elizabeth Leseur, Lucy Menzies says that Elizabeth's doctrine of suffering developed from her own heartaches and anguish over the atheism of her husband and also her own illness, during which she came to know that "all human souls are deeply interconnected . . . we cannot only pray but suffer for each other. . . . Nothing is more real than this interconnection, this gracious power put by God himself into the very heart of our infirmities." (*Mirrors of the Holy*, p. 304) Elizabeth Leseur "grew into this doctrine more and more," adds Lucy Menzies. She wished in herself to make amends by her own personal distress and sacrifice and thus gave suffering a supernatural intercession. Suffering was for her creative.

The Radiance in a Constant Cross

Christ's Cross is literally everywhere, in the passion flower that blooms on sunny walls and grows on hill and in vale, also atop church spires and gleaming in the night sky, where the Southern Cross of five stars serves as a pointer to the South Pole.

We cannot escape crosses, either physically or emotionally. When we seek to become too comfortable in our way of living and too complacent about the moral tone of our world, when we fail to identify with the poor, the depressed, and those who have never known social justice, we know nothing of the real crosses that Christ would have us carry for others.

We sometimes consider our own crosses too heavy to bear. But are they? Look about. The story is told of a woman who was weary with her heavy cross and wished she might choose another instead of her own. In a dream, she had that choice, when she was confronted with many crosses of different shapes and sizes. The first that impressed her was a little one set with jewels, and she sighed, "Ah, I could wear that one with comfort." But when she took it up she discovered it was much heavier than it appeared. She turned to pick up another cross, but the flowers beneath it were pierced with thorns which tore her flesh. At last she came upon a plain cross without either jewels or carvings. She took it up and was surprised to find it was bathed in a certain radiance. It was her own that she had been carrying, and it was the lightest and most suited to her of all. Similar experiences of others illuminate this poem, "O Constant Cross," by Violet Alleyn Storey, in *A Treasury of the Cross*, edited by Madeleine S. Miller:

> "O constant cross,
>   Would I might put you down," I said,
> "The road I walk so burdened
>   Lies so beautiful, ahead
>
> "Without you, I'd go proudly,
>   Without you, I might run,
> Here on the loveliest road of all,
>   Straight toward the sun."

A voice spoke from the cross,
   And light became my load:
"Save that you bore me bravely,
    You had not found the road."

CHAPTER THIRTY-THREE

THEIR SERVICE TO HIS CHURCH

From the time of Christ's Ascension, women filled an active and faithful role in support of Christ's Church, leaving an inspiring legacy to churchwomen today. Some of these women adherents to the faith, along with his most devoted men disciples, were among the first to return to Jerusalem and to proceed to the "Upper Room" to form the new church.

In these times an upper room was in a home, and it is probable that this one was in the home of a prayerful woman, Mary, mother of John Mark, for it is later recorded that "he [Peter] came to the house of Mary the mother of John, whose surname was Mark; where many were gathered together praying" (Acts 12:12).

After the Ascension, the disciples proceeded to an upper room together, for Jesus had told them before his Ascension that "ye shall receive power, after that the Holy Ghost is come upon you: and ye shall be witnesses unto me both in Jerusalem, and in all Judaea, and in Samaria, and unto the uttermost part of the earth" (Acts 1:8).

It is remarkable that after this gathering of the disciples, it is related that "These all continued with one accord in prayer and supplication, with the women, and Mary, the mother of Jesus, and with his brethren" (Acts 1:14).

Woman's Home, a Cradle for Church

If this upper room where they gathered may be called "the cradle of the church," this Mary as its hostess was the church's first "nursing mother" and the first to preside over a Church of the Household. It is reasonable to suppose that this same upper room in Mary's house was where Christ appeared after the Resurrection. It also may have been the scene of the Last Supper and the place of the advent of the Holy Spirit.

This house no doubt became an important rendezvous for the Church at Jerusalem, and this Mary one of its most devout members. Paul refers to her son Mark, "the cousin of Barnabas," who sold a field which belonged to him, and brought the money and laid it at the apostles' feet, an indication that the family had prosperous connections in Jerusalem.

Had it not been for the zeal and faithfulness of these early devotees, both men and women praying together, the Church could not have become what Paul later described as Christ's body. It is no wonder that when the day of Pentecost came, they were prepared for the wonders that followed, the harvest of about three thousand souls into the new church and the descent of the Holy Spirit upon the disciples, when they began miraculously to speak in other languages, "as the Spirit gave them utterance." The miracle is described as speaking in "cloven tongues of fire," analogous to the "burning bush" at Sinai. And all this happened fifty days after Christ's redemption of the world. A part of the miracle was that women were not excluded but with the men were witnesses to these first miracles.

WOMEN AMONG FIRST CONVERTS

Women also were among the first converts of the new church, for the record declares, "And believers were the more added to the Lord, multitudes both of men and women" (Acts 5:14). When Philip, the evangelist, preached the good news about the Kingdom of God and the name of Jesus Christ, "they were baptized, both men and women" (Acts 8:12). Before Philip's coming the men and women of Samaria "from the least to the greatest" had fallen victim to the delusions of Simon the Sorcerer, but the women as well as the men turned to the message of the evangelist and went forth and were baptized.

Samaria became an early stronghold of Christianity after the witness of the Woman of Samaria with Jesus at the well at Sychar. She was the first to proclaim that the Savior had come, not alone for the Jews but for all the people.

The Book of Acts refers also to collective groups of women in the Apostolic Church living in other areas of Judaea, where Paul began his work. When Paul and Barnabas set forth on their first missionary journey to Antioch, to bring the good news of the Resurrection, the Jews publicly spoke of their contempt of Christ and of his doctrine and law. Paul then turned to the Gentiles, who glorified the word of God. And when the message spread, "the Jews stirred up the devout and honourable women and the chief men of the city, and raised persecution against Paul and Barnabas, and expelled them out of their coasts" (Acts 13:50). Here we have an example of how Gentile women, who had served Christ's church so faithfully, now were quickly incited to turn against his servants, Paul and

Barnabas. Their emotional outburst probably influenced Paul in being a little hard on women occasionally. At the same time, their temperamental reaction is a good example of how easy it is for faithful women as well as the faithless to be led astray.

THOSE AT THESSALONICA, TYRE

At Thessalonica women in turn took a leading role in the new church. In a Jewish synagogue Paul reasoned with them regarding the scriptures, telling them that "this Jesus, whom I proclaim to you, is the Christ. And some of them were persuaded, and joined Paul and Silas; as did a great many of the devout Greeks and not a few of the leading women" (Acts 17:3-4, RSV).

A third mention of the participation of groups of women in the new church took place at Tyre in Syria. While Paul's ship unloaded its cargo, he stayed there with the believers for seven days, and then as he prepared to set sail from this rocky isle, he says, "they all brought us on our way, with wives and children, till we were out of the city: and we kneeled down on the shore, and prayed" (Acts 21:5). As they kneeled together, wives, husbands, and children, there was a new sense of solidarity in the church at Tyre.

THOSE AT SEAPORT OF JOPPA

At Joppa, a seaport of Jerusalem, there was yet another group of churchwomen led by Dorcas (Tabitha). When she directed the women "in good works and acts of charity" (Acts 9:36, RSV), she kept alive a needed service for early believers. We do not know whether those she aided were dependent widows in the church, who in turn gave their time and labor, or whether they were a group of influential women of which Dorcas was the head. But we are certain that the work of Dorcas was well known in the church at Joppa and that her death was a grave loss to its women.

When her death was reported to Peter, he came and raised her from the dead, "and it was known throughout all Joppa; and many believed in the Lord" (Acts 9:42). Probably the most ardent believers were those women who had first summoned Peter to the bedside of Dorcas.

In the Church at Philippi

At Philippi, a city of East Macedonia, a few miles inland from the Aegean Sea, was another church worker, Lydia, described as a "worshiper of God" (Acts 16:14, RSV). What more reverent term could we use to describe an ardent Christian? A native of Thyatira, Lydia sold her wares at Philippi and seemed to have been the inspiration of another group of women, who worshiped by the banks of the Gangites River and to whom Paul spoke. In this place of prayer Paul first preached the gospel with the result that the Lord opened Lydia's heart to Paul's words, and afterward she and her household were baptized; and at her invitation Paul and Silas stayed at her house while they were in Philippi. She later offered hospitality to the slave girl, whose deliverance by Paul from a "spirit of divination" brought about his and Silas's arrest. On their release from prison they went again to Lydia's house and there visited the converts before departing.

We can imagine that these dedicated women at Philippi, especially Lydia, Paul's first convert in Macedonia (Europe), were among those of whom Paul, later writing to the church at Philippi, said, "Now ye Philippians know also, that in the beginning of the gospel, when I departed from Macedonia, no church communicated with me as concerning giving and receiving, but ye only" (Phil. 4:15).

This Philippian church continued to attract these very Christians. In describing two other women there, Euodias and Syntyche, Paul makes us wonder if they could have belonged to that first group led by Lydia. It appears that Euodias and Syntyche had disagreed over a church matter.

Chrysostom, one of the fathers of the fourth-century Greek church, comments that these two women may well have been leaders of congregations meeting in their own houses. It could be that the controversy, which they were advised to lay aside, was in connection with the teaching given at meetings in these house churches. Too often commentators have assumed that they had disagreed over something personal. The greatest compliment Paul paid these two women was that they "laboured with me" (Phil. 4:3), suggesting dedicated and courageous service in his work.

HELPERS IN ATHENS, CORINTH, EPHESUS, ROME

In the city of Athens, where Paul preached his great sermon, "For in him we live, and move, and have our being" (Acts 17:28), he found another woman believer, Damaris (v. 34), who was probably one of the best-educated women in this ancient city of culture.

Paul tells of still another church member, Priscilla, who along with her husband, Aquila, worked with him, first at Corinth, where Paul lodged in their home, and later at Ephesus and Rome, where they accompanied Paul on his journey. Priscilla and Aquila remained at Ephesus while Paul sailed on to Caesarea, but when he returned the following year, it is natural to suppose that again he stayed in their house. He could have written the first Epistle to the Corinthians while there. At the close of that letter, Paul said, "The churches of Asia send greetings. Aquila and Prisca, together with the church in their house, send you hearty greetings in the Lord" (I Cor. 16:19, RSV). Some ancient manuscripts insert after the names of these two the words, "with whom I am lodging."

The eminent Chrysostom, filled with admiration for Priscilla's character and work, contrasted her fame with the oblivion into which empresses fall, and declared that "as the sun looks over the whole earth, so the glory of this woman overruns the world."

"A Helper of Many" at Cenchreae

At Cenchreae, a port of Corinth on the Saronic Gulf, connected with the commercial center of central Greece by a system of forts, Paul came upon another servant of the church, Phebe, who gave liberally of her substance to Christians there. It is also thought that she took Paul's Epistle to the Romans at Rome from her port city.

Afterward, Paul commended Phebe to the church at Rome and as "a helper of many and of myself as well" (Rom. 16:1, RSV). He singled her out as a deaconess of the church at Cenchreae and asked the church in Rome to "receive her in the Lord as befits the saints" (Rom. 16:2, RSV).

Chrysostom says of Phebe, along with Priscilla, "these were noble women, hindered in no way by their sex . . . and this is as might be expected, for in Christ Jesus there 'is neither male nor female,'" a statement first made by Paul.

The Faithful Household of Apphia

Another noble woman, Apphia, also had a Church of the Household, maybe at Colossae, or, more probably, close by at Laodicea. Paul addressed a short letter to Philemon, "and to our beloved Apphia, and Archippus our fellow-soldier, and to the church in thy house" (Philem. 2). Apphia is thought to have been Philemon's wife, Archippus, their son, and Onesimus, their slave who ran away. Paul asked this family to receive Onesimus back, no longer as a slave but as a brother in Christ. So personal is Paul in his entreaty that he says, "I am sending him back to you, sending my very heart. I would have been glad to keep him [Onesimus] with me, in order that he might serve me on your behalf during my imprisonment for the gospel; but I preferred to do nothing without your consent in order that your goodness might not be by compulsion but of your own free will" (Philem. 12–14, RSV). Paul concludes by asking Apphia and Philemon to prepare a guest room for his coming.

Here in a few words we have the picture of a noble woman, one who is so hospitable that Paul felt free to request a room in her house. She and her husband possessed such Christian love and faith that Paul's heart was filled with joy and comfort at the thought of them. In fact, he was so certain of their brotherly love that he knew they would receive back into their home Onesimus, the man who had been their slave, as a true brother in Christ.

OTHER BELIEVERS IN ROMAN CHURCH

Paul honored four women in the Roman Church by describing them as ones who labored in the Lord. They are Mary (another Mary who is not identified elsewhere; Rom. 16:6); "Tryphena and Tryphosa, who labour in the Lord . . . the beloved Persis, which laboured much in the Lord" (Rom. 16:12). The fact that Mary's name occurs to Paul, along with those of Priscilla and Aquila and Epaenetus, the latter, Paul's first Asian convert, suggests she was one of the prominent persons in the community. Paul also stressed she too had worked hard in the Lord. The similarity in the names of Tryphena and Tryphosa suggests they were sisters, maybe twins.

The women of those days, again writes Chrysostom, "were more spirited than lions, sharing with the apostles their labors for the Gospel's sake. In this way they often traveled with them and performed small ministries, such as supplying the material needs of their brethren, as well as participating in the missionary work."

Paul saluted another woman in the Roman Church, Rufus's mother, who doubtlessly had shown him some kindness and probably had entertained him in her house during his stay in Ephesus.

PHILIP'S DAUGHTERS AT CAESAREA

Some years later, at Caesarea, a sumptuous Roman city, we come upon Philip again, the evangelist of Samaria. This was Paul's third missionary journey, and this time when he stopped at Samaria he was accompanied by Luke. Among those who greeted Paul and Luke here were Philip's four unmarried daughters, who prophesied. They may also have assisted their father in distributing relief to the poor, as this was one of an evangelist's duties to a growing church. It could be that they predicted the troubles awaiting Paul in Jerusalem, or that they even tried to dissuade him from going. Their work as witnesses was significant, because it was at Caesarea that Paul first preached to the Gentiles. Afterward the Holy Ghost fell upon all of those gathered there.

These daughters, it seems, had remained unmarried, in order to devote their full time to the church and the exercise of prophetic gifts. They probably felt, as Paul wrote to the Corinthian Christians some years before his visit there, that "the unmarried careth for the things that belong to the Lord . . . but he that is married careth for the things that are of the world" (I Cor. 7:32–33). Christ's own example and approval of the celibate way of life gave such women, like Philip's unmarried daughters, a position of independence they had never enjoyed before.

They fulfilled the Pentecostal promise that women would share in the gift of prophecy. In the spirit-filled church this gift was for all, but some possessed it in a higher degree than others and devoted their lives to its exercise. These daughters of Philip probably spoke words of comfort to Paul, for he later described one who prophesies as one who "speaks to men for their upbuilding and encouragement and consolation." . . . Also, as one who "edifies the church" (I Cor. 14:3–4, RSV).

All of these women who served the early Church, from the time of Pentecost to the establishment of Paul's many churches, live on as valiant Christian witnesses, continuing to inspire because they were imbued with the Holy Spirit. Because they gave of themselves so fully to Christian causes and considered it all labor of love for the Lord. Because they prayed and believed and had such power that their acts continue to uplift and inspire. Because some of them not only cradled the first church of Christ but also had Christendom's first Churches of the Household. Because they prophesied and believed so fully in the message of Christ.

We can see them trudging on to difficult tasks, riding over bumpy roads or walking about the small villages in their softly flowing apparel of lovely colors, and wearing in their faces a radiance that only this new Christianity could give them. Many were their problems, and yet they had so much to fill them with enthusiasm and wonder: the conversion and baptism of unbelievers, first, Saul of Tarsus but after his conversion, called Paul, fellowship with those who had witnessed Christ's own healing and preaching, and with his disciples who had walked with him daily, even to the Cross. No Christians ever bore so many burdens and yet no Christians ever knew such miraculous blessings as these in the first New Testament churches.

CHAPTER THIRTY-FOUR

IMPERISHABLE LEGACY—The Fruits of the Spirit

The women in that first band of New Testament Christians were so imbued with the Holy Spirit that they spoke of being filled with it, of walking, living in, and bearing witness to its divine essence, of being stopped and led by it. Some of these women were completely transformed when they realized that the Holy Spirit came directly from God, a God eternal and changeless. Their knowledge of the exercise of the Holy Spirit gave boldness to the shy, courage to the timid, a magnetic personality to the unattractive, eloquence to the illiterate, and plenty to the poor.

There are many references to the Spirit of God in the Old Testament but Jesus was the first to declare that "God is a Spirit," as illustrated earlier in his discourse with the Woman of Samaria. God therefore is a spiritual manifestation invisible to our physical senses, and the source of the fruits of the Spirit, while Christ is the fruit bearer.

Paul lists the nine fruits of the Spirit in Galatians 5:22–23 as love, joy, peace, longsuffering [patience, RSV], gentleness [kindness, RSV], goodness, faith [faithfulness, RSV], meekness [gentleness, RSV], temperance [self-control, RSV]. Paul did not arrange these in casual order.

Like the seasons of the year, each progresses toward the other in natural sequence.

LOVE, THE SEED OF ALL OTHERS

Eternal womanhood at its best represents these fruits of the Spirit, all proceeding again and again from the one point, love, the strongest force in a woman's life. The unloving woman is out of touch with God, but the loving woman fulfills the law of God, for love is God and God is love. The outpouring of the Holy Spirit is really the outpouring of God's love, "and he that dwelleth in love, dwelleth in God, and God in him" (I John 4:16).

God's love might be likened to that of a mother's bounteous love for her child. To give happiness and to devote herself, even to the point of self-surrender, is a stronger need in a mother's life than in a father's. A noble mother plays a role akin to Jesus, who "having loved his own which were in the world, he loved them unto the end" (John 13:1). Love is a mother's richest legacy from God and can be her most fruitful gift to her children. In his second Epistle, John commends "the elect lady and her children" for loving one another. To "walk after his commandments" is love, he adds.

Those who represented the purest mother love in the Bible have lighted the paths of mothers down the centuries. Included among these others are Helena, the mother of the first Christian emperor, Constantine; Anthusa, the mother of the fourth-century John Chrysostom, one of the Fathers of the Greek Church; Susanna Wesley, the mother of John Wesley, founder of Methodism.

Like the self-denying mother, all of us have to be self emptied so that the beauty and perfection of God can fill us. The Spirit within then becomes the creative force, yielding these other fruits of the Spirit. It is easy to understand that they will die in an unloving heart, just as a seed dies in rocky soil.

The fourteenth-century Flemish mystic and writer, the blessed John Ruysbrück, trained in religious devotion by his mother, said, "When love has carried us above all things . . . we receive in peace the incomprehensible Light, enfolding us and penetrating us. What is this Light, if it be not a contemplation of the Infinite, and an intuition of Eternity? We behold that which we are, and we are that which we behold, because our being, without losing anything of its own personality, is united with Divine Truth."

A noble woman typifies love and loveliness. The eternal ideal for woman embodies grace, charm, beauty, physical and intellectual creativity, resourcefulness, courage, and honor. But, again, love is first.

The more a woman is filled with love, the more fully the life of God will possess her. Inevitably, love, which is creative, will bring forth the other fruits, all tenderly nurturing the soul.

JOY AND ITS INDEFINABLE STRENGTH

One of the first results of love is joy, this second fruit of the Spirit, which signifies more than outward exhilaration. The most intense joy manifests itself in an exultant delight in God. The woman who finds her joy in God and Christ's doctrine possesses a divine radiance. Christ found super-abundant joy in his communion with his Father and in the knowledge of his power.

Joy, we discover, has many facets. There is joy in a good conscience, in work well done, in good tidings, in right-eousness, in hope, and, as an old chorale says, in the glory of the skies, human love, mystic harmony, gentle thoughts, beauty of earth.

Joy can spring also from the beauty of God all about us, the sudden emergence of ostrich fern in the pathless woods, or new wild ginger when the landscape laughs around it, or a robin's nest with the sunlight on it. There is much joy too in the mystery, stillness, and enchantment of the deep forest, or the abrupt disclosure of a great mountain, or the culminating moment in a magnificent concerto. Each floods us with joy because we feel in it something beyond ourselves and leading straight to God. Such joy shows us not only the beauty of God but the action of and the being of God. Suddenly we come to know that such joy is indescribable, for it is a sudden response from a loving God.

And yet joy need not spring from outward beauty alone. Those women, who actually walked with Christ, found joy in his presence, his Sermon on the Mount, his Beati-tudes, his miracles and other wonders, including his tri-umph over evil.

PEACE, THE SPIRIT OF ACCEPTANCE

The third fruit, peace, called the Spirit of tranquil ac-ceptance, suggests total well-being, soundness, prosperity, and success, both in the material and spiritual realms.

Writing to the Philippians one of his most joyful epistles, Paul spoke of "the peace of God, which passeth all understanding," and then he admonished his followers, "whatsoever things are true, whatsoever things are honest, whatsoever things are just, whatsoever things are pure, whatsoever things are lovely, whatsoever things are of good report; if there be any virtue, and if there be any praise, think on these things. Those things, which ye have both learned, and received, and heard, and seen in me, do: and the God of peace shall be with you" (4:8–9). Some of Paul's most devout Philippian women no doubt devoured this message, written from prison. It is difficult to understand how he could express himself so joyfully inside prison walls, but Paul's peace came from within.

Many other women experienced real peace of different kinds in Bible times. Deborah, for example, brought peace to her people when she led them to victory against a powerful enemy. Naomi understood the solitary peace of a grandmother in the birth of her first grandchild, Obed. Elisheba, the wife of Aaron, first head of the Hebrew priesthood, knew peace in the sacred service of her husband and two of her sons, who ministered in the tabernacle and who taught the people the law of God. Jerusha, one of the queen mothers of the Hebrew Monarchy, found peace in her son, King Jotham, who did "right in the sight of the Lord."

In his discussion of *Where to Find Peace*, the writer Boris Pasternak tells us that in this era of world wars and atomic energy values have changed, and that we can discover peace only within. "This means, as I see it, a departure from the materialistic view of the Nineteenth

Century. It means a reawakening of the Spiritual world, of our inner life, of religion."

PATIENCE, A SPECIAL NEED OF WOMEN

The fourth fruit of the Spirit, patience, is one of the most admirable qualities in womanhood. And the Bible presents several unusual examples of patience in women, who probably would not be remembered had they not possessed this quality, which seemed inexhaustible.

Watching for five long months over the dead, unburied bodies of her two sons and Saul's five grandsons, all of whom had been hanged and accursed after King Saul's death, Rizpah, his concubine, showed infinite patience. She, who had worn regal robes, now sat silently, alone and weary on a rock, with death all around her until King David learned of her sacrifice and then had her loved ones buried in a family grave. Although she suffered long and tragically, her patience never faltered.

One of the Bible's meekest daughters, identified only as Jephthah's daughter, accepted her father's pledge with great patience. A commander of the Israelites in a battle against the Ammonites, Jephthah made the reckless vow that if God would give him victory, he would make a burnt offering of whatsoever first came from his house to meet him. After subduing the enemy, he returned to his home at Mizpah, and who should be the first to greet him but his much beloved daughter, his only child. She came forth playing timbrels and dancing. No child ever accepted so patiently and so lovingly her fate. This daughter only requested one favor, to be alone for two months, and when she returned, her father did with her as he had vowed.

In these dark days of the judges of Israel, this story would have been forgotten, had it not been for the willingness of this young woman to suffer patiently and to accept meekly a fate she could not change. She was neither hasty in spirit nor angry at her father but quietly bore the yoke that had been placed upon her.

UNWAVERING GENTLENESS (KINDNESS)

The fifth fruit of the Spirit, gentleness (kindness), can be one of the qualities most becoming to a woman. Of the excellent wife in Proverbs, it is said, "in her tongue is the law of kindness." Shakespeare tells us that "kindness in women, not their beauteous looks, shall win my love." Like a golden chain, gentleness binds a woman to others who cross her path, if only for a brief moment.

The woman who possesses this quality radiates day after day the best and enables others to see characteristics they never thought of in connection with their own spiritual lives. In turn she helps others, less godlike, to find their pathway to God.

Of the two sisters, Rachel and Leah, mothers of the Twelve Tribes of Israel, Leah was the gentle one. She was unsought, undesired, plainer. The well-favored Rachel was Jacob's favorite wife. But Leah had an inestimable asset. She was clothed with humility. Through both her trials and her blessings, she learned to praise God fervently.

Jesus was gentle but firm with Salome, ambitious mother of James and John, who asked if one of her sons might sit to his left and the other to his right. Jesus answered her, saying that this privilege would be given to those prepared by God. In trying to be a good shepherd to her children, this mother exceeded the bounds of good taste.

GOODNESS, NEXT TO GODLINESS

The sixth fruit, goodness, like godliness, arises from faith in God and a willingness to be obedient to him. Peter says that godliness includes more than "holy living." It means walking in the light and giving light to others.

The woman who expresses goodness is not merely good. Like the excellent woman of Proverbs, cited earlier, she is good for something.

Real goodness is not transitory but enduring. A woman who is good does much by her example alone. She not only does good but is willing to suffer for the good she does. She possesses a kind of divinity within. She learns to trust goodness and magnifies it in every word and action.

FAITHFULNESS, AN INHERITANCE FROM GOD

The seventh fruit, faith, or faithfulness, as explained in Chapter Twenty-eight, is an inheritance from God. Eunice and Lois, the mother and grandmother of Timothy, were so faithful in the training of Timothy that Paul praised them, saying, "When I call to remembrance the unfeigned faith that is in thee, which dwelt first in thy grandmother Lois, and thy mother Eunice; and I am persuaded that in thee also" (II Tim. 1:5).

Christ said that "He that is faithful in that which is least is faithful also in much" (Luke 16:10). The woman who possesses this kind of faithfulness continues quietly in the hardest of tasks, not yielding to a restless desire for change.

She is the mother of the severely crippled child, whom she must serve constantly. She is the nurse tending the destitute dying. She is the woman crucified by long-suffering with cancer and accepting her fate quietly to the end. She is the medical missionary working on another continent among those who neither speak her language nor understand her sacrificial service. She is the selfless wife of a missionary, the untiring servant of the poor, whose many philanthropies are a constant witness to her Christian spirit. Faithfulness to all of these is the steady acceptance and performance of the common duty without any consideration of personal preference.

MEEKNESS, AN INDESTRUCTIBLE JEWEL

The eighth fruit of the Spirit, meekness, is a "precious jewel" for a woman to wear. In God's eyes it is far more to be desired than outward adornment. Elisabeth, meek and lowly toward her cousin Mary, the mother of Christ, never put herself first as the mother of the great John the Baptist but acknowledged Mary as the mother of a greater one than she.

Hroswitha, the eminent tenth-century canoness of the

Benedictine monastery at Gandersheim, Saxony, always belittled self. She is the earliest poet known in Germany. Although her works still have an important place in medieval literature and do honor to a woman and the Dark Ages in which she lived, she spoke meekly of her accomplishments as a poet, and admitted her shortcomings. She asked readers to give credit to God, if her work was at all worthy, and at the same time ascribe "all the blemishes to my lack of care."

As the Blessed Angela of Foligno, mentioned in another chapter, lay gravely ill, she urged her sons to shun power and honor, to remain humble and meek. On her deathbed her disciples asked for a last message. She, whose visions of the being of God are among the greatest of the medieval mystics, had only this to say in her farewell: "Make yourselves small! Make yourselves very small."

The powerful Queen Isabella of Spain, who had often appeared before her people in a robe of woven gold cloth and wearing a crown, asked to be buried in a coarse Franciscan robe, so meek was she and so disinterested in regal power. She felt it wrong for Christians to waste too much on "vain and transitory things." As St. Teresa of Avila, the beloved woman of the Carmelites, lay dying at Alba, she was asked if she wished to be buried in her own convent at Avila, her birthplace. Meek to the very end, she whispered back to the priest, "Will they not give me a little earth here?"

All of these women have survived the centuries, not only because of their accomplishments but largely because of their meek qualities of character.

SELF-CONTROL, AN EXCEPTIONAL QUALITY

Although self-control (temperance) is the last-named fruit of the Spirit, it is none the less significant. Only in exercising resolute self-control can we know the selflessness of God. If a woman lacks the quality of temperance, she may destroy herself in alcoholism, narcotic addiction, immorality, a violent temper, or other iniquities.

Lot's wife had no self-control when she looked back on the material possessions she had left behind in Sodom after God had directed her and her husband and daughters into a new land. Had Lot's wife been willing to forsake the past and move faithfully into an unknown future, she could have gone forward with her husband and daughters into a new and freer life. Instead she turned to look back, and as she did, she was encrusted with salt in an erosion of the earth that came out of Sodom as fire and brimstone rained upon it. She died on the spot without even touching again what she longed to possess once more.

Because Herodias could not control her hatred for the beloved John the Baptist, who had opposed her incestuous marriage to Herod, she instigated his beheading. Her hatred for him took on such a violent quality that she could not stand the sight of him.

Neither of these women could ever become inheritors of the Kingdom of God, because of their worldly desires: immorality, licentiousness, idolatry, enmity, and strife. These, like unextinguishable fires, burned within them and prompted their outward actions.

The entirely opposite qualities, the fruits of the Spirit,

can become elemental forces for good in a woman's life. "He who sows to the Spirit," says Paul, "will from the Spirit reap eternal life." These qualities have no connection with our material selves, therefore they are indestructible, a part of God himself.

Summing it all up, the fruits of the Spirit represent love in its many forms, and since woman at her best represents love at its best, all who walk into such a woman's presence see more clearly what God wants them to be, the inheritors of a rich legacy from him and his son, Jesus Christ.

BIBLIOGRAPHY

(INCLUDING ALL BOOKS OF
QUOTED MATERIALS)

ALLWORTHY, T. B., *Women in the Apostolic Church*, W. Heffer and Sons, Ltd., Cambridge, 1917.

BABER, ADIN, *Nancy Hanks, The Destined Mother of a President*, Arthur H. Clark Co., Box 230, Glendale, Calif. (no publication date).

BAILEY, ALBERT EDWARD, *Daily Life in Bible Times*, Charles Scribner's Sons, New York, 1943.

BARRIE, JAMES M., *Margaret Ogilvy*, By Her Son, Charles Scribner's Sons, New York, 1896.

BUCK, PEARL S., *To My Daughters, With Love*, The John Day Co., Inc., New York, 1967.

BUDGE, WALLIS, translator, *The Kebra Negast*, Glory of the Kings of Ethiopia, including the Queen of Sheba, sixth century A.D., The Medici Society, London, Liverpool, Boston, 1922.

BURROWS, MILLAR, *The Dead Sea Scrolls*, The Viking Press, Inc., New York, 1955.

———, *More Light on the Dead Sea Scrolls*, The Viking Press, Inc., New York, 1958.

CLEMENT, CLARA ERSKINE, *Heroines of the Bible in Art*, L. C. Page & Co., Boston, 1907.

CRAVEN, THOMAS, *Men of Art*, Simon and Schuster, Inc., New York, 1931.

DE CHARDIN, PIERRE TEILHARD, *The Future of Man*, Harper & Row, Publishers, New York, 1964.

DEEN, EDITH, *All of the Women of the Bible*, Harper and Brothers, New York, 1955.

———, *Great Women of the Christian Faith*, Harper and Brothers, New York, 1959.

DODD, M. E., *The Prayer Life of Jesus*, The Sunday School Board of the Southern Baptist Convention, Nashville, Tenn., 1923.

DUCKAT, WALTER, *Beggar to King, All the Occupations of Bible Times*, Doubleday & Co., Garden City, New York, 1968.

EMERSON, RALPH WALDO, *Complete Writings*, Wm. H. Wise & Co., New York, 1929.

FREE, JOSEPH P., *Archaeology and Bible History*, Scripture Press, Wheaton, Ill. (no publication date).

GEIKE, JOHN CUNNINGHAM, *The Life and Words of Christ*, revised edition, D. Appleton & Co., New York and London, 1905.

GIBRAN, KAHIL, *The Prophet*, Alfred A. Knopf, New York, 1942.

JÖRGENSEN, JOHANNES, *Saint Catherine of Siena*, Longmans, Green & Co., London, New York, Toronto, 1938.

KELLER, WERNER, *The Bible As History*, William Morrow & Co., New York, 1956.

KOHLER, LUDWIG, *Hebrew Man*, Abingdon Press, New York and Nashville, 1957.

LE FORT, GERTRUD VON, *The Eternal Woman*, translated from latest revised German edition, Bruce Publishing Co., Milwaukee, 1965.

MACE, DAVID R., *Hebrew Marriage*, Philosophical Library, New York, 1953.

McMILLEN, S. I., M.D., *None of These Diseases*, Fleming H. Revell Co., Westwood, N.J., 1963.

MARSHALL, PETER, *Mr. Jones, Meet the Master, Sermons and Prayers of Peter Marshall*, Fleming H. Revell Co., New York, London, and Glasgow, 1949.

MENZIES, LUCY, *Mirrors of the Holy, Ten Studies in Sanctity*, A. R., Mowbray and Co., London and Oxford, 1928.

MILLER, MADELEINE, *A Treasury of the Cross*, Harper and Brothers, New York, 1956.

MORRISON, JAMES DALTON, editor, *Masterpieces of Religious Verse*, Harper and Brothers, New York and London, 1948.

MOULD, ELMER W. K., *Essentials of Bible History*, third edition, revised by H. Neil Richardson, Robert F. Berkey, The Ronald Press Company, New York, 1966.

PEPPER, CURTIS BILL, "The Making of a Saint," *Look* magazine, March 4, 1969, vol. 33, pp. 34–36.

PORTER, KATHERINE ANNE, *The Days Before*, essay, "Marriage Is Belonging," Harcourt, Brace & Co., New York, 1952.

PRITCHARD, JAMES B., *Ancient Near Eastern Texts, Relating to the Old Testament*, Princeton University Press, Princeton, N.J., 1950.

SHEEN, FULTON J., *The Quotable Fulton Sheen*, edited by F. Gulfhurst, Droke Co., Anderson, S.C., 1967.

SMITH, CHARLES RYDER, *The Bible Doctrine of Womanhood*, The Epworth Press, London, 1923.

TOYNBEE, ARNOLD J., *A Study of History*, 12 vols., Oxford University Press, London, New York, Toronto, 1961.

UNDERHILL, EVELYN, *Mysticism*, E. P. Dutton Co., New York, 1930.

UNWIN, J. D., *Sex and Culture*, Oxford University Press, London, 1934.

WALSH, WILLIAM THOMAS, *Saint Teresa of Avila*, Bruce Publishing Co., Milwaukee, 1944.

WEGENER, G. S., *6000 Years of the Bible*, Harper and Row, Publishers, New York, 1963.

REFERENCE BOOKS

BARNHART, CLARENCE L., editor, *The New Century Cyclopedia of Names*, Appleton-Century-Crofts, Inc., New York, 1954.

BUTTRICK, GEORGE, editor, *The Interpreter's Dictionary of the Bible*, 4 vols., Abingdon Press, New York, Nashville, 1962.

———, *The Interpreter's Bible*, 12 vols., Abingdon Press, New York, Nashville, 1957.

DURANT, WILL, *The Story of Civilization*, 10 vols., Ariel Durant, co-editor of last 3 vols., Simon and Schuster, Inc., New York, 1954–1967.

GROLLENBERG, L. H., editor, *Nelson's Atlas of the Bible*, Thomas Nelson and Sons, New York, London, 1957.

HASTINGS, JAMES, *Dictionary of the Bible*, Charles Scribner's Sons, New York, 1948.

HASTINGS, SELBIE, JOHN A., and LAMBERT, JOHN C., A *Dictionary of Christ and the Gospels*, T & T Clark, Edinburgh, 1906.

MILLER, MADELEINE S. and LANE, J., *Harper's Bible Dictionary*, New York, Harper and Brothers, 1952.

NAVE, ORVILLE J., *Topical Bible*, Moody Press, Chicago, 1921.

ORR, JAMES, general editor, *The International Standard Bible Encyclopedia*, 5 vols., William B. Erdman's Publishing Co., Grand Rapids, 1941.

STRONG, JAMES, *Exhaustive Concordance of the Bible*, Abingdon Press, New York and Nashville, 1953.

THOMPSON, J. A., *The Bible and Archaeology*, Wm. B. Erdman's Publishing Co., Grand Rapids, 1962.

YOUNG, ROBERT, *Analytical Concordance of the Bible*, Wm. B. Erdman's Publishing Co., Grand Rapids, 1936.

Apocrypha, The Books Called, authorized version, Oxford University Press, London, Toronto (no publication date).

Holy Bible, King James Version (basic text used), Harper and Brothers, New York.

Holy Bible, Revised Standard Version, edited by Harold Lindsell, Ph.D., D.D., Harper and Row, Publishers, New York, Evanston, and London, 1952.

Holy Bible, Douay Version, translated at the English Catholic University, Douay, France, 1582.

The Bible, translated by James Moffatt, D.D., D.Litt., Harper and Brothers, New York, 1954.

Interpreter's Bible, by Nolan B. Harman, editor, Abingdon Press, 1951–55.

The New English Bible, Oxford University Press, Cambridge University Press, 1961.

Index

Aaron, 22, 82, 313; resentment of Zipporah, 118

Abel, 21

Abel, woman of, 98–99

Abigail, 24, 39, 231; beauty of, 134, 137–38

Abimelech, 85–86, 156

Abishag, 133–34

Abraham, 134, 231, 257; and angels, 13–14; steward of (*see* Eliezer of Damascus)

Absalom, 94, 96, 97

Achsah, 53

Acts, 298–304 *passim*; **1:8**, 253, 298; **1:14**, 298; **2:18**, 239; **4:35** (stewardship), 251; **5:9, 11** (stewardship), 251, 252; **5:14** (converts), 300; **8:12**, 300; **9:4, 6** (Paul's conversion), 247; **9:36, 42** (Dorcas), 113, 301, 302; **12:12**, 298; **13:48, 50** (Paul and Barnabas at Lystra, Antioch), 113, 300; **16:14** (Lydia), 78, 302; **17:3–4** (Thessalonica), 301; **17:28, 34** (Athens), 303; **21:5** (Tyre), 301; **26:18, 29** (trial of Paul), 169, 170

Adam, 51, 144

Adjectives, 103–13

Adultery, 106, 152, 177, 181–88; Cato on, 222; in heart, 278–

79; Jesus and the Sinful Woman, 275–76; laws of pagan nations, 226

Agassiz, Elizabeth Cary, 9

Agassiz, Jean Louis, 9

Agricultural activities, 39–40, 41–42, 72–73

Ahab, 75, 178, 179

Ahasuerus, 54, 82, 90, 134, 141; and Vashti, 140

Ahaziah, 179

Ahimaaz, 96–97

Ahinoam, 165

Aholah, 217–18

Aholibah, 217–18

Ai, excavations at, 44–45

Alabaster, woman with, 276

Aldrin, Edwin E., Jr., 19

Allen, Dr. Charles L., 7–8

Allworthy, T. B., 282–83

Amaziah, 195

Amenhoptep, 128

Amnon, 154–55, 165

Amos, 189–96; **2:6, 7, 8**, 194; **3:15**, 191; **4:1, 2–4**, 191, 192; **5:2**, 194; **5:8**, 195; **5:14–15, 24**, 193; **6:6**, 194; **7:14–15**, 195; **8:5–6**, 194

Ananias, 247, 251–52

Ancient Near Eastern Texts, 223

Angela of Foligno, Blessed, 27–29, 318

Angelico, Fra, 133
Angels, 12–19, 280
Anna, 241–42, 265
Anthusa, 310
Antioch, 300
Apocrypha, 92, 109–11
Apollo missions, 19
Appearance, 123–24; face and emotions, 122
Apphia, 305–6
Appiani, Andrew, 137
Aquila, 79, 304
Arabs, 157
Archippus, 305
Aristotle, 7, 222
Ark of the Covenant, 60, 121
Armstrong, Neil A., 19, 238
Armstrong, Viola, 238
Art, artists, 5–7, 133, 135–36 ff.
Asa, 178
Asenath, 52
Asherah, 178–79
Ashtaroth, 173–74, 175
Assyrians, 223, 226
Astronauts, 19
Astronomy, 270–71
Athaliah, 35, 71, 75–76, 179, 198
Athens, 223, 303
Augustine, St., 9
Augustus, Caesar, 222
Aztecs, 158

Baal, 173 ff.
Baber, Adin, 93–94
Babylonians, 223 ff. See also specific Books of the Bible
Bahurim, woman from, 40, 97
Barabbas, 252
Barak, 87, 167
Barnabas, 78, 113, 300–1
Barrie, Sir James, 132, 138
Baruch, 209

Bath-sheba, 44, 54, 134, 139–40, 186–87
Beauty, 132–42. See also Appearance; Cosmetics
Bees, 40
Beggar to King, All the Occupations of Biblical Times, 72
Beiberkraut, Professor, 135
Bellini (painter), 133
Benedictus, 243
Benjamin, 69, 137, 146, 166
Bernice, 167, 169–70
Bible Doctrine of Womanhood, The, 197
Bible as History, The, 125–26, 172
Bibliography, 321–26
Bigio, Francia, 140
Bilhah, 116
Bloy, Leon, 10
Blum, Sarah, vii
Boaz, 23, 72, 73, 108; and romantic love, 146
Book of the Covenant, The, 224. See also Exodus
Book of Divine Consolation, The, 28–29
Booth, Catherine, 274
Booth, William, 274
Braun, Wernher von, 19
Bread, 42–43; parable of leaven, 273; shewbread, 63–64
Bronze mirrors, 63
Buck, Pearl, 153, 181
Burrows, Millar, vi

Caesar and Christ, 222
Caesarea, 307–8. See also Paul
Cain, 21
Caleb, 53
Carriage (of women), 124
Catherine of Siena, 252–53, 294
Cato of Rome, 222

Cenchreae, 304–5
Chapin, Edwin Hubbell, 17
Chardin, Berthé de, 236–37
Chastity, 152–57 ff., 225
Chemosh, 177
Childbirth, 67–71, 124
Chinese proverb, 46
Chronicles, First (I), 54; **2:35,** 52–53; **7:24** (women in construction work), 73; **25:5–6, 8** (music), 65
Chronicles, Second (II), **22:3, 23:13** (fertility cults), 179; **24:7** (fertility cults), 180; **35:25** (lament for Josiah), 65
Chrysostom. See John Chrysostom
Church, the (See also Sanctuary), service to, 298–308
Chuza, 281, 283
Cignaroli, Giovanni, 137
Civilization, status of women and degree of, 55–56
"Civilization" (Emerson), 55
Clement, Clara Erskine, 137
Cleophas, 287
Clothing, 76–77, 124–27 ff.; Isaiah's denouncement, 200–1
Coin, parable of lost, 273
Colonna, Vittoria, 9
Colors, 125–26. See also Dyeing
Commission on the Status of Women, 57–58
Communication with God, 12–17
Constantine, 310
Construction work, 73–74
Contentiousness, 106–7
Corinth, 304. See also Corinthians
Corinthians, First (I), **7:32–33** (marriage), 307; **11:14–15** (hair), 124; **14:3–4** (one who prophesies), 308; **15:14–15** (Christ rising, faith), 269; **15:40, 49** (Transfiguration),

268; **16:19** (Aquila and Priscilla), 304
Corinthians, Second (II), **12:2–4,** 244; **12:9–10** (thorn in flesh), 293
Cosmetics, 128, 129
Cozbi, 167
Craven, Thomas, 5–6
Creation, the, 3–11
Crosses, bearing of, 289–97
Curie, Marie, 253–55
Curie, Pierre, 253–54

Damaris, 303
Dancing, 68
Daniel, 27, 265; **2:22,** 27
Dante, 8–9
Darius, 111
Daughters, 226–27 (See also specific Books of the Bible, persons); status of, 52–54
David, 40, 134, 177; and Abigail, 24; and Abishag, 133, 134; and Bath-sheba, 44, 139–40, 186–87; and handmaids, 231–32; and helpers during Absalom's rebellion, 94–98 passim; impatience of first wife, 120–21; lament for Saul and Jonathan, 125, 208; and Rizpah, 314; and temple musicians, 65
Days Before, The, 152
Dead, raising the, 260–61, 262, 266–68, 281
Dead Sea (Qumran) Scrolls, vi, 17, 127, 135
Death (See also Dead, raising the; specific persons), parable on, 273
Deborah, 35, 82, 83, 85–88, 91, 167, 313; Victory Ode of, 54
Deborah (nurse of Rebekah), 71
Delilah, 77

Demosthenes, 222
Deuteronomic Code, 224. *See also* Deuteronomy
Deuteronomy, 89, 160; **4:7,** 83; **4:44,** 224; **5:1–21,** 224; **17:17** (multiple wives), 176; **22:5** (clothing), 125; **22:13–21** (chastity), 158, 182; **22:16, 22:22** (adultery), 226; **22:23–26** (parallel to laws of Hammurabi), 225; **22:28–29,** 53, 225; **23:17** (prostitution), 182; **24:1–4** (divorce), 225; **25:5–9,** 183
Dinah, 155–56
Discretion, 105
Disease. *See* Sickness
Divine Comedy, The, 8–9
Divorce, 225–26
Dodd, M. E., 245–46
Doorkeepers, 80
Dorcas (Tabitha), 113, 301–3
Douay Version, 109
Driver, Samuel Rolles, 144
Drusilla, 167, 169–70
Ducket, Walter, 72
Durant, Will, 175, 222
Dyeing, 78–79; hair, 129

Ecclesiastes, **7:26–29,** 5, 106, 163–64; **9:9,** 146; **12:12,** viii
Ecclesiasticus, adjectives in, 109–10; **26:1–3, 13–14, 15–16, 23–26,** 110; **26:6–10, 23–25, 27,** 109–10
Ecumenical Council (1962), 17
Edict of Nantes, 253
Educated women, 57
Eli, 69
Eliezer of Damascus (Abraham's steward), 34–35, 40, 127, 249–50
Elijah, 25, 179, 261–62

Elisabeth, 31–32, 242–43, 317
Elisha, 25–26, 70, 100, 262
Elisheba, 313
Elkanah, 120
Emerson, Ralph Waldo, 55–56, 171
Emotional conflicts, 113–22
Energy, monogamy and, 158–60
Enos (Enosh), 22
En Rogel, 96–97
Epaenetus, 306
Ephesians, **6:6,** 234
Ephesus, 304
Equality, women and, 56–57
Esau, 52, 115, 257
Esdras, **I:4:18–20, 22, 26–27,** 110–11
Essentials of Bible History, 174
Esther, 54, 82, 83, 89–91; beauty of, 133, 134, 141–42; **1:11,** 140; **1:18,** 112–13; **2:7,** 134; **2:15,** 17, 141–42; **4:13–14,** 16, 90
Eternal Woman, The, 36–37
Ethbaal, 178
Eunice, 316–17
Euodias, 80, 303
Euripides, 74
Eusebius of Caesarea, 172
Eustochium, 9
Eve, 3, 5, 21–22, 164–65; marriage of, 144; status of, 51
Evil. *See* Wickedness; specific types
Exodus, **1:15–21** (midwives, childbirth), 70–71, 124; **2:16–17, 19–20** (Moses and shepherdesses), 93; **4:25** (Zipporah and circumcision), 117; **15:13, 17–18,** 84; **15:21** ("Sing Unto the Lord"), 83; **15:26** (diseases), 119; **20–23,** 224; **20:14** (adultery), 182; **21:7–10** (daughters), 52, 227; **22:16–17,** 53, 225; **25:30** (shewbread), 63;

Exodus (cont'd)
28:30, 60; 28:32 (weaving),
76; 34:12–27, 224; 35:22, 25–
26, 60–61; 38:8, 63; 40:38, 64
Ezekiel, 212–20; 13:17–19, 214;
16:1–14, 32–34, 44, 216–17;
23:11, 17, 48–49, 217–18; 24:
18, 218; 28:13, 127–28;
33:28–29, 33, 213; 36:26–27,
215
Ezra, 2:61, 53

Fabrics, 126–27. See also Weaving
and spinning
Face (See also Appearance; Beauty;
Cosmetics), as barometer, 122
Faith, 256–62, 316–17
Felix (procurator of Judea), 169
Fertility cults, 173–75 ff.
Fig Tree and the Bramble, the, 85–
86
Flowers, 41, 128
Food, 44 (See also Agricultural ac-
tivities; Kitchen equipment;
specific items); served after re-
ligious services, 64
Foolishness, 107
Fortunetellers, 213–15
Foundling girl, allegory of, 216–17
Francis of Assisi, 291–92
Fry, Elizabeth, 253
Fuller, Ethel Romig, 247–48

Galatians, 4:4–5, 227; 5:22–23
(fruits of spirit), 309–10
Galileo, Galilei, 9
Geike, John Cunningham, 285
Genesis, 3, 4, 115, 164, 249; 2:18,
20, 22, 23, 24 (romantic love,
marriage), 143–44; 4:1 (Eve),
21, 144; 4:25, 26 (Eve and
descendants), 22; 12:11–14
(beauty of Sarah), 134; 18:6

(bread of the Presence), 63;
18:14, 14; 20:9, 156; 21:17–
18 (Hagar), 14; 23:23 (Jeremiah), 27; 24:16 (beauty of
Rebekah), 133; 24:22 (gifts to
Rebekah), 127; 24:59 (Rebekah's nurse), 71; 24:63–67
(marriage of Isaac and Rebekah), 145; 28:16 (Jacob),
26; 28:17, 38; 29:11 (beauty
of Rachel), 136; 29:17, 133,
136; 29:18, 20, 137, 145;
30:1, 2, 14, 15, 23 (Rachel's
emotional conflicts), 116–17;
34:7, 155; 34:31, 156; 35:18
(birth of Benjamin), 69; 37:3
(Joseph's robe), 115; 38:16,
18–19 (Tamar), 183–84; 38:
26 (Tamar), 107, 183–84; 38:
28 (birth of Tamar's twins),
69; 39:7–9 (Joseph and Potiphar's wife, 185
Gentleness, 315–16
Gibran, Kahlil, 249
Gideon, 85
Giordano, Luca, 137
Goats, 40
God, 143, 240 ff.; communication
with, 12–17; and Creation, 3–
11; Jesus and (see Jesus
Christ); relations of women to,
20–30; and the sanctuary,
59 ff.; Spirit of, fruits of, 309–
20; and status of women as national leaders, 83
Goddesses, influence of pagan, 172–
80
Goethe, Johann Wolfgang von, 180
Gomer, 187
Goodness, 316. See also specific
persons, writers
"Gracious," 104
Greece, 223; Athens, 223, 303

Hagar, 14–15, 51, 231
Hair, 124, 129
Haman, 82, 90
Hammurabi, Code of, 223–24, 225–26
Hamutal, 165
Hanks, Abraham, 94
Hanks, Nancy, 93–94
Hannah, 23–24, 35, 232–33; Song of Praise, 54; taunted by husband's other wife, 120
Harems, 191–92
Harlotry. See Prostitution
Hawthorne, Nathaniel, 262
Healing, 259–60
Hebrew Man, 124
Hebrew Marriage, 154
Hebrews, **1:14** (angels), 13; **11:3**, 256; **11:4** (Abel) 21; **11:11, 20, 21, 22,** 257; **11:23,** 258; **11:31,** 77, 257; **11:33–34** (faith), 262; **12:2** (Jesus and faith), 259
Hegai, 141
Helena, 310
Heman, 65
Henry IV (Henry of Navarre), 253
Herbs, 42, 128–29
Herod Agrippa I, 169
Herod Agrippa II, 169
Herod Antipas, 168, 282
Herod of Chalcis, 169
Herod the Great, 169
Herodias, 167–69, 319
Herod Philip, 167
Heroines of the Bible in Art, 137
Higginbotham, Ella, vi
Historia Ecclesiastica, 172
Hittites, 223, 226
Hoffer, Eric, 271
Holiness Code, 224. See also Leviticus
Holmes, Oliver Wendell, 67

Homosexuality, 152
Hosea, 187
Hospitality, 44
Houses, 44–45
Hroswitha, 317–18
Hughes, Rupert, 100
Huldah, 35, 80, 82, 83, 88–89, 91

Ichabod, 69
Incest, 225
Interpreter's Bible, 78–79, 179
Irving, Washington, 132
Isaac, 14, 35, 51–52, 249, 250; painting of, 135–36; and romantic love, 144–45
Isabella of Spain, 235–36, 318
Isaiah, 4, 197–204; luxuries, 128; and many heavens, 244; songs about servant of the Lord, 232; **3:16–17,** 199; **3:18–23,** 200; **3:24–26,** 201; **4:1,** 201; **4:4,** 199; **5,** 39–40; **5:20,** 198; **32:9,** 14, 108, 202–3; **32:15–18,** 203; **33:15–16,** 204; **42:1–4,** 232; **47:5, 7** ("lady"), 112; **49:1–6,** 232; **50:4–9,** 232; **52:13–15,** 232; **53:1–12,** 232; **61:1–4,** 232; **61:6,** 239; **65:8** (harvest), 40; **65:22** (labor), 81
Ishmael, 14, 51

Jacob, 26, 52, 115, 257; and Rachel's beauty, 136–37; and Rachel's resentment, deceit, 116–17; and romantic love, 145–46; and Shechem, 156
Jael, 126, 166–67
James, 316
James I, King, 104
Jeanne d'Albret, 253
Jehoahaz, 165
Jehoahaz II, 209

Jehoiachin, 209, 212
Jehoiakim, 209
Jephthah's daughter, 35, 314–15
Jeremiah, 65, 205–11; **3:6,** 205; **5:8,** 207; **8:18, 21,** 205; **9:17–18, 20, 21,** 207; **17:13,** 211; **23:23,** 27; **25:30–31,** 208; **44: 15, 16–18,** 210; **44:24–25,** 211; **52:1–2** (Hamutal), 165
Jerome, St., 9
Jerusalem, walls of, 73–74
Jerusha, 313
Jesus Christ, 115, 227; and angels, 16–17; and clothing, 130; example of prayer and worship, 240–48; example of steward- ship and witness, 249–55; and faith, 256–62, 317; and fruits of the Spirit, 309 ff.; gentle- ness of, 316; gifts of, 272– 79; and married love, 150; and ministering women, 280–88; mother as handmaid, 232–34; service to His Church, 298– 308; spiritual revelations to women, 263–71; suffering for, 237–39, 289–97; women in Matthew's genealogy of, 54; women's legacy from, 229–320
Jethro's daughters, 40, 72
Jewelry, 127–28
Jezebel, 75–76, 178–79, 198; cos- metics, headdresses, 129
Joab, 98–99, 179
Joan of Arc, 235
Joanna (wife of Chuza), 281 ff.
Joash, 71
Job, 4, 121, 244; **9:11,** 27
Jochebed, 22, 258
Joel, 239
John, 150, 244, 263, 316; and min- istering women, 281–82, 283; and white raiment, 131; **4,** 264; **4:23,** 241; **8:7, 10, 11** (the Sinful Woman), 275; **11** (Martha), 265–66; **13:1** (love), 310; **13:16,** 234; **19:17–18** (Cross), 289; **20,** 268; **20:13,** 290–91
John the Baptist, 31, 168–69, 242– 43, 319
John Chrysostom, 303 ff., 310
John, First (I), **4:16,** 310
John Mark. *See* Mark
John, Second (II), 113, 310
John XXIII, Pope, 17
Jonathan, 95, 96–97
Joppa, 301–2
Jörgensen, Johannes, 294
Joseph (father of Jesus), 16
Joseph (Old Testament), 52, 115, 257; and Potiphar's wife, 185– 86; and Rachel's emotional conflict, 116, 117
Joseph of Arimathea, 286
Joshua, **2:1, 11,** 77, 257
Josiah, 65, 80, 82, 89, 175, 180, 209
Jotham, 85, 313
Joy, 311–12
Judah, 107, 183–84
Judges, **1:14** (Caleb's daughter), 53; **2:13** (fertility cults), 173; **4:5, 14** (Deborah), 86; **5:1– 31** (Deborah), 54, 87, 88, 112, 126; **5:29** ("lady"), 112; **9** (Abimelech), 85; **10:6** (fer- tility cults), 173; **13:3, 22,** 15; **16:13–14** (Samson's hair), 77; **19:24** (daughters made prosti- tutes by fathers), 227; **20:6,** 166; **21:6, 23,** 166

Kebra Nagast, The, 74
"Keeper of the Springs," role of, 38–47

Keller, Werner, 125–26, 172

Kennedy, John F., 57–58

Kindness, 315–16

King James Version (KJV), vi–vii, 104. *See also* specific Books

Kings, First (I), **1:1–4** (Abishag), 133, 134; **10:6–9** (Queen of Sheba), 75; **11:1–8** (Solomon's marriages), 176; **15:10, 13** (Maacah), 178; **16:32–33,** 178; **17:24,** 25; **18:19** (Ahab and Jezebel), 178

Kings, Second (II), **4:3–7,** 25; **4:8,** 108; **4:32–36** (birth of Shunammite's child), 70; **5:1–4** (Naaman), 99; **8:6,** 26; **11:3** (hiding of Joash), 71; **22:14–20** (Huldah), 89

Kitchen equipment, 42–43

Kohler, Ludwig, 124

Laban, 136

"Lady," 112–13

Lamentations, **4:10,** 108

Lamps, 43

Lapidoth, 86

Lazarus, 266–68, 281

Leah, 52, 116–17, 136, 315

Leatherwork, 80

Leaven, parable of, 273

Le Fort, Gertrud von, 36–37, 164–65

Leonardo da Vinci, 6–7, 133

Leseur, Elizabeth, 294–95

Leviticus, 160, 224; **18:1–30,** 152, 224–25; **19:1–35,** 182, 224; **20:10** (adultery), 226; **20:11–12, 19–21** (incest), 225; **20:13** (homosexuality), 152; **21:9, 14,** 182

Life and Words of Christ, The, 285

Lighted Lamp, parable of, 284

Lloyd George, David, 246

Lois, 316–17

Look magazine, 237, 238

Lord's Prayer, 244, 245

Lot's wife, 319

Love, as fruit of Spirit, 310–11; romantic, 143–50

Lower Beth-horon, 73

Luke, 16, 281 ff., 307; **1:6** (Elisabeth), 32; **1:15** (Elisabeth), 242; **1:38,** 233; **1:42** (Elisabeth), 242; **1:46–55,** 54, 233; **1:67–80** (Elisabeth), 243; **2:37–38** (Anna), 242; **4:25–26** (Elijah and Zarephath), 261–62; **7:12–15** (widow of Nain), 260–61; **7:40–48** (Woman with Alabaster), 276; **8:1–3,** 280, 281, 283; **8:5–8, 11** (Sower of the Seed), 284; **8:16–17** (Lighted Lamp), 284; **8:48** (faith and healing), 259; **12:42** (stewards), 249; **12:47–48,** 234; **13:12–13** (faith and healing), 259; **13:20–21** (parable of leaven), 273; **14:27** (the Cross), 289; **15:8–10** (parable of coin), 273; **16:10** (faithfulness), 317; **17:6** (sycamine tree miracle), 262; **18:3–5** (widows), 278; **20:46–47** (widows), 278; **21:1–4** (widow's mites), 250; **22:27** (service), 275; **23:8** (trial of Jesus), 282; **23:34,** 284; **23:46, 49, 55–56** (death of Christ), 285, 286; **24:6–7, 34** (risen Christ), 286, 288

Lydia, 78, 302

Maacah, 177–78

Mace, David R., 154

Machir, 95

McMillen, Dr. S. I., 119

Magnificat, the, 54, 233
Mahlah, 53–54
Maidservants, 96–97, 99–100
Manasseh, 209
"Manners" (Emerson), 55–56
Manoah, 15
Margaret of Navarre, 253
Mari, 225
Mark, 281, 298, 299; **6:25, 26** (John the Baptist), 168; **9:23–24** (faith), 260; **12:29–31**, 227; **12:41–44** (widow's mites), 250; **14:9** (Mary of Bethany), 281; **15:40–41** (ministering women), 280; **16:14** (rising of Christ), 287
Marriage (See also Sex; Wives; specific persons), monogamy, 158–59; romantic love, 143–50
Marshall, Peter, 46–47
Martha of Bethany, 263–64
Mary, Romans: **16,** 306
Mary (Salome; mother of James and Mark), 280–81, 298, 299, 316
Mary, Queen, 62
Mary, Virgin, 115, 227, 231–35, 242–43, 272, 281 ff., 298; and angels, 16–17; artists and, 133; and the Cross, 290; Magnificat of, 54, 233; Pietá, 6
Mary of Bethany, 266, 290
Mary Magdalene, 245, 263, 264, 268–69; and Cross, rising of Christ, 290–91; as ministering woman, 280 ff.
Masterpieces of Religious Verse, 248 n
Matthew, 54, 281; **4:11** (ministering angels), 280; **5:28** (adultery in heart), 278–79; **6:5–8** (Sermon on the Mount), 243–44; **6:9–13** (Lord's Prayer),

244; **6:25** (and clothing), 130; **14:19** (grace at meals), 245; **15:28** (faith and healing), 260; **17:20** (faith), 258–59; **19:13** (blessing of children), 245; **21:31–32** (Jesus and the Pharisees), 277; **24:42** (parable on death), 273; **27:19** (Pilate's wife), 252; **27:55–56** (ministering women), 280–81, 285; **28:5–10** (rising of Christ), 286–87
Meekness, 317–18
Men of Art (Craven), 5–6
Menzies, Lucy, 28, 295
Mephibosheth, 95–96
Micah, **6:4,** 83–84
Michal, 120–21
Michelangelo, 5–6, 9, 187–88
Midian, daughters of, 92–93
Midwives, 69–71
Milcah, 53–54
Mill, John Stuart, 9–10
Miller, Madeleine S., 296
Milton, John, 17, 147
Ministering women, 280–88
Miriam, 22–23, 82, 83–84, 91, 258; prejudice of, 118–19
Mirrors, bronze, 63
Mirrors of the Holy, 28, 295
Moffatt, James, translation, vii. See also specific Books
Mohammed, 157
Moloch, 177, 179
Mona Lisa, 6
Monica (mother of Augustine), 9
Monogamy, 158–59
Moors, 159–60
Mordecai, 89, 90, 141
Moses, 22, 23, 59, 82, 223–24; bad temper of wife, 117; exhortation on God, 83; and faith, 257–58; and fine linen of

Moses (cont'd)
    Egypt, 127; and Jethro's daughters, 40; and shepherd-esses, 92–93; and whoredoms, 167; and Zelophehad's daughter, 53, 54
Mothers, 35–37 (See also specific Books of the Bible, persons); and love, 310–11
Mould, Elmer W. K., 174
Mourning women, 207–8
Mr. Jones, Meet the Master, 46
Murders, 165–67
Murillo, Bartolomé, 135
Music, 64–66, 68, 208
Mysticism (Underhill), quoted, 28–29

Naaman, 99–100, 231
Nain, widow of, 260–61
Names, daughters and, 52–53
Nancy Hanks, the Destined Mother of a President, 93–94
Naomi, 23, 71, 72, 146; and peace, 313
National Cathedral (Washington, D.C.), 62
National leaders, 82–91
Nebuchadnezzar, 89, 211
Needlework, 61–62
Nehemiah, 2:17, 18 (walls of Jerusalem), 73; 5:5 (bondaged daughters), 226; 7:63 (Barzillai's daughter), 53; 7:67, 65–66; 13:26 (pagan women, marriage), 108
New English Bible, vii. See also specific Books
Nicodemus, 286
Noah (daughter of Zelophehad), 53–54
Noglah, 53–54
None of These Diseases, 119

Numbers, 12:2, 10–12, 13 (Miriam's prejudice against Zipporah), 118; 15:38 (weaving), 76–77; 25:15 (Cozbi), 167; 26:59, 22; 27:4–11 (Zelophehad's daughters), 53
Nurses, 71–72, 94–97

Obed, 71, 146, 313
"O Constant Cross," 296–97
Ogilvy, Margaret, 138
Oil, 42, 43
Ointments, 128–29
Olives, 42
Onesimus, 305, 306
Othniel, 53
Outcast women (See also Wickedness), Christ and, 275–77

Pagan cultures, status and, 222–23
Pagan goddesses, influence of, 172–80
Pasternak, Boris, 313–14
Pasteur, Louis, 9
Patience, 314–15
Patriarchs (See also specific Books, Patriarchs), status of wives, 51–52
Paul, 227, 234, 269, 299 ff., 320 (See also specific Epistles); and battle between flesh and spirit, 264–65; and bishops as God's stewards, 250; on clothing, 130; and faith of Eunice and Lois, 316–17; and fruits of the Spirit, 309; Lydia and, 78, 302; and many heavens, 244; and peace, 313; and prayer, 244 ff.; and suffering on behalf of Christ, 291; and thorn in flesh, suffering, 293; and Transfiguration, 268; trial in Caesarea, 169–70; and woman of

Paul (cont'd)
high principle, 111–12, 113
Paula, aid to St. Jerome by, 9
Peace, 312–14
Peninnah, 120
Penni, Francesco, 135–36
Pepper, Curtis Bill, 237, 238
Persis, 306
Peter, 80; and Dorcas's death, 302; on godliness, 316; Pentecostal sermon, 239; and rising of Christ, 287; and Sapphira and Ananias, 251
Peter, First (I), **3:3–5**, 113, 142; **3:14** (suffering), 291; **4:10** (stewards), 250
Pharaoh's daughter, 258
Phebe, 304–5
Philemon, 305; **2**, 305; **12–14**, 305
Philip the Evangelist, 80, 300; daughters of, 307–8
Philippi, 302–3. See also Philippians
Philippians, **1:29**, 291; **4:3**, 303; **4:8–9** (peace), 313; **4:15**, 303
Philo Byblius, 172
Phinehas, 69, 167
Pietá (Michelangelo), 6
Pilate, 252, 284, 286
Pilate's wife, 252
Plato, 222
Porter, Katherine Anne, 152
Potiphar's wife, 185–86
Poussin, Nicolas, 135
Prayer, 240–48
Prayer Life of Jesus, The, 245–46
Priestly Code, 224
Priscilla, 79, 80, 304
Pritchard, James B., 223
Prophet, The, 249
Prostitution (harlotry), 181 ff., 216 ff.; courtesans of Rome and Greece, 223; daughters

made prostitutes by fathers, 227; and influence of pagan goddesses, 172 ff.
Proverbs, 5, 31–36, 39 ff., 103–4 ff., 127, 128, 152–53, 315; on contentiousness, 105, 106; on foolishness, wisdom, 107, 185; on wickedness, 106–7, 184, 185; **2:17**, 106–7; **6:25–26**, 106; **7:1–4** (wisdom), 185; **7:5, 10, 13**, 106, 107; **7:16–18, 21–23, 27** (harlotry), 184, 185; **9:13**, 107; **11:16** ("gracious"), 104; **11:22** (discretion), 105; **12:4**, 104; **13:14**, 107; **14:1**, 107; **16:16**, 107; **19:14** (prudence), 105; **24:20**, 179; **25:24**, 105; **27:15**, 106; **30:18–19** (romantic love), 143; **30:20, 22–23** (unloveliness), 106; **31:10–31**, 31–36, 39 ff., 104
Prudence, 105
Psalms, **8:3–5**, 19; **9:9**, 25; **34:7**, 15; **36:7**, 32; **43:3**, 21; **45**, 128; **45:10–11**, 139; **45:13**, 108, 126, 138–39; **51**, 187; **51:7**, 42; **53:1**, 21; **65:9–13**, 40–41; **73:25–26**, 65; **78:72**, 80–81; **86:16**, 231; **9:11**, 13; **95:6**, 240; **103:7**, 224; **104**, 3–4; **105:1–3**, 66; **116:16**, 231; **119:105**, 11; **123:2**, 232; **126:6**, 45; **128:2**, 81; **136:5**, 27; **139:7–10**, 18; **144:12, 15**, 156–57; **147:5**, 27
Purple, 79

Queens, 75–76. See also specific persons
Qumran Scrolls. See Dead Sea (Qumran) Scrolls
Quotable Fulton J. Sheen, The, 290

Rachel, 35, 52, 69, 206, 315; beauty of, 133, 136–37; resentment, deceit of, 116–17; and romantic love, 145–46

Rahab, 54, 77, 257

Ramsay, William Mitchell, 283

Raphael, 133, 135, 137, 139

Ras Shamra, 173

Rebekah, 34–35, 40, 115–16; beauty of, 133, 135–36, 137; gifts to, 127; and herbs, 42; nurse of, 71; and romantic love, 144–45; status, 51–52

Reed, Dr. William L., vi

Rehoboam, 177

Rembrandt van Rijn, 140

Reni, Guido, 135

Revelation, 244; 3:5, 131; 21:2, 150

Revised Standard Version, vii. See also specific Books

Rights and privileges, 51–58

Rizpah, 314

Roberts, Versie, viii

Romans, Epistle to the, 8:6–10, 265; 16:1, 2 (Phebe), 304, 305; 16:6, 306; 16:12, 306

Romantic love, 143–50

Rome, ancient, 222–23, 304. See also specific rulers

Rubens, Peter Paul, 137

Rufus's mother, 306

Ruth, 23, 35, 53; agricultural duties, 72–73; and romantic love, 146; son born, 71; worthiness of, 108; 2:20, 23; 3:11, 108; 4:15, 71

Ruysbrück, John, 311

Sailmaking, 79, 80

Saint Catherine of Siena, 294

Saints, 291–94

Salome (daughter of Herodias), 168

Salome (mother of James and Mark). See Mary (Salome; mother of James and Mark)

Salvation Army, 274

Samaria, 300

Samaria, woman of, 241, 263–65, 269, 300, 309

Samson, 15, 40, 77

Samuel, 24

Samuel, First (I), 1:6–7, 120; 1:11, 233; 2:1–10, 23–24, 54; 4:19–20 (Ichabod's birth), 69; 7:3 (fertility cults), 173; 12:10 (fertility cults), 173; 25:3 (Abigail's beauty), 138; 25:28–31 (David and Abigail), 24

Samuel, Second (II), 1:24 (David's lament for Saul and Jonathan), 125, 308; 4:4 (Jonathan's son), 95; 6:16 (impatience of David's wife), 121; 9:7–10 (Jonathan's son), 95–96; 11:2 (David and Bathsheba), 139; 11:4, 5 (David and Bath-sheba), 186; 12:23 (David's lament for son), 187; 13:1 (beauty of Tamar), 133; 13:12–14 (Tamar), 154–55; 13:18 (Tamar), 125; 17:17, 96–97; 20:18–22, 98; 22:29, 43

Sanctuary, women's status in the, 59–67

Sandals, 130

Sapphira, 251–52

Sarah, 13–14, 35, 231, 257; Abimelech and, 156; beauty of, 134, 137; status, 51

Saul, King, 94–95, 96, 125, 314

Schaeffer, Claude F. A., 173

Schnorr von Karolsfeld, Julius, 135

Schrader, Julius, 141

Seduction, 53. See also Chastity

Self-control, 319–20
Seneca, 94
Sermon on the Mount, 243–44
Seth, 22
Sex (chastity; seduction), 151–60, 181–88, 225–26 (*See also* Adultery; Prostitution; Romantic love); and clothing, 124–25
Sex and Culture, 157–60
Shakespeare, William, 133, 315
Shallum (husband of Huldah), 88
Shallum (Jerusalem ruler), daughters of, 73–74
Sheba (Benjamite), 97–98
Sheba, Queen of, 74–75, 127
Shechem, 155–56
Sheen, Fulton J., 290
Sheep, 40
Shepherdesses, 92–93
Sherah, 73
Sheshan, 53
Shewbread (showbread), 63
Shiprah, 69–70
Shunem, woman of (The Shunammite), 25–26, 38–39, 70, 108, 262
Sickness (illness), 119–20, 259–60
Silas, 301, 302
Simon the Pharisee, 276
Simon the Sorcerer, 300
Sin. *See* Wickedness; specific sins
Sinful Woman, the, 275–76
Sisera, 87, 126, 167
6000 Years of the Bible, 135
Skin, 124
Slaves, slavery, 52, 231
Sleep, sleeping, 19, 44
Smith, Charles Ryder, 197
Social welfare, 68–69
Socrates, 138, 222
Solomon, 108, 134, 175–77; and music in temple, 65; and Queen of Sheba, 74–75, 127

Song of Solomon (Song of Songs), 147–50; **1:2**, 147; **1:8**, 148; **1:13**, 128; **1:15–16**, 147; **2:5, 6, 7**, 147; **2:10–14, 16**, 147–48; **3:4**, 149; **3:5**, 147; **4:3**, 128; **4:9–11**, 149; **7:7**, 124; **8:4**, 147; **8:6–7**, 149–50; **8:14**, 150; **21:2**, 150
Sower of the Seed, 283–84
Spinning and weaving, 39, 76–78
Spirit, fruits of the, 309–20
Stanton, Elizabeth Cady, 170
Status, 51–58; and national leadership, 82–91; pagan cultures and, 222–23; in sanctuary, 59–67
Stewardship, 249–52
Storey, Violet Alleyn, 296–97
Story of Civilization, The (Durant), 175, 222
Story of History (Toynbee), viii
Suffering, 237–39, 289–97. *See also* Sickness; specific persons
Susanna (healed by Jesus), 281
Swann, Dr. W. F. G., 246
Syntyche, 80, 303

Tabitha. *See* Dorcas
Tamar, 54, 69, 107, 125, 133, 154–55, 165, 183–84
Teaching, 80
Teilhard de Chardin, Pierre, 236–37
Tentmaking, 79–80
Teresa of Avila, St., 292–93, 318
Teresa of India, 237–38
Tertullian, 130
Thessalonians, 81
Thessalonians, First (I), **2:7**, 72; **5:3** (childbirth), 124
Thessalonica, 301. *See also* Thessalonians
Thomas, doubting, 268–69
Thomas à Kempis, 94

Thutmose III, 129
Timothy, 111–12, 316
Timothy, First (I), **2:9–10** (clothing), 130; **3:11,** 112
Timothy, Second (II), **1:5,** 317; **3:6–7,** 112
Tintoretto, 141
Tirzah, 53–54
Titus, 111, 285; **1:7–8,** 250; **2:3–5,** 112
To My Daughters, With Love, 153, 181
Torquato Tasso, 180
Toynbee, Arnold, viii
Treasury of the Cross, A, 296
Trees, 41–42
Tryphena, 306
Tryphosa, 306
Tyre, 301

Underhill, Evelyn, 28–29
Unloveliness, 107
Unwin, J. D., 157–60
Upper Beth-horon, 73
Ur, 128
Uriah, 134, 140, 186
Uzzen-sherah, 73

Van Eyck, Jan, 133
Vashti, 89, 134, 140
Vecchio, Palma, 137
Veronese, Paolo, 135, 141

Vineyards, 39–40

Walsh, William Thomas, 293
Water, 40–41
Weaving and spinning, 39, 76–78
Wegener, G. S., 135
Wesley, John, 310
Wesley, Susanna, 310
Where to Find Peace, 313–14
White, 131
Wickedness, 106–7, 163–220. See
    also specific evils, prophets
Widows (*See also* specific persons),
    Jesus and, 277–78
Wisdom, 107
Wisdom of Solomon, **6:7,** 92
Witnessing, 249, 252–55
Wives, 104–5 ff. (*See also* Marriage;
    specific persons); status of patriarchs', 51–52
"Woman" (Emerson), 171
Woman in the Apostolic Church,
    282–83

Yahweh. *See* God

Zacharias, 31, 242
Zarephath, widow of, 25, 262
Zedekiah, 165, 209
Zelophehad, 53–54
Ziba, 96
Zipporah, 93, 117